MARKSTRAT
2

MARKSTRAT 2

by

Jean-Claude Larréché
INSEAD

&

Hubert Gatignon
The Wharton School

 The Scientific Press • 507 Seaport Court • Redwood City, CA 94063-2731 • (415) 366-2577

MARKSTRAT 2
Jean-Claude Larréché and Hubert Gatignon

Printed in the United States of America

10 9 8 7 6 5 4 3

ISBN 0-89426-124-X (with 5¼" MS/DOS Disk)
ISBN 0-89426-164-X (with 3.5" MS/DOS Disk)

Publisher: The Scientific Press
Text design & production editor: Gene Smith
Cover design: Rogondino & Associates
Cover photograph: Ed Malles

CONTENTS

THE MARKSTRAT2
SIMULATION SOFTWARE

The MARKSTRAT2 software has been developed and is distributed by STRAT*X, a company specializing in strategic marketing training. The student disk provided with this book includes the software allowing teams to access the MARKSTRAT results, to enter their decisions and to make financial projections. It does not include the simulation model which is available only to instructors.

How to Have Access to the MARKSTRAT Simulation

- **Universities.** Professors can obtain a license to use the MARKSTRAT2 software for courses offered by their university.

- **Corporate licensing.** Corporations can obtain a license to use the MARKSTRAT2 software for their own internal training programs.

- **Corporate seminars.** Management development seminars on strategic marketing are offered for corporate executives, based on the MARKSTRAT2 software.

- **Individual use.** The MARKSTRAT2 software has been designed to be used exclusively in a class situation under the supervision of qualified instructors. Another simulation MARKOPS (Marketing Operations and Strategy), has also been developed for individual training in marketing.

To obtain more information on the MARKSTRAT2 and MARKOPS simulations, please contact:

STRAT*X International
222 Third Street
Cambridge, MA 02142
U.S.A.

Tel. (617) 494-8282
Fax. (617) 494 1421

STRAT*X S.A.
73 rue Victor Hugo
77250 Veneux les Sablons
France

Tel. (33 1) 60 70 58 80
Fax. (33 1) 60 70 33 69

MARKSTRAT2 is a combination text and manual which replaces the previous MARKSTRAT manual. Chapters 1–4 detail the technical aspects of the MARKSTRAT simulation in greater depth. Chapters 5–9 discuss the marketing strategy concepts illustrated in the simulation, which were not covered at all in the previous manual.

The basic structure of the MARKSTRAT simulation has not been changed. Instructors familiar with the previous MARKSTRAT program will find scenario A.0 in the MARKSTRAT2 software instantly and completely familiar. The structure has, however, been completely reprogrammed onto separate student and instructor PC diskettes to enhance the student/instructor interaction and the overall ease of use, flexibility, and processing speed.

The MARKSTRAT simulation is now widely used in business schools around the world as part of their graduate or executive development programs. A number of companies have organized MARKSTRAT seminars for several hundred of their executives. This accumulated experience indicates that in today's increasing competitive situation, the MARKSTRAT simulation is an effective tool to develop a strategic market orientation.

The MARKSTRAT simulation has been specially designed for learning, practicing and testing marketing strategy concepts. Compared to the more traditional marketing management games, its main features are:

1. a longer term perspective

2. an emphasis on strategic concepts such as competitive analysis, product portfolio, market segmentation, product positioning and repositioning issues

3. the opportunity to manage and expand the product line through the modification of existing brands and the introduction of new ones

4. the availability of a comprehensive set of fifteen marketing research studies

5. the graphical representation of brand similarities and preferences through perceptual mapping

6. a more dynamic environment, reflected by different product/market life cycles, the creation of a new market, inflation, price controls, and changes in the level of productivity.

For maximum effectiveness, the MARKSTRAT simulation should be integrated in a course emphasizing strategic marketing concepts. At the graduate level, the simulation is best suited for the end of a basic marketing management course, or for more advanced marketing strategy courses. At the executive level, it can be a valuable component of marketing or general management programs. MARKSTRAT has been extensively used, with consistent success, in in-company training programs aimed at developing strategic marketing skills or a marketed-oriented culture.

MARKSTRAT2 reflects the experience which has been gained since the introduction of the MARKSTRAT simulation. In particular, the present edition communicates necessary information more effectively. We separate into several parts the information which is required to start the simulation and additional information which becomes relevant only later in the simulation. From a conceptual standpoint, this new edition emphasises the strategic orientation of MARKSTRAT. The main strategic concepts that are illustrated during a MARKSTRAT simulation are discussed in new chapters. This additional material provides the students with references to strategic concepts in marketing that can be expected during the simulation. These new chapters are not intended to replace a text on these issues, but they should offer a better perspective and a greater opportunity to investigate strategic issues that are illustrated during the course of a MARKSTRAT simulation.

To facilitate the student/instructor interface with the simulation, we have augmented this manual with a diskette for the personal computer version of MARKSTRAT. Each team can use the diskette included in this manual to interact with the game administrator. Decisions are entered and results are received by the means of this diskette. In addition to providing an easy means of communication, the software checks for inconsistent decisions at the time of data entry. Consequently, all mechanical errors and basic checks such as expenditures being within the limit of the allocated budget are greatly reduced. Instructions on the usage of this part of the MARKSTRAT software are included at the end of this manual.

The original development of the MARKSTRAT simulation was a three-year project conducted by the authors at the European Institute of Business Administration (INSEAD) and at the European Center for Continuing Education (CEDEP) in Fontainebleau.

Since then the authors have benefitted from the support of their respective institutions, Jean-Claude Larréché from INSEAD and Hubert Gatignon from The Wharton School, University of Pennsylvania. Part of MARKSTRAT2 was written while Hubert Gatignon was Visiting Professor at the EIASM (Brussels) and at the FUCAM (Belgium).

Since 1984 the rights to the MARKSTRAT software and trademark have been transferred to STRAT*X, a company specializing in strategic training software and services. STRAT*X is now responsible for the licensing of the simulation on a worldwide scale. STRAT*X has redesigned the MARKSTRAT software for use on microcomputers. It is committed to continuously improve the simulation, provide related products, and support the implementation of MARKSTRAT management development programs.

Over the years, the MARKSTRAT simulation has benefited from the comments of Professors Gert Assmus at Dartmouth College, Harper W. Boyd, Jr. at the University of Arkansas, Thomas C. Kinnear at the University of Michigan, Reza Moinpour at the University of Washington, David B. Montgomery at Stanford University, Victor Cook and Edward C. Strong at Tulane University, Barton A. Weitz at the University of Florida, Marian Burke at Duke University and Reinhard Angelmar, Philippe Naert, Christian Pinson, Vikas Tibrewala, and David Weinstein at INSEAD. Business executives and students all around the world have provided constructive feedback on successive versions of the simulation. Sharon Klammer at General Electric has been the first adopter of the microcomputer version and has continuously been an enthusiastic supporter of the MARKSTRAT simulation. At STRAT*X, Laurent Bonnier, Dominique Garval, Scott Imperatore, Nic Simon, Mark Spelman, and James Thorne have contributed to improving the simulation based on their extensive experience with in-company executive training programs. Finally, the programming of this version of the MARKSTRAT simulation has been entirely realized by STRAT*X under the leadership of Gérard Rincent. To all of them we would like to express our gratitude.

J. C. Larréché & H. Gatignon

ORGANIZATION OF
THE MARKSTRAT MANUAL

CHAPTER 1

Why a Simulation?

In the MARKSTRAT simulation, a team of individuals form a company that they will manage. This company faces a competitive environment in which four other firms operate similarly. The management of each firm is especially concerned with the company marketing strategy. Therefore, long term strategic issues involving product design, distribution, pricing, advertising and sales force strategies are the basis of each firm's actions. These decisions are made under uncertainty as to the market conditions, including competitors' moves.

Given the complexity of strategic decisions in marketing, this simulation offers a unique learning experience which cannot be gained by traditional, static educational material.

THE PURPOSE OF A SIMULATION

In general, the purpose of a simulation is to test alternative actions without incurring the cost or the risk of implementing them in real settings. The use of a simulation requires a model that is a simplified representation of reality. Although models can be expressed in several forms (such as physical, graphical, or verbal), they are most frequently represented by mathematical relations. The structure of the model, the mathematical equations used, and the values of its parameters are defined from data relevant to the situation being modeled.

The huge number of variables interacting in a social or business situation cannot all be included in a model (even when they can be defined) because it would be impractical and technically difficult to attempt to do so. The art of modeling, therefore, lies in the selection of only the most important variables in a given process and in the definition of their relationships. The resulting model can, then, be programmed and run on a computer to economically test alternative actions and to answer "what if" types of questions.

There has been extensive development of simulation models in marketing. They are, by definition, incomplete representations of reality and cannot incorporate unexpected competitive actions or drastic changes in the environment. They are, however, empirically based, and good models have high enough predictive validity that a satisfactory plan, tested on a simulation model, may be implemented with success in the real situation.

PEDAGOGICAL GAMES

Pedagogical games are a particular type of simulation for which the main objective is to learn and to practice concepts, techniques, and decision-making processes. Pedagogical games have been developed for such diverse areas of application as political science, economics, history, psychology, sociology, and business. The simulation model used in a business game represents a business situation in such a way that the *learning* of concepts, techniques and decision-making processes can be transposed onto real business situations. Games, however, as opposed to the decision-making simulation models used in companies, are not based on specific empirical data. They usually simulate a fictitious industry and use synthetic data, so that the *numerical results* obtained in the process of playing the game cannot be transposed to real life situations.

In a typical business game, several companies are in competition in a given industry, and each company is managed by a group of students. Each group makes decisions about various aspects of their company's management for a given period of "simulated time," which may run from one month to one year. When all groups have independently made their decisions, they are entered in a computer-based simulation model. The results of each company are returned to the corresponding group. Often information may be purchased, including information on competing companies. The game is, thus, played over several simulated periods in which each team tries to maximize its objectives (for instance, sales, market share, or profits). The objectives are, of course, achieved much more systematically and successfully by considering and applying concepts previously developed in lectures.

In participating in a pedagogical game, one is immediately immersed in a dynamic competitive situation. Many months of activity are simulated in a short time, and rapid feedback is obtained on all decisions. Learning in the new situation takes place through trial and error and through the acquisition of additional information. The behavior of competitors also affects results and must, accordingly, be taken into account. Finally, one must cooperate with the other members of the "management" team.

A simulation in the form of a business game is a pedagogical device wherein learning takes place in a stimulating competitive environment. Compared to the more traditional case study approach, a simulation provides a more dynamic situation within which actions are to be tested and modified. Compared to practice in a real business situation, a game satisfactorily reproduces the main aspects of reality while providing faster feedback at lower cost and lower risk.

_____ **THE MARKSTRAT SIMULATION**

MARKSTRAT is a training simulation and, as such, has the following characteristics:

1. It is a simplification of reality. The computerized model used in MARKSTRAT contains a set of relationships that simulate real business phenomena, particularly strategic marketing phenomena. However, in order to maximize its pedagogical effectiveness, it includes only the main elements of those phenomena.

2. It represents a specific business environment: the MARKSTRAT world. This environment possesses its own characteristics in terms of products, market sizes, distribution channels, etc. Accordingly, decisions should be based solely on information gathered in MARKSTRAT and not on data obtained from existing markets or products, which would not be compatible with the situations modeled in MARKSTRAT.

3. It provides a realistic learning setting. In MARKSTRAT, it is possible to test various propositions gathered through prior business education or practice. The experience gained during the course of the simulation can then be transferred to real business situations.*

MARKSTRAT is, however, different in several respects from other business games that you may know. It has been designed primarily to apply and test marketing _strategy_ concepts. Because of the availability of essential strategically relevant information, MARKSTRAT provides an opportunity to experience the marketing strategy development process. Students have available to them all the information necessary to perform a strategic marketing analysis using tools that they are acquiring in accompanying lectures and readings or tools that they have acquired previously. The result of that strategic analysis is a thorough evaluation of the various possible strategic alternatives. Here again the various strategy evaluation approaches, such as portfolio analysis or empirically based methods, can be applied.

MARKSTRAT goes beyond strategy formulation, as the strategic plan needs to be implemented through decisions at the tactical level. The implementation of the marketing plan is in itself a challenge typically not provided by other more traditional pedagogical methods. In particular, the ability to assess the success or failure of marketing implementation over time is an important benefit of MARKSTRAT.

Specifically, MARKSTRAT focuses on the various marketing functions of the firm and on the elements of the environment that have the greatest impact on these functions. Particular emphasis is placed on the main elements of marketing strategy: segmentation and positioning. Other strategic analyses that should be performed to assess strategic opportunities and

_____

*In recent years, a number of research studies have been performed in university and business corporations on the MARKSTRAT simulation. For an example of such studies, see the December 1987 issue of the _Journal of Business Research_, edited by Professor Victor J. Cook and entirely devoted to the MARKSTRAT simulation.

evaluate alternative strategies are (1) competitive analysis leading to defensive or offensive strategies, (2) analysis of the dynamics of productivity as markets evolve, and (3) environmental analysis. The decisions concerning the allocation of resources across products/markets are enhanced by product/market portfolio analysis. Marketing mix allocation is made more effective by evaluating individual marketing variables and their synergies. Product, distribution, price, advertising and salesforce policy are considered as the means of implementing an overall marketing strategy that is formulated at the corporate level.

This strategy emphasis is supported by the length of the simulated periods, which are of one year's duration. The simulation is usually run over six to ten periods, which provides the longer time horizons necessary for adequately testing marketing strategies. Other functions of the firm (such as finance, production, and R&D) intervene only as support for or constraints upon the firm's marketing strategy.

The MARKSTRAT simulation also incorporates a large number of market research studies, which may be purchased by the competing companies to assist in decision making. In addition to classical studies (such as consumer surveys, consumer panels, distribution panels, and market forecasts), MARKSTRAT makes available more sophisticated information (such as perceptual maps, salesforce experiments, and advertising experiments).

THE MARKSTRAT MANUAL

The general setting of MARKSTRAT is presented in Chapter 2, "The MARKSTRAT World." Chapter 3 presents the information which can be obtained via market research. Chapter 4 describes in detail how to operate one of the MARKSTRAT companies, how to report decisions, and how to interpret yearly results. Finally, Chapters 5 through 9 introduce strategic concepts in marketing and discuss how they are integrated in MARKSTRAT. Chapter 5 discusses segmentation and positioning strategies and illustrates several examples of segmentation strategies that can be used in MARKSTRAT. The interface between marketing and research and development is discussed in Chapter 6. In that chapter, we cover issues of how to communicate with the R&D department and we present strategic concepts involving new product development. Chapter 7 introduces concepts of competitive strategies. We discuss how to assess the competition in a given market, and the implications of various strategies in different competitive environments are illustrated with vivid examples from MARKSTRAT simulations. Chapter 8 covers the decisions about what market(s) and what product(s) the firm should put its resources into. This chapter integrates many of the marketing strategic issues examined in previous chapters from the perspective of the portfolio of markets/products of the firm. Chapter 9 deals more specifically with functional strategies. Each element of the marketing mix is examined and methodologies for decision making are presented. This last chapter also presents an integrated perspective of the main effects contained in the MARKSTRAT simulation.

In each of these chapters, many examples of situations are given in the context of the competitors' strategies. These examples enhance the experiences gained in using MARKSTRAT because participants can better expect and predict certain types of competitive behaviors. Consequently, a more thorough examination of the competitive environment and a better understanding of market behavior is achieved. This manual is the only text which presents sets of marketing strategy principles in the same environment. Typically, each principle is illustrated by analyzing different industries with different characteristics, which are determinants of behavior according to the principles. By using a simulation that can reproduce different market conditions depending on competitive behavior, a better understanding of the principles are achieved because the comparison across competitive behaviors is easier, given that everything else is constant. As a result, this manual can be used as a reference for an inventory of marketing strategy principles.

The manual does not need to be read in its entirety before starting the MARKSTRAT game. In fact, only the first four chapters are essential to start making decisions for the first period. Chapters 5 and 6 can then be read before making the next decisions. The last chapters can be used as the game progresses to enhance marketing strategy decision making.

FINAL CONSIDERATIONS

After you read chapters one through four, you will be ready to participate in the MARKSTRAT simulation. You certainly will not yet have assimilated all the information contained in these chapters, and the main purpose of the first decisions will be to familiarize yourself with the MARKSTRAT world and the mechanics of the simulation. At the beginning of the simulation exercise, you will be assigned to a firm, and you will receive the company report of your firm for period 0. You will notice that each firm markets two brands. You are able, from the company report information and the information in this manual, to evaluate the relative market strength of your firm compared to your competition. Even though you might have a fair amount of information, there are still many uncertainties that will decrease when *you* make the decisions and *your competitors* make their moves. Consequently, you should not take inconsiderate risks for your first decision.

For your first decision, you should concentrate on the management of your two existing brands and your sales force. In the process of reaching your decisions for that first period, you should analyze the actions of your firm's previous management team. It is not wise at this stage to drastically change their advertising, pricing, salesforce, and production policies since you probably cannot yet make a sound decision about the direction and the degree of the change. On the other hand, you may consider purchasing Market Research Studies, which will be made available for your next set of decisions.

During the first sets of decisions, it is essential that you rapidly develop good working relationships in your group. It is important that each member of your group should be involved in the discussion of all issues and should develop a grasp of the total situation. Therefore, it is important to avoid the natural tendency for each member to concentrate in his or her area of expertise. Later in the simulation—when everybody will have a common understanding of the strategic issues and the management of the firm will become more complex in terms of the number of brands, the R&D interface, the market developments, and the intensity of competition—some specific problem areas can be delegated to individuals. In this way, the group should learn to work efficiently, and each of its members should benefit equally from the MARKSTRAT experience.

In previous administrations of the MARKSTRAT simulation, it has also been found that you will gain more from the learning experience by paying particular attention to the following advice:

- **Emphasis on strategic issues.** Concentrate your efforts on strategic issues and long-term planning. The simulation purposely does not consider short-term activities, such as promotions or the design of advertising research studies. In addition, some adjustments are automatically performed within a simulated period to relieve the burden of some operational problems, such as production planning.

- **Importance of analysis.** Before making decisions, be sure that you understand the behavior of the market. Do not jump to the first explanation, or conclusion, that you may have reached when faced with a problem: it may be incomplete. Be careful that at various points in the simulation, as the warning about railroad crossings has it: "one train may hide another one." The detailed analysis of Market Research Studies, of your own situation and of past competitive behavior should help you reach more robust decisions.

- **Group time allocation.** Make sure that you allocate your discussion time sensibly between problem areas. You will be under pressure to submit your decisions by a given deadline, and you should avoid making decisions hastily in the last minutes available. Do not waste time on discussion of a $100,000 issue if it will force you to rush through other decisions where millions are at stake.

- **Administrative errors.** Your team will have to bear the consequences of administrative errors made in filling out the Decision Form or in inputting your decisions using the MARKSTRAT software. These errors cannot be corrected retroactively. In particular, be careful to specify your decisions in the specified units and to save your decisions when using the MARKSTRAT software.

- **Artificial accuracy.** Avoid artificial accuracy in quantifying your decisions. All of your decisions should be in rounded numbers. For instance, a specified price of $546.15 will certainly not have an impact much different than a price of $546.00. This artificial accuracy may only give you a feeling of false confidence or may draw your attention too much toward the numbers themselves, while the main issues are in the strategic options that lie behind the numbers.

- ■ *Role of the administrator.* The MARKSTRAT administrator does not manipulate the simulation parameters in the course of the game. The MARKSTRAT simulation has been designed to automatically generate environmental changes. The markets will evolve mainly according to the actions taken by the competing firms. There will, thus, be no interference by the administrator in favor of or against any firm, and you should feel entirely responsible for your firm's performance.

In the final analysis, even though extensive marketing information is available to you that will allow you to systematically analyze market situations, you will soon realize that your judgment will have to play an important role in making your decisions. As in most real cases, there is no single specific solution to any of the problems that you will encounter. There are, however, alternatives that will clearly appear inferior after good analysis of the situation. There are other alternatives that will appear satisfactory but for which the relative merits depend mainly on the uncertainties of competitive actions. You will have, in this case, to use your judgment of competitive behavior and to make choices under uncertainty. Over a series of decisions, sound analysis and good judgment will inevitably bear fruit.

We hope that participating in the MARKSTRAT simulation will give you a better understanding of marketing strategy concepts, and that you will enjoy this learning experience. We wish you success in the management of your firm.

CHAPTER 1 SUMMARY

Effective Pedagogical Simulations

- are a simplification of reality
- represent a specific business environment.
- provide a realistic and dynamic learning setting.

MARKSTRAT's *Main Characteristics Are:*

- It is designed to illustrate marketing *strategy* concepts.
- Each simulated period corresponds to one year.
- The objectives of the firm are long term.
- Marketing acts as a profit center.
- Firms operate in a competitive environment.
- Marketing strategy is designed around basic segmentation and positioning concepts.
- Marketing mix decisions are secondary to strategic decisions.

CHAPTER 2

The MARKSTRAT World

The MARKSTRAT simulation does not claim to accurately represent a particular industry or market. It relates to an artificial community of approximately 250 million inhabitants whose monetary unit is the MMU (MARKSTRAT Monetary Unit, symbolized by $). This MARKSTRAT world behaves globally like most markets, and all general marketing principles accumulated either through experience or from marketing textbooks are relevant. However, MARKSTRAT, like any specific country, market or industry, also has its own peculiarities. It is, thus, important both to read carefully the description of the MARKSTRAT world that follows and to interpret the information you will receive in the course of the simulation concerning the peculiarities of the products you are about to manage and the environment in which you are to operate.

THE INDUSTRY

The MARKSTRAT world consists of five competing companies that manufacture and market a consumer durable good comparable to an electronic entertainment product. Each firm is managed by a team. At the beginning, each firm markets two brands but can modify or withdraw existing brands and introduce new ones as the simulation evolves. In any year, a company may commercialize up to five brands altogether. Each firm may start from a different initial situation in terms of market shares, consumer awareness levels, and distribution coverage of the brands. The marketing strategy of each firm should be adapted to its peculiar situation within the industry. For the same reason, the performance of the different companies over the successive periods of the simulation cannot be compared in absolute terms; but, more appropriately, with respect to their initial situation. In spite of these differences in the characteristics of the firms, no one has a systematic advantage over the other firms. Each company has an equal opportunity to develop an appropriate strategy, which, although different for each competitor, will lead to successful performance.

9

ORGANIZATION OF THE FIRM

In each of the five firms, the marketing department is considered to be a profit center, responsible for the design and implementation of marketing strategy as well as for marketing operations. In this privileged situation, the marketing department is responsible for the overall orientation of the company to its markets, and it must interact with other departments of the firm. In each period, it must request a certain level of production for each of its brands from the production department. The quantities requested and produced are charged to the marketing department at an internal transfer price corresponding to the production cost and including profit margin for the production department which also operates as a profit center. The marketing department is also responsible for inventory holding costs incurred from over-production. In a similar fashion, the marketing department may ask the R&D department to work on specific projects, in which case it bears the expenditures involved within its budget.

The performance of the marketing department as a profit center is appraised as the *net marketing contribution* represented in Figure 2.1. This *net marketing contribution* is defined as total revenues from sales, minus: cost of goods sold (based on transfer prices), inventory holding costs, R&D, advertising, sales force, and market research expenditures. Inventory holding costs

Figure 2.1: The Marketing Department as a Profit Center

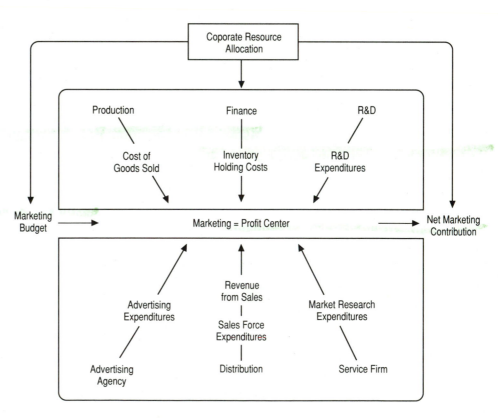

are taken out of the net marketing contribution because the quantity to be produced—and therefore the level of inventory—is seen in MARKSTRAT as a marketing strategic decision. Marketing managers must make a tradeoff between the likelihood and amount of lost sales versus the risk of incurring additional costs due to holding inventory.

The marketing department is given a budget for the following period to cover R&D, advertising, sales force, and market research expenditures. The budget shows the funds available to spend in the next year. If total spending exceeds the allocated budget for a period, expenses will be automatically cut, starting with advertising expenditures. This allocated budget is automatically assigned, partly based upon the net marketing contribution in the preceding period, but firms may also sometimes negotiate changes with the administrator, on the basis of a well-defined marketing plan. Although the budget allocated to the marketing department is linked to the success of the department in terms of net marketing contribution, the relationship between the budget and the net marketing contribution is not linear. The percentage of the net marketing contribution allocated back to the budget decreases when the net marketing contribution increases so that resources can be allocated to other businesses of the company under a different management organization.

A minimum budget is always provided in case of insufficient performance. Because of the resource allocation decision rule, a firm might be given a much larger budget than would be really needed to maximize the firm's performance. In such a situation, the firm should certainly not automatically spend its entire allocated budget. Theoretically, the firm should only spend an additional MMU if the return is at least equal to the MMU spent. Note, however, that if the entire allocated budget is not spent in the current period's move, the leftover is not entirely added to next year's budget. The MMUs that are not spent will increase the firm's net marketing contribution (or at least would not be an expense deducted from revenues). Consequently, the budget for the following period would be higher than if the entire budget had been spent without increasing net marketing contribution by an at least equal amount.

The marketing departments in MARKSTRAT have a considerable influence upon the general strategy of their firms. They can give directives to other departments, such as production and R&D, but they are responsible for the inefficiencies that may result. They are not concerned with other activities of the firm such as credit management, capital investments, financial reporting, purchasing, or plant management. These services are performed by other departments, also acting as profit centers. For instance, increases in production capacity are made by the production and finance departments, according to the requirements of the marketing department. The net marketing contribution is used at the corporate level to cover these activities, as well as fixed costs, financial charges, and profits. As far as the marketing department is concerned, the net marketing contribution only represents a measure of performance, while its yearly budget represents available funds that can be used freely to attain self-assigned objectives. Consequently, MARKSTRAT companies should develop strategies that take into consideration the cash flow over time associated with such strategies. Growth strategies that involve large resources and only a long term pay back might be infeasible because of the decreased budget that would follow in the short term.

Because of this organizational structure within the firm, some agreements have been made between the various departments regarding their interactions and internal profit computations. A particularly important agreement has been made between the marketing and the production departments concerning two issues: the magnitude of possible adjustments of production schedules and transfer pricing.

The requested production level is automatically adjusted during a given year according to the potential sales that the brand could obtain during that year. These adjustments are, however, limited to plus or minus 20%. Beyond that level, the production department organization would be overly affected by the disruption of drastic shifts.

The marketing and production departments have agreed to transfer units of products at a transfer price according to the following rules:

1. Transfer prices benefit from the experience gained in production costs.

2. Only the units sold are charged to the marketing department.

3. Although in case of over-production the transfer price benefits from the total accumulated production experience, the finance department charges inventory holding costs. The surplus will be transferred during succeeding years at the current transfer cost, which is subject to inflation.

4. The base transfer price agreed upon by the production, R&D, and marketing departments deals with the average unit cost for a 100,000 unit batch. When a smaller first batch is produced, fixed costs have to be allocated to fewer units. Consequently, the actual transfer price, in constant MMU's, will be higher than the base cost until accumulated production reaches 100,000 units.

5. The transfer price increases with inflation.

MARKET STRUCTURE AND ITS ENVIRONMENT _____

The MARKSTRAT market has grown consistently over the last twenty years. After several significant technological breakthroughs, the products have increasingly appealed to a wider audience, and the market has recently achieved an even greater rate of growth. It is now a well structured market with five principal competitors and established channels of distribution. Over the years, the firms have acquired an understanding of consumer behavior, industry practices, and characteristics of the environment similar to the information presented in this manual.

Products_____

The product currently available in the MARKSTRAT market is called the "Sonite," a consumer durable good comparable to an electronic entertainment product. It is relatively sophisticated technically but, in contrast with what has occurred in the last twenty years, no major basic technological changes are expected in the future. Sonite brands are differentiated mainly in terms of six physical characteristics, and only these principal characteristics will be considered in the course of the simulation. They are:

1. Weight (Kg)
2. Design (index)
3. Volume (dm^3)
4. Maximum frequency (1000 hz)
5. Power (W)
6. Cost ($)

All these characteristics can be measured for a given Sonite, either by standard measurement instruments or by well-defined procedures. The level of accuracy considered is in integer numbers of the specified units. The cost characteristic of a given Sonite represents the average unit cost on its first production run, assuming a production batch of 100,000 units.

Each firm currently distributes two brands. The ten Sonite brands, which are available at the start of the simulation, and their characteristics are listed in Table 2.1. It is easy to recognize the origin of the brands from their names. Each brand name is made up of four characters, and the first letter is "S" for Sonite. The second letter of the brand name identifies the company in the following way, "A" for company 1, "E" for company 2, "I" for company 3, "O" for company 4 and "U" for company 5. The last two characters are letters or numbers selected by each firm to generate different brand names. It is, for instance, easy to recognize that brands "SIRO" and "SIBI" in Table 2.1 belong to company 3.

It is generally thought that the MARKSTRAT firms will modify their brands and introduce new ones in the coming years in order to better meet the needs

Table 2.1: Physical Characteristics of Brands Commercialized at the Start of the Simulation

Brand Name	Physical Characteristics					
	Weight (kg)	Design (index)	Volume (dm^3)	Maximum Frequency (1000 Hz)	Power (W)	Unit Cost ($)
SAMA	10	8	30	25	10	100
SALT	12	9	37	25	30	125
SEMI	17	7	50	30	80	160
SELF	15	5	60	40	90	200
SIRO	10	3	50	20	10	50
SIBI	11	8	35	25	20	100
SOLD	17	7	50	30	70	165
SONO	10	3	70	20	90	180
SUSI	10	3	50	25	20	70
SULI	15	6	40	20	70	175

of the market segments. These changes will represent variations on the six main characteristics described above. Brand improvements and new brand introductions naturally depend upon the willingness and ability of the firms to launch R&D projects. All new Sonite brand names should follow the conventions previously described, namely: the first letter should be "S," the second letter should identify the company, and the last two letters can be freely selected as long as all brands have different names. The selected name has no influence on the market response to the brand.

More recently, there has been talk in the industry about a completely new product, the "Vodite." The idea for the product comes from a basic technological breakthrough made in the space industry under government contracts. The MARKSTRAT industry is certainly the most likely to manufacture and distribute the Vodite because of its technological and marketing expertise.

Although the scientific bases are known and available, substantial R&D efforts are required for the development of a Vodite brand. From preliminary information available, its main physical characteristics would be:

1. Autonomy (m)
2. Maximum frequency (1000 Hz)
3. Diameter (mm)
4. Design (index)
5. Weight (g)
6. Cost ($)

The Vodites would satisfy an entirely different need than that of the Sonites, and there would be no interaction between the two types of products at the sales level. They could be distributed, however, through the same channels, although the appropriateness of each channel differ for the Sonite and the Vodite markets. If a Vodite brand is developed and launched, the reaction of the market to this new product, the rate of adoption, and the equilibrium level of sales would remain entirely unknown at the present time, although development of the Vodite market may be similar to the historical development of the Sonite markets. Vodite brand names follow the same convention as the Sonite brand names, except that the first letter should be a "V," for Vodite.

Each MARKSTRAT firm can market a maximum of *five* brands per year. These five brands can be either Sonites or Vodites, so that a company could, for example, have 3 Sonites and 2 Vodites or 5 Vodites and no Sonites. The number of brands marketed varies over time as a function of the strategy of the firm and according to their R&D activity. MARKSTRAT companies should at least market one brand. It is not allowed for a firm to disappear completely from the market, even during only a limited period. The minimum allocation rule for the budget guarantees the survival of the business because the market opportunities are worth the investment from the corporate management perspective.

Consumers

The target markets in MARKSTRAT are households and individuals over 18 years of age. The opinion of experts, confirmed by several studies undertaken by the firms, is that one can distinguish five segments with different characteristics and significantly different purchasing behavior.

- *Segment 1: The Buffs.* Persons who are enthusiastic and very knowledgeable about the products. They are primarily concerned with quality and technical features.

- *Segment 2: The Singles.* Persons who live alone. Although they are less technically competent than the Buffs, they demand good performance from a product that they may use more than the average consumer.

- *Segment 3: The Professionals.* Persons who have a higher level of education and high incomes. They tend to be more independent in their occupation and to engage in many social activities. Their purchase of the product is partially motivated by social status needs.

- *Segment 4: The High Earners.* Persons who have high incomes but do not possess the higher level of education or occupational independence of the individuals in Segment 3.

- *Segment 5: Others.* Persons who do not belong to the above groups. This segment represents the largest proportion of the population. However, in the past it has known a significantly lower penetration of Sonite products than other segments.

The order of these groups corresponds to the priority of attribution of an individual to a segment. For instance, the persons in the "High Earners" group are those who have high incomes but do not qualify as members of the three preceding segments: "The Buffs," "The Singles," or "The Professionals." The resulting segmentation is thus mutually exclusive and exhaustive.

"The Buffs" currently constitute the largest segment in terms of Sonite unit sales, and represent 30% of the market. They are followed by Segment 3 (20%), Segment 5 (19%), Segment 4 (16%) and Segment 2 (15%). It is, however, common knowledge in the industry that the five segments are at different stages in their development. This is partly reflected by different growth rates. While the overall Sonite market has enjoyed an average annual growth rate of 35% over the last three years, Segment 1 has been stagnant, Segments 2 and 5 have grown at 25–30%, and Segments 3 and 4 have grown at twice that rate.

Distribution

All products may be directly distributed through three different channels:

- *Channel 1: Specialty stores.* They make an important proportion of their sales from Sonite-type products and provide specialized services.

- *Channel 2: Electric appliances stores.* They carry Sonites only as an addition to their main electric appliances lines.
- *Channel 3: Department stores.* They handle a wide variety of merchandise and may have a department carrying the Sonites.

It is estimated that there are 3,000 specialty stores, 35,000 electric appliances stores, and 4,000 department stores in MARKSTRAT, all of which can potentially distribute the Sonite and Vodite brands. Each of the channels differs in terms of penetration of Sonite brands and attraction of different types of clientele. Differences exist between the margins obtained by the stores in each of the three types of channels, and they are mainly due to differences in the service level and the quantities purchased. These margins, expressed as a percentage of the recommended retail price, are approximately constant across brands for a given channel type. Their values are 40%, 35% and 40% respectively for channels 1, 2 and 3. These margins represent an equilibrium that has evolved over the years, and neither distributors nor Sonite manufacturers have any motivation to disrupt the equilibrium.

Pricing

The MARKSTRAT companies provide recommended retail prices for each of their brands. These prices are generally respected by all channels except for promotions. These promotions are of short duration and represent only a small proportion of sales. The average retail price in any one year is, thus, close to the recommended retail price. Over the last three years, prices of Sonites have increased regularly and have followed inflation.

If the recommended retail price becomes very high compared to the unit cost of a given product, consumers and consumer unions may react negatively. The same negative reactions may also occur in the case of a sudden high price increase or decrease. In these cases, the recommended retail price will be automatically adjusted to limit the negative effect of these adverse reactions.

Sales Force

The sales force of a MARKSTRAT company is organized around markets, not products. Specifically, the sales force is organized by channel type in order to better meet the specific needs of the channels. Each salesperson carries the company's entire line of brands. A company may naturally change the size of its sales force at a cost representing training, firing, and salary expenses. These costs are provided each period in the newsletter section of the output. Changes in the number of salespersons are expected to have an influence on the distribution coverage of the company's brands. In addition, each year a company may modify the allocation of its sales force to specific distribution channels at no significant cost, since the sales force is knowledgeable about all the products of the company.

Advertising

The practice in the MARKSTRAT industry is to advertise specific brands, rather than the company name. Therefore, even though a firm might market several brands, possibly including several brands to the same segment, these brands do not benefit from the company's identity and image. Advertising is primarily used as a communication device to get consumers to know about the brand name and about the characteristics of the brand. Brand awareness is therefore directly related to advertising expenditures. In the absence of advertising, consumers tend to forget about the brand. In addition, when a brand is withdrawn from the market, even for as short a time as one year, consumers' awareness of the brand drops to become insignificant, due to the competitive nature of the market. The persuasive power of advertising is also substantial in MARKSTRAT, as advertising is used to position and reposition brands so that consumers are convinced that the product offerings correspond to their needs and wants. When a product is modified but marketed under an existing brand name, the new characteristics will be perceived almost immediately because of the high involvement in the purchase decision.

Advertising can also develop primary demand for a whole product class. As potential consumers know more about the existence of products and their characteristics, they are likely to give a greater consideration to the purchase of these products. The size and growth rate of specific market segments and of the total market is consequently influenced by the total amount of advertising spent in the industry. Furthermore, advertising may have an impact on the motivation of the sales force, on the decisions made by distributors, and creates barriers to entry against competitors.

Advertising expenditures for Sonite brands are of two types. The bulk of the advertising budget is devoted to the purchase of media space and time. The rest of the budget is spent on advertising research. On average, the MARKSTRAT companies spend six percent of their sales on advertising. In general, five percent of their advertising budgets are allocated to advertising research, performed by their advertising agencies and concerned mainly with creative work, media selection studies, and copy testing. They may try to change the allocation between media expenses and research expenditures in an effort to improve advertising effectiveness. The greater the advertising research, the more likely it is that the message will be communicated to the right audience with minimum communication miscomprehension.

Market Research

Fifteen studies can be purchased by the MARKSTRAT companies from outside marketing service firms. They are described in the next chapter. When a firm orders a study, the study is performed during the simulated period and the results are made available at the end of the period, providing information for the next period's decisions. The costs of these studies are provided every period in the newsletter section of the company report.

Research and Development

The marketing department of a firm may request the R&D department to develop specific projects in order to improve existing brands or to introduce new ones. Although a complete coverage of R&D strategies and procedures is included in Chapter 5, we now give an overview in order to appreciate the full extent of control that the marketing department has to develop and implement a marketing strategy.

A request to the R&D department consists of a project name, a budget, and values of the physical characteristics that the researched product should possess. The names of R&D projects are made up of five characters. The first character is always the letter "P," for Project. The second character identifies the type of product being developed: the letter "S" for Sonites, and "V" for Vodites. The last three characters can be selected by the firms to identify specific projects. "PSETA" and "PVOTE" are, for instance, valid names for projects concerning a Sonite and a Vodite, respectively. There is no need for the name of an R&D project to correspond to the name of an existing or planned brand, and all current and past R&D projects must have different names. More specifically, an R&D project name is structured as follows:

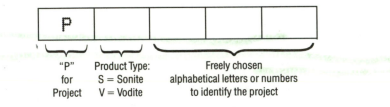

An example of an R&D project code name could be:

P	V	O	X	3

This R&D project is a Vodite. The last three characters identify the project according to the desires of the team. Consequently the letter following the product type (letter "O" in this example) does not mean that this project is developed by firm 4 as it is the case for brand names. In the past, each firm has successfully completed two R&D projects corresponding to the brands commercialized in Period 0. Their names are made of the letter "P" followed by the corresponding brand name. For instance, the R&D project corresponding to the existing brand SAMA is called PSAMA.

The budget for a given project represents the investment that marketing is ready to make for the R&D department to try to develop that specified product in the coming year. It will, naturally, be subtracted from the marketing budget. This is natural because the marketing department uses the R&D

output to implement their strategy. Therefore the performance of the marketing department depends on the effective use they make of the R&D department. Note that the R&D effort does not concern fundamental research but instead involves specific products.

In specifying the physical characteristics of the desired product, the marketing department should, obviously, evaluate the market opportunities for any alternative offerings. The values of the physical characteristics for R&D projects should be prescribed in integer numbers of the relevant units, and the feasible ranges for each of the first five dimensions are indicated in Table 2.2. The sixth characteristic, both for Sonites and Vodites, represents the transfer price corresponding to the average unit production cost of manufacturing the first 100,000 units of the new product. It does not have any upper limit, and its lowest level depends on the first five physical characteristics of the product.

Therefore, the R&D department has to develop a product with given physical characteristics, but it also has to find the raw materials and the technology that will allow production at the specified cost. Obviously, the more stringent this economic constraint, the more difficult it will be for the R&D department to develop the corresponding product. If the product is eventually marketed, the original (i.e. launching period) transfer price will be determined on the basis of this cost which is associated with the completed project. If the team waits several periods to launch the brand, it can be expected that the basic cost increases with inflation. Post introduction, the cost may vary as a function of the quantities produced due to the experience curve effects, as well as due to inflation.

Up to four projects may be simultaneously given to the R&D department during a given year. If a project is not successfully completed in one year and is unlikely to be completed in the future (because the product specifications are too stringent), this will be indicated in a message from the R&D department. If a project is not successfully completed for lack of funds, the R&D

Table 2.2: Feasible Ranges of the Physical Characteristic Values for
Sonites and Vodites

	Physical Characteristics	Feasible Range
Sonites:	Weight (*Kg*)	10–20
	Design (*index*)	3–10
	Volume (*dm³*)	20–100
	Maximum Frequency (1000 *Hz*)	5–50
	Power (*W*)	5–100
Vodites:	Autonomy (*m*)	5–100
	Maximum Frequency (1000 *Hz*)	5–20
	Diameter (*mm*)	10–100
	Design (*index*)	3–10
	Weight (*g*)	10–100

department will supply an estimate of the additional budget that it would need to bring the project to completion. If an R&D project is not successfully completed in one year, it may be pursued in the following periods. The likelihood of the success of a project depends primarily on the *cumulative* expenditures incurred and the degree of similarity between the desired product and the firm's existing ones. The R&D department is also a profit center and, thus, will use all funds provided to it in the course of the year.

Conceptually, R&D project expenses include not only the expense required to develop the prototype but also the research and evaluation necessary to find components and potential suppliers, make technical evaluations, provide production line planning, and produce prototypes. In period 1, a successful R&D project for a Sonite would generally cost between $100,000 and $1,000,000, depending upon the degree of difference between the desired characteristics of the project and the characteristics of existing products. In order to develop a Vodite, industry experts believe that it will be necessary to spend a minimum of $2,000,000 on R&D.

Productivity Gains

The manufacturing costs of the products tend to decrease as a result of productivity improvements gained through experience, although this effect may be offset by inflation. Greater changes in manufacturing costs may be obtained by undertaking appropriate R&D projects, for which it is necessary to change only the cost characteristics of an otherwise unmodified product. Both of these effects are conceptually represented in Figure 2.2.

Figure 2.2: Productivity Gains

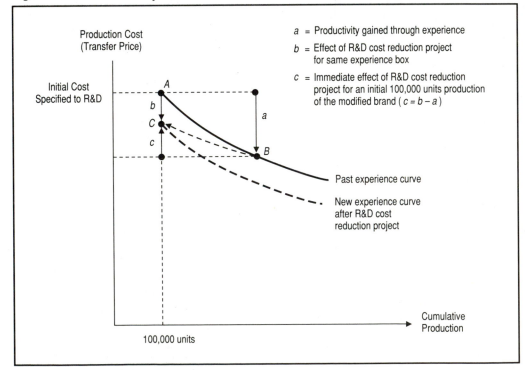

Point *A* on Figure 2.2 indicates the previous cost on transfer price for the initial batch of 100,000 units. As cumulative production increases, resulting productivity gains cause transfer price to decrease to point *B*. The curve on which points *A* and *B* are found is the original experience curve for that product. The R&D department might, however, complete a project with identical product characteristics, but at a lower cost. This is represented on Figure 2.2 by point *C*, which reflects an initial transfer price lower than the original cost (point *A*) but higher than the unit cost previously obtained through experience effects (point *B*). In this example:

- the unit cost has been reduced through experience (*a* is negative)
- the R&D project has reduced the unit cost for the same experience basis (*b* is negative)
- but the immediate effect of the R&D project for an initial 100,000 units of production is to increase unit cost (*c* is positive).

The experience curve corresponding to the new R&D project is represented on Figure 2.2 by the dotted line. The actual transfer price for the product resulting from the new R&D project will be somewhere on that curve, according to the production schedule of that product.

Economic Environment

The MARKSTRAT industry operates in an economy that is currently subject to an average inflation rate of two percent. This inflation affects the manufacturing, advertising, sales force, R&D, and market research costs of the companies. In addition, price controls may be imposed on all brands by the government in order to try to reduce inflation if it was reaching much higher levels in the future.

The Gross National Product (GNP) provides management with information about trends in the entire MARKSTRAT economy. In the recent past, the entire economy has been growing at a rate of four percent.

CHAPTER 2 SUMMARY

Management Responsibilities of a MARKSTRAT Team

1. Advertising	4. Market research
2. R&D	5. Production forecast
3. Sales force	6. Inventory

Budget

The budget is spent on:

- Advertising expenditures
- R&D expenditures
- Sales force expenditures
- Market research expenditures.

Gross Marketing Contribution

Retail sales (unit retail price × units sold)

minus   Distribution margins

---

equals   Company revenues

minus   Cost of goods sold (unit transfer price × units sold)

minus   Inventory holding cost

minus   Advertising expenditures

---

equals   **Gross Marketing Contribution**

Net Marketing Contribution

Gross marketing contribution

minus   R&D expenditures

minus   Sales force expenditures

minus   Market research expenditures

minus   Exceptional cost or profit

---

equals   **Net Marketing Contribution**

Brand Naming Conventions

Brand names consist of four characters

- The first letter is "S" for a Sonite product
  and "V" for a Vodite product.

- The second letter identifies the company.

- The last two characters may be freely chosen by a company
  when launching a new brand, as long as all brands
  commercialized by the company have different names.

The brand name should have the following structure:

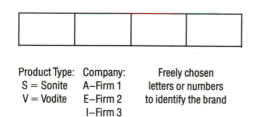

Product Type:	Company:	Freely chosen
S = Sonite	A–Firm 1	letters or numbers
V = Vodite	E–Firm 2	to identify the brand
	I–Firm 3	
	O–Firm 4	
	U–Firm 5	

and should look like the following example:

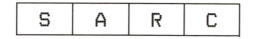

SARC is a Sonite produced and marketed by Firm 1.

R&D Project Name Conventions

- R&D project names consist of five characters.

- The first characters is always the letter "P."

- The second character identifies the type of product that is being searched for ("S" for Sonites and "V" for Vodites).

- The last three characters may be freely chosen by a company, as long as its projects (current and past) have different names.

- The R&D project name bears no relationship to the commercialized brand name. Thus, "PSUZZ" may be used to improve existing brand "SULI" or to create a new brand "SUZI."

An R&D project name should be structured as follows:

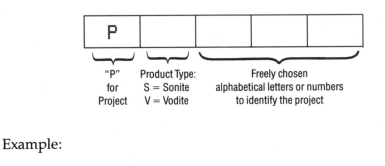

Example:

| P | V | O | X | 3 |

This R&D project is a Vodite. The last three characters identify the project and consequently the letter following the product type (letter "O" in this example) does not mean that this project is developed by firm 4.

General Background Information

1. Average annual inflation rate over last 3 years: 2%

2. Average annual price increases in the Sonite market over the last 3 years: 3%

3. Percent of Sonite unit sales by segment in the last year:

   Segment 1:   30%
   Segment 2:   15%
   Segment 3:   20%
   Segment 4:   16%
   Segment 5:   19%

4. Average annual increases of Sonite unit sales over the last 3 years:

   Segment 1:   5%
   Segment 2:   25%
   Segment 3:   50%
   Segment 4:   60%
   Segment 5:   30%

   Total: 35%

5. Total number of potential distributors of Sonites or Vodites:

   Channel 1:   3,000
   Channel 2:   35,000
   Channel 3:   4,000

6. Average margins of distributors as a percentage of retail price:

   Channel 1:   40%
   Channel 2:   35%
   Channel 3:   40%

7. Average advertising expenditures as a percentage of sales over the last 3 years: 6%

8. Average advertising research expenditures as a percentage of total advertising expenditures over the last 3 years: 5%

CHAPTER 3

Market Research

The design and implementation of a marketing strategy requires gathering information on the competitive market situation. This may be achieved in several complementary ways. The first way is by carefully reading and assimilating the information contained in this manual, particularly the first four chapters. The second way is by trying out various marketing actions in succession and learning through experience. This corresponds to experimentation in the market place to improve knowledge and to reduce uncertainties. The third way is by buying market research information from outside marketing service firms.

Given some knowledge of market structure and behavior, a marketing strategy may be designed in terms of repositioning existing brands and positioning new brands with respect to the five consumer segments. Actions must then be taken at the level of the marketing mix elements, R&D projects, and production planning in order to implement the marketing strategy selected. It should be clear from this three-stage process—gathering of information, design of a marketing strategy and implementation of this strategy—that the management of the marketing mix should not be an end in itself but only a means of achieving a strategy. However, in order to understand consumers' behavior, to measure the impact of marketing mix actions and to evaluate past actions, market research should provide management with information dealing with different types of analysis done at various stages of the decision process, whether at the strategy design or at the strategy implementation stage.

The companies in the MARKSTRAT industry may buy up to 15 different market research studies in one annual period. The costs of these studies in the initial period are indicated in Table 3.1, and they are expected to increase with inflation in the course of the simulation. The results from these studies have different levels of errors attached to them, according to the methodology used and the sample size. The reports for each of the fifteen studies concern the information at the end of the period for which the decisions have been made, i. e., at the end of the simulated period.

Table 3.1: Initial Cost of Market Research Studies

		Initial Cost
Study 1:	Consumer Survey, Sonite Market	$ 60,000
Study 2:	Consumer Panel, Sonite Market	$100,000
Study 3:	Distribution Panel, Sonite Market	$ 60,000
Study 4:	Semantic Scales, Sonite Market	$ 10,000
Study 5:	Perceptual Mapping of Brands Similarities and Preferences, Sonite Market	$ 35,000
Study 6:	Market Forecast, Sonite Market	$ 20,000
Study 7:	Consumer Survey, Vodite Market	$ 40,000
Study 8:	Consumer Panel, Vodite Market	$ 70,000
Study 9:	Distribution Panel, Vodite Market	$ 50,000
Study 10:	Semantic Scales, Vodite Market	$ 10,000
Study 11:	Market Forecast, Vodite Market	$ 20,000
Study 12:	Competitive Advertising Estimates	$ 30,000
Study 13:	Competitive Sales Force Estimates	$ 15,000
Study 14:	Sales Force Experiment	$ 24,000
Study 15:	Advertising Experiment	$ 35,000

STUDY 1: CONSUMER SURVEY—SONITE MARKET

Study 1 (Figure 3.1) is a survey questionnaire administered to 3000 individuals at the end of the simulated period. It gives brand awareness, shopping habit data and purchase intentions for each of the five segments. The brand awareness figures represent the proportion of individuals who have unaided recall of a brand's name, and they are given for each Sonite brand currently on the market. The shopping habit data give, for each channel type, the proportion of individuals who would choose this channel when shopping for a Sonite. The purchase intentions figures represent the proportion of individuals who would select a brand as their first choice if they were buying one within a year. These figures are also represented for each Sonite brand currently on the market.

STUDY 2: CONSUMER PANEL—SONITE MARKET

This study (an example of which is shown in Figure 3.2) provides the market shares, based on units sold, for each Sonite brand in each channel. The industry sales in each segment are also indicated, in thousands of units (KU).

Figure 3.1

```
--------------          STUDY 1 : CONSUMER SURVEY - SONITE MARKET   ----------------

                            BRAND AWARENESS (%)

    SAMA :  61.3   SALT :  54.4   SALU :  30.2   SARO :  24.3
    SEMI :  73.4   SELO :  38.5
    SIRO :  66.0   SIBI :  72.9
    SOLD :  78.6   SONO :  62.2   SOFT :  66.1
    SUSI :  60.3   SULI :  76.6   SULZ :  54.6   SUSZ :  28.7   SUS2 :  28.7


                            SHOPPING HABITS (%)

            Segment    Channel 1    Channel 2    Channel 3    Total
               1          58.6         12.7         28.7       100.0
               2          43.2         21.6         35.2       100.0
               3           7.4         61.5         31.1       100.0
               4          21.9         47.8         30.4       100.0
               5          14.8         30.8         54.4       100.0


                          PURCHASE INTENTIONS (%)


    Brand   Segment 1   Segment 2   Segment 3   Segment 4   Segment 5   Total
    SAMA       1.3         2.6         0.1         1.2        28.3        7.3
    SALT       1.9         1.1         0.4        12.6         1.5        4.3
    SALU       2.4         0.4         1.6         1.2         0.4        1.0
    SARO       5.1         1.7         0.3         3.1         1.0        1.9
    SEMI       8.2         1.4        32.9         7.3         1.3        9.0
    SELO       0.7         1.0         0.1         0.5         4.3        1.4
    SIRO       1.1         1.7         0.1         1.0        12.9        3.6
    SIBI       5.8         2.0         1.3        40.5         2.0       12.9
    SOLD       6.9         1.3        59.6         7.5         1.3       13.7
    SONO       9.0         1.4         0.6         1.7         1.2        1.8
    SOFT       4.1        60.1         0.2         1.6        10.8       18.6
    SUSI       1.0         1.5         0.1         0.7         6.6        2.1
    SULI      39.4         3.3         1.6         7.3         2.2        6.3
    SULZ      10.9         2.2         1.2        12.6         1.7        5.4
    SUSZ       0.5         1.0         0.0         0.4        19.8        4.7
    SUS2       1.7        17.5         0.1         0.8         4.8        5.9
```

Figure 3.2

```
--------------          STUDY 2 : CONSUMER PANEL - SONITE MARKET   ----------------

                    MARKET SHARES BASED ON UNIT SALES (%)

    Brand   Segment 1   Segment 2   Segment 3   Segment 4   Segment 5   Total

    SAMA       1.0         2.5         0.1         1.1        28.8        6.8
    SALT       1.3         1.0         0.3        10.9         1.5        4.0
    SALU       1.6         0.4         1.4         1.0         0.4        0.9
    SARO       3.5         1.5         0.2         2.6         1.0        1.6
    SEMI       8.2         1.6        28.7         6.9         1.3        9.8
    SELO       0.6         1.1         0.0         0.4         4.0        1.2
    SIRO       1.0         1.9         0.1         1.0        13.7        3.5
    SIBI       5.8         2.4         1.3        41.8         2.2       14.4
    SOLD       8.6         1.9        64.4         8.7         1.6       18.6
    SONO       8.7         1.6         0.5         1.5         1.1        1.7
    SOFT       3.1        54.3         0.1         1.1         8.4       12.9
    SUSI       1.0         1.8         0.1         0.7         7.3        2.1
    SULI      41.9         4.3         1.6         7.7         2.6        7.0
    SULZ      11.7         2.9         1.2        13.6         2.0        6.2
    SUSZ       0.5         1.1         0.0         0.3        19.2        4.3
    SUS2       1.5        19.7         0.1         0.7         4.8        5.1


                            MARKET SIZE

    Sales KU    193         545         638         854         570       2800
```

STUDY 3: DISTRIBUTION PANEL—SONITE MARKET —————————————————

This study (Figure 3.3) provides the market shares, based on units sold, for each Sonite brand in each channel. The industry sales in each distribution channel are also indicated, in thousands of units.

Figure 3.3

```
--------------    STUDY 3 : DISTRIBUTION PANEL - SONITE MARKET    --------------

                      MARKET SHARES BASED ON UNIT SALES (%)

           Brand    Channel 1      Channel 2      Channel 3      Total

           SAMA       3.0            5.8            10.5          6.8
           SALT       2.8            5.0             3.8          4.0
           SALU       0.2            1.3             1.0          0.9
           SARO       1.5            1.6             1.6          1.6
           SEMI       7.1           12.4             9.1          9.8
           SELO       1.5            0.6             1.6          1.2
           SIRO       2.1            2.9             5.2          3.5
           SIBI      13.2           17.2            12.3         14.4
           SOLD       9.5           26.4            17.4         18.6
           SONO       3.6            0.7             1.4          1.7
           SOFT      21.5            8.7            10.7         12.9
           SUSI       1.8            1.6             2.9          2.1
           SULI      13.2            3.5             5.9          7.0
           SULZ       8.6            5.3             5.3          6.2
           SUSZ       2.3            3.4             6.7          4.3
           SUS2       8.1            3.6             4.6          5.1


                                  MARKET SIZE

           Sales KU    749           1032            1020         2800
```

STUDY 4: SEMANTIC SCALES—SONITE MARKET —————————————————

This study (illustrated in Figure 3.4) is based on a semantic differential questionnaire administered to a sample of 600 individuals. Several semantic scales, such as the following one corresponding to the physical characteristics of Sonites, were presented to the respondents:

Lightest   1   2   3   4   5   6   7   Heaviest

Respondents were asked to rate each brand according to the way they perceived the brand on that characteristic. They were also asked to indicate their most preferred (or "ideal") point on each scale, and to rank the scales in terms of their importance to them. The reported results are the mean scale values for each brand and for the segment ideal points on the three scales which were ranked as most important.

Figure 3.4

```
--------------    STUDY 4  : SEMANTIC SCALES - SONITE MARKET   --------------

        * The three semantic differential scales perceived as
          most important are : 1) PRICE, 2) POWER, 3) DESIGN

        * High ratings correspond to high price, high power and
          high design.

        IDEAL VALUES        PRICE       POWER       DESIGN

        Segment  1          4.45        6.22        5.26
        Segment  2          2.92        4.76        5.72
        Segment  3          5.94        5.66        5.18
        Segment  4          5.30        4.02        5.68
        Segment  5          2.04        3.30        5.71

    BRAND PERCEPTION

            SAMA            2.63        2.33        6.16
            SALT            5.24        2.99        6.27
            SALU            6.16        6.32        6.31
            SARO            4.33        4.68        5.12
            SEMI            5.91        5.53        5.57
            SELO            2.30        2.59        2.32
            SIRO            2.59        1.83        5.98
            SIBI            5.24        4.28        6.34
            SOLD            6.06        5.58        5.48
            SONO            4.80        6.52        2.58
            SOFT            2.52        4.46        4.88
            SUSI            1.94        2.61        2.49
            SULI            4.77        5.51        4.95
            SULZ            4.93        4.86        5.60
            SUSZ            1.90        2.57        5.03
            SUS2            2.71        4.29        6.39
```

STUDY 5: PERCEPTUAL MAPPING OF BRANDS SIMILARITIES AND PREFERENCES—SONITE MARKET

This study provides a joint space configuration obtained by non-metric multi-dimensional scaling (Figure 3.5. Note that the printout has been slightly rearranged to print the material on a single page in this manual; a facsimile printout appears in Appendix A, pp. 164–65.) It relies on similarity and preference data on the complete set of Sonite brands obtained through interviews with a sample of 200 individuals. It first gives the minimum number of dimensions that were sufficient to provide a good fit to the data, as well as a likely interpretation of the axes based on semantic scale responses. The study then provides the graphical representation in this space of the perceptual positioning of the Sonite brands and the segments' ideal points. An example of such a perceptual map and further details on its interpretation will be given in chapter 5.

Figure 3.5

```
---  STUDY 5 :  PERCEPTUAL MAPPING OF BRANDS SIMILARITIES AND PREFERENCES  ---

          * Study realized on a random sample of 200 individuals.
          * No significant differences in perceptions have been
            observed between segments.
          * Statistically significant results on two dimensions.
          * Based on semantic scales, the most satisfactory inter-
            pretation of the axes is :
            Axis 1 : PERCEIVED PRICE
            Axis 2 : PERCEIVED POWER


                     COORDINATES                              COORDINATES
     IDEAL POINTS    Axis 1   Axis 2        BRAND PERCEPTION  Axis 1   Axis 2

     Segment  1        2.6     13.9          A : SAMA          -9.6    -10.3
     Segment  2       -8.1      4.2          B : SALT           9.2     -5.8
     Segment  3       12.7     10.3          C : SALU          13.8     15.6
     Segment  4        8.3      0.0          D : SARO           2.4      5.2
     Segment  5      -13.9     -4.9          E : SEMI          12.1     10.2
                                             F : SELO         -12.1     -9.6
                                             G : SIRO         -10.3    -14.7
                                             H : SIBI           8.6      2.8
                                             3 : SOLD          13.4      9.8
                                             I : SONO           4.5     15.9
                                             J : SOFT          -9.4      4.0
                                             * : SUSI         -13.8    -10.0
                                             K : SULI           4.7      9.5
                                             L : SULZ           5.9      6.2
                                             * : SUSZ         -14.0    -10.1
                                             M : SUS2          -8.3      2.9
```

```
                        HIGH PERCEIVED POWER

                               +                          IDEAL POINTS
                               !                          1 : SEG. 1
                               !                          2 : SEG. 2
                               !   I        C             3 : SEG. 3
                               +                          4 : SEG. 4
                               !  1                       5 : SEG. 5
                               !
                               !
                               !                          FIRM 1
                               +   K      E3              A : SAMA
                               !                          B : SALT
                               !                          C : SALU
                               !   L                      D : SARO
                               + D
                       J2      !
                       M       !     H                    FIRM 2
                               !                          E : SEMI
    LOW                        !                  HIGH    F : SELO
    PERCEIVED +----+----+----+----+----+--4-+----+----+  PERCEIVED
    PRICE                      !                  PRICE
                               !
                               !                          FIRM 3
                               !                          G : SIRO
                       5       +                          H : SIBI
                               !     B
                               !
                               !                          FIRM 4
                    * F A      +                          3 : SOLD
                               !                          I : SONO
                               !                          J : SOFT
                               !
                       G       +
                               !                          FIRM 5
                               !                          * : SUSI
                               +                          K : SULI
                                                          L : SULZ
                        LOW PERCEIVED POWER                * : SUSZ
                                                          M : SUS2
```

STUDY 6: MARKET FORECAST—SONITE MARKET

This study provides an estimate of the expected Sonite market size (in thousands of units) and market growth (in percentage), for the next period and gives a breakdown by segment (Figure 3.6). It relies on market extrapolation and assumes stable marketing action on the part of the competitors.

Figure 3.6

```
--------------    STUDY 6  : MARKET FORECAST - SONITE MARKET    ----------------


                             EXPECTED                 VOLUME
                           MARKET  SIZE           GROWTH  RATE
                           NEXT   PERIOD          NEXT   PERIOD
                             (KU)                     (%)

              Segment 1        184                   -5.0
              Segment 2        763                   40.0
              Segment 3        702                   10.0
              Segment 4       1110                   30.0
              Segment 5        684                   20.0

                Total        3443                    22.9
```

STUDY 7: CONSUMER SURVEY—VODITE MARKET

The description of this study for the Vodite market corresponds to the description of Study 1 for the Sonite market.

STUDY 8: CONSUMER PANEL—VODITE MARKET

The description of this study for the Vodite market corresponds to the description of Study 2 for the Sonite market.

STUDY 9: DISTRIBUTION PANEL—VODITE MARKET

The description of this study for the Vodite market corresponds to the description of Study 3 for the Sonite market.

STUDY 10: SEMANTIC SCALES—VODITE MARKET

The description of this study for the Vodite market corresponds to the description of Study 4 for the Sonite market.

STUDY 11: MARKET FORECAST—VODITE MARKET _____

The description of this study for the Vodite market corresponds to the description of Study 6 for the Sonite market.

These last five studies (7 to 11) are the counterparts for Vodites of Studies 1 to 6, with the exception of the Perceptual Mapping of Brands Similarities and Preferences, which is not available for the Vodite market. It is indeed expected that the number of Vodite brands will not be high enough in the course of the simulation to make a non-metric multidimensional scaling study feasible. When no Vodite brand is available on the market, study 10 will only give the perception of ideal values on the semantic scales for each segment, and would be used primarily for R&D planning. In the same situation, study 11 will give a forecast of the potential market for the next period if a Vodite brand were introduced, based on declared purchase intentions obtained from a sample of individuals. It should be noted that in this case the market forecast obviously does not rely on history and tends to be less accurate and generally somewhat optimistic. Studies 7, 8 and 9 are irrelevant when no Vodite brand is available on the market, and their request would result in wasting the corresponding expenditures.

STUDY 12: COMPETITIVE ADVERTISING ESTIMATES _____

Estimates of the total advertising expenditures for each competitive brand are provided by an advertising research firm (an example is provided in Figure 3.7). These estimates are also given for the brands of the company requesting the study as a reference to control for estimation errors.

Figure 3.7

```
--------------    STUDY 12 : COMPETITIVE ADVERTISING ESTIMATES   --------------

                        ALL NUMBERS IN THOUSAND $

   SAMA: 1684     SALT: 1265     SALU: 1669     SARO: 1366

   SEMI: 3172     VEVO: 3755     SELO: 4621     VEVU: 7254

   SIRO: 3328     SIBI: 3551

   SOLD: 6264     SONO: 0        SOFT: 6777     VOLT: 3493

   SUSI: 1535     SULI: 2852     SULZ: 2526     SUSZ: 2839     SUS2: 3021
```

_____ STUDY 13: COMPETITIVE SALES FORCE ESTIMATES

Estimates of the sales force sizes of competitive companies and their breakdown by channel of distribution are obtained from a specialized market
research firm (see Figure 3.8 for an example). The same estimates are also
given for the sales force of the company requesting the study as a reference
to control for estimation errors.

Figure 3.8

```
-------------     STUDY 13 : COMPETITIVE SALES FORCE ESTIMATES   --------------

                        NUMBER OF SALESPERSONS

                  Channel 1     Channel 2     Channel 3      Total

        Firm  1       13            42            37           92
        Firm  2       29            26            33           88
        Firm  3       24            36            42          102
        Firm  4       41            36            40          117
        Firm  5       32            47            43          122
```

_____ STUDY 14: SALES FORCE EXPERIMENT

A sales force experiment is set up in regional test markets by increasing the
number of salespersons per channel. The experimental results (an illustration
is given in Figure 3.9) are then used to estimate the number of distributors
and market share each of the company's brands would have had in the entire
market if the sales force directed to each channel had been increased as
indicated.

Figure 3.9

```
-------------------     STUDY 14 : SALES FORCE EXPERIMENT   --------------------

        EXPECTED RESULTS IF SALES FORCE INCREASED BY 10 IN EACH CHANNEL

                                Channel 1     Channel 2     Channel 3

        SAMA   Number of distr.    970          14979          1595
               Market share (%)    4.3             6.4           11.8

        SALT   Number of distr.    969          14959          1593
               Market share (%)    4.3             5.5            4.2

        SALU   Number of distr.    993          15323          1632
               Market share (%)    0.7             1.4            1.1

        SARO   Number of distr.    991          15289          1628
               Market share (%)    2.6             1.7            1.8
```

STUDY 15: ADVERTISING EXPERIMENT

An advertising experiment is conducted, increasing the advertising budget in selected regional test markets. The experimental results are used to project what the level of brand awareness and the share of market would have been for each of the company brands by segment if the advertising budget had been increased for that brand by the indicated percentage over the actual expenditures. As can be seen in the example in Figure 3.10, the estimates are also broken down by segment. The experiment tests only size of budget, not changes in other parts of advertising strategy such as advertising research or positioning objectives.

Figure 3.10

```
--------------------   STUDY 15 : ADVERTISING EXPERIMENT   --------------------


   EXPECTED RESULTS IF ADVERTISING BUDGET INCREASED BY 20 % FOR GIVEN BRAND

                                               SEGMENT
                                     1      2      3      4      5     Total
       SAMA     Awareness %        62.9   61.9   60.8   62.2   62.4   61.9
                Market share %      1.0    2.6    0.1    1.1   30.1    7.1

       SALT     Awareness %        56.3   56.3   54.6   54.5   55.9   55.3
                Market share %      1.4    1.0    0.3   11.2    1.5    4.1

       SALU     Awareness %        31.7   32.3   31.9   32.0   32.9   32.2
                Market share %      1.7    0.4    1.5    1.1    0.4    0.9

       SARO     Awareness %        26.8   25.9   26.1   26.1   26.5   26.2
                Market share %      3.7    1.6    0.2    2.8    1.1    1.7
```

CHAPTER 3 SUMMARY

Market Research Studies for the Sonite Market

Study 1: Consumer Survey: Sonite Market

- Brand awareness for each brand

- Shopping habits by channel for each segment

- Purchase intentions by segment for each brand

Study 2: Consumer Panel: Sonite Market

- Market shares based on unit sales, total and by segment, for each brand

- Industry sales by segment

Study 3: Distribution Panel: Sonite Market

- Market shares based on unit sales, total and by channel, for each brand

- Industry sales by channel

Study 4: Semantic Scales: Sonite Market

- Ideal values of each segment on three most important product characteristics

- Average evaluation of each brand on three most important product characteristics

Study 5: Perceptual Mapping of Brand Similarities and Preferences: Sonite Market

- Ideal values of each segment on two-dimensional perceptual space

- Average position of each brand on two-dimensional perceptual space

Study 6: Market Forecast: Sonite Market

- Expected market size by segment for next period

- Expected market growth by segment for next period

Market Research Studies for the Vodite Market

Study 7: Consumer Survey: Vodite Market

- See Study 1

Study 8: Consumer Panel: Vodite Market

- See Study 2

Study 9: Distribution Panel: Vodite Market

- See Study 3

Study 10: Semantic Scales: Vodite Market

- See Study 4

Study 11: Market Forecast: Vodite Market

- See Study 6

General Market Research Studies

Study 12: Competitive Advertising Estimates

- Estimated total advertising expenditures of each brand

Study 13: Competitive Sales Force Estimates

- Estimated number of salespersons by channel for each firm

Study 14: Sales Force Experiment

- Estimated number of distributors and expected market share by channel for each brand if sales force had been increased in each channel

Study 15: Advertising Experiment

- Expected awareness and market share by segment for each brand if the advertising budget had been increased

Operating Instructions

Each of the five MARKSTRAT companies is managed by a team, and these five teams can organize themselves as they wish. It is, however, desirable that each team elect a chairperson or a coordinator to facilitate communications with the administrator. For each period, a deadline will be set for each team to submit a Decision Form on a microcomputer diskette representing their company's decisions for the current simulated year. The decisions for the five companies will then be used as inputs to the MARKSTRAT computerized simulation model. Each team will then receive the Company Report, a document containing their results for the period, general market information, and the market research studies they requested. The MARKSTRAT simulation will usually be played over six to ten simulated years.

To help the teams in the management of their companies, two additional documents are provided: the Budgeting Form and the Planning Form. The Budgeting Form is designed to facilitate computation of the estimated net marketing contribution in the next period, and the planning form is designed to appraise a company's performance over time. At the beginning of the simulation, each team uses the Company Report corresponding to Period 0 operations, which represents their company's initial situation. Thus, their first decisions deal with Period 1. These four documents (the Company Report, the Decision Form, the Budgeting Form, and the Planning Form) will now be described in detail.

THE COMPANY REPORT

The printout of a sample Company Report for Firm 1 in Period 5 of a simulation is presented in the following pages. It is given for descriptive purposes only, and the specific figures indicated should not be used in making decisions. The data have nothing to do with your run of MARKSTRAT . The Company Report is made of seven parts that are discussed in turn: Decisions, Messages, General Results, Marketing Results, Research and Development, Cumulative Results, and the Newsletter.

Figure 4.1

```
┌─────────────────────────────────────────────────────────────────────┐
│                                                                       │
│  -----------------------  D E C I S I O N S  -----------------------  │
│                                                                       │
│                       PRODUCT   MANAGEMENT                            │
│            Name of   Product.  Advert.  Advert.    Rec.      Percept. obj. │
│    Brand   R & D     planning  budget   research   retail   (-20 to 20 or 99) │
│    names   project   KU        K$       %          price $  Axis 1   Axis 2 │
│                                                                       │
│    SAMA    PSALM     350       2000     10         270      -11      -5   │
│    SALT              150       1500     6          380      99       0    │
│    SALU    PSALA     150       2000     10         480      99       13   │
│    SARO              140       1700     10         345      99       5    │
│                                                                       │
│                            SALES FORCE                               │
│            Distribution channels         One     Two     Three       │
│            Number of salespersons        13      40      35          │
│                                                                       │
│                      RESEARCH AND DEVELOPMENT                        │
│       Project   Expend-    --------- Physical characteristics --------- │
│       name      itures     1      2      3      4      5      6       │
│                                                                       │
│       PSARA     100        13     6      50     25     65     130     │
│                                                                       │
│                      MARKET RESEARCH STUDIES                        │
│          1   2   3   4   5   6   7   8   9   10  11  12  13  14  15   │
│          Y   Y   Y   Y   Y   Y   N   N   N   N   N   Y   Y   Y   Y    │
│                                                                       │
│       Administrator's change in exceptional cost or profit :    0 K$  │
│       Administrator's change in budget .................. :     0 K$  │
│                                                                       │
│  ------------------------  M E S S A G E S  ------------------------  │
│                                                                       │
│                  MESSAGE(S) FROM THE SIMULATION                      │
│                                                                       │
│   * YOU DID NOT RESPECT YOUR BUDGET CONSTRAINT.                      │
│   YOUR BUDGET HAS BEEN REDUCED ON : - ADVERTISING                   │
│                                                                       │
│   * OBSOLETE INVENTORIES FOR DELETED OR MODIFIED BRAND(S) CHARGED AS AN │
│   EXCEPTIONAL COST AT 10 % OF TRANSFER COST.                        │
│                                                                       │
└─────────────────────────────────────────────────────────────────────┘
```

Decisions

This section is a recapitulation of the decisions made by the firm. Its purpose is only to provide you with a record of the data which was actually used by the simulation. In the example in Figure 4.1, Firm 1 has four brands, two of which have just been modified with new R&D projects. One can also observe that it has a total of 88 salespersons, it pursues one R&D project and has bought all market research studies relevant to the Sonite market. Any changes agreed between the administrator and the firm in exceptional cost or profit or in the budget are also indicated at the end of this section.

Messages

Messages are sometimes given to the companies, mainly when corrective action has been taken. For instance, if the assigned budget has been exceeded, arbitrary cuts in marketing expenditures will be indicated*; if the price of a

---

*In such a case, advertising expenditures are cut first. If this is insufficient to maintain the expenditures within the budget, sales force expenditures are cut next, then R&D projects budgets are cut and finally marketing research studies would be deleted one by one until the expenses are within the budget limit.

given brand is increased to such a level that market response is very unfavorable, downward adjustments are automatically performed and reported; if a firm tries to use an R&D project that has not yet been completed to modify an existing brand or to launch a new one, it will be reported that the brand introduction or modification could not be implemented. Figure 4.1 gives an example of a message due to exceeding the budget. It also shows a case where obsolete inventories had to be disposed of for deleted or modified brands resulting in an exceptional cost. Each message is explained in the manual in chapters corresponding to the issue. Note that many of these messages would occur only if the team fails to consider the warning messages provided by the software for entering the decisions. Indeed, the software has been designed to catch errors of that nature. Some actions are clearly incompatible with the current status of the firm operations. In these cases, the software for entering the team decisions will not accept such input. However, in other cases, only a warning message will be flashing on the screen of the decision input software. It is advised not to ignore these messages, and to take appropriate action wherever desirable and possible. Other messages sent by the administrator to all firms or to a specific firm may also sometimes be present in this section.

General Results

This section shows the performance of the firm during the simulated period. See Figure 4.2. The gross marketing contribution is computed for each brand as revenues less identifiable brand expenses (that is, cost of goods sold, inventory costs, and advertising expenditures). The average selling price used in the computation of revenues depends on the way brand sales are split among the three distribution channels, since channel margins are different. The unit transfer cost is the price that the marketing department was charged for the units sold.

The marketing department is also charged for the inventory holding costs, because it is responsible for production volume. The inventory is valued at transfer prices and its holding costs are computed as a percentage of its value, according to the rate given in the newsletter at the end of the Company Report for the previous period. If the marketing department wants to drop a brand, any remaining inventory for this brand will be written at a cost of 10% of its transfer price. These costs will appear in the "extraordinary cost" account. When a brand is improved, the same procedure will apply to the inventory of the old product in order to avoid the possibility of having two products with the same brand names simultaneously available on the market. It should be pointed out that this exceptional cost does not affect the budget for the current period.

The expenditures that are not allocated by brands (that is, R&D, Sales Force, and Market Research costs) are then subtracted from gross marketing contribution to give the net marketing contribution. The budget available for the next period is shown at the end of the General Results section. The Advertising, Sales Force, R&D, and Market Research expenditures for the

Figure 4.2

```
------------------  G E N E R A L   R E S U L T S  --------------------


                                SAMA      SALT      SALU      SARO

    Units sold     Units      189627    111617     24497     44087
    Production     Units      280000    120000    120000    112000
    Inventory      Units       90373      8383     95503    139248

    Retail price     $           270       380       480       345
    Av. selling price $         166       236       297       212
    Unit transf. cost $          99        98       177       147

    Revenues        K$        31478     26342      7276      9346
    Cost of goods sold K$    -18773    -10938     -4336     -6481
    Inv. hld. cost  K$         -775       -71     -1465     -1774

    Advertising     K$        -1645     -1234     -1645     -1399

    Gross marketing
      contribution  K$        10290     14122      -181      -314


    Gross marketing contribution .    23917 K$
    Research and development .....     -100 K$
    Sales force .................    -1964 K$
    Market research .............     -440 K$
    Exceptional cost or profit ...   -2798 K$
    Net marketing contribution ...   18614 K$

    Next period budget ..........    8061 K$



------------------  M A R K E T I N G   R E S U L T S  --------------------


    Brands                    SAMA      SALT      SALU      SARO

    Market share  % Units      6.8       4.0       0.9       1.6

    Number of distributors
       Channel 1               634       641       658       662
       Channel 2             13358     13348     13682     13640
       Channel 3              1377      1379      1409      1422
```

next period are to be made within this budget. The authorized budget is a function of the net marketing contribution generated in the previous period. There is, however, a minimum budget level allowing sustained marketing activities even when the net marketing contribution is low or negative. There is also a maximum budget level to avoid excessive marketing spending when the net marketing contribution is very high.

Marketing Results

For each of the company's brands, its market share and the number of distributors carrying the brand in each channel are given. The market share is computed on the basis of units sold. The lower part of Figure 4.2 shows an example of the Marketing Results in the company report.

Research and Development

All R&D projects which the firm has pursued in the current and past periods are listed in this section (Figure 4.3). These projects include those which already existed in the firm at the beginning of the simulation (PSAMA and PSALT in the example). For each R&D project, the following information is given:

- Name
- Availability: YES if the project has been successfully completed and is therefore available to introduce or modify brands, NO otherwise.
- Physical characteristics: the specifications of each project on all six physical characteristics.
- Cumulative expenditures: the total expenditures made on each project up to its completion or to the current period.

In addition, for R&D projects which are not yet successfully completed, this section provides an indication of the additional investment which would be required to complete them. If the requested unit cost (physical characteristic 6) is unrealistically low, the minimum realistic unit cost for this R&D project is also indicated. These messages from the R&D department on additional investment required and minimum realistic unit cost are further explained in Chapter 6 on the Marketing and R&D interface.

Figure 4.3

```
-------------    R E S E A R C H   &   D E V E L O P M E N T   -------------


  Project   Avail.          Physical           Cumul.    Addition.    Minimum
  name                    characteristics       expend.   invest.     realistic
                                                          required     unit cost
                      1    2    3    4    5    6    K$        K$           $

   PSAMA     YES     10    8   30   25   10  115    2000
   PSALT     YES     12    9   37   25   30  144    1500
   PSALU     YES     12    9   37   25   90  249    2200
   PSARO     YES     13    6   50   25   65  184    1550
   PSALM     YES     10    8   30   25   25  130     500
   PVAMA     NO      30   15   50    6   60  108     100       7603         231
   PSALA     YES     12    9   37   25   90  191     900
   PSARA     YES     13    6   50   25   65  134     600
```

Cumulative Results

Cumulative results obtained by the company since the beginning of Period 0 are presented in this section (Figure 4.4). For brands available at the start of the simulation the cumulative results include the results of Period 0. No R&D projects are in progress and no market research studies are available in Period 0.

Figure 4.4

```
----------------- C U M U L A T I V E   R E S U L T S  -------------------

        Results Units Retail
        since   sold  sales    Revenues    CGS      IHC    Advert.     GMC
Brand   period  KU     K$         K$        K$       K$       K$        K$
-----   ------  ----- --------  --------  --------  -----   --------  ---------
SAMA      0     1013   272165    167408    81344     1401    11806     72678
SALT      0      473   186595    115422    51284     1194    11208     51757
SALU      4       46    22252     13725     9320     3109     3645     -2353
SARO      4       85    29443     18049    13353     2738     2899      -929
-----   ------  ----- --------  --------  --------  -----   --------  ---------
TOTAL           1618   510455    314603   155302     8443    29558    121154

Research & development expenditures  (K$) ......................     5850
Sales force expenditures  (K$) ................................     9492
Market research expenditures  (K$) ............................     1598
Exceptional cost or profit  (K$) ..............................     2798
Net marketing contribution  (K$) ..............................    101415
```

Newsletter

The newsletter (Figure 4.5) gives information that would normally be known to the industry at the end of the year. It first indicates the Gross National Product growth rate and inflation rate for the current period as well as the

Figure 4.5

```
----------------------- N E W S L E T T E R  ----------------------------

G N P growth rate this period ............................     4.0 %
G N P growth rate estimation next period .................     4.0 %
Inflation rate this period ...............................     2.7 %
Estimated inflation rate next period .....................     3.4 %
Inventory holding cost per annum (% of transfer cost) ....     8.7 %
Cost of a salesperson next period ........................   23000 $
Cost of firing a salesperson next period .................    5700 $
Cost of training a new salesperson next period ...........    3600 $


        COST OF MARKET RESEARCH STUDIES NEXT PERIOD (K$)

    1 :   70     2 :  117     3 :   70     4 :   12     5 :   41
    6 :   23     7 :   47     8 :   82     9 :   59    10 :   12
   11 :   23    12 :   35    13 :   18    14 :   28    15 :   41


NEW BRANDS OR PRODUCT MODIFICATIONS  INTRODUCED OVER THE LAST PERIOD

         ---- Physical  characteristics ----
Brands    1     2     3     4     5     6    Retail price

 SAMA     10     8    30    25    25   126      270
 SALU     12     9    37    25    90   186      480
 SELO     10     3    50    25    20    84      170
 VEVU     75    10    50     5    40   310      640
 SIRO     10     8    50    20    10    93      250
 VOLT     50    15    50     6    65   362      800
 SUSZ     10     6    50    25    20   103      200
 SUS2     17     9    50    20    50   155      280
```

Figure 4.5 (*continued*)

```
------------------------   N E W S L E T T E R   --------------------------

                        INFORMATION ON SONITE MARKET
                  Unit       Market      Retail       Retail     Market
      Brands     sales  U    share  %U   price  $     sales  K$  share  %$

       SAMA      189627      6.8         270          51199      5.0
       SALT      111617      4.0         380          42414      4.2
       SALU       24497      0.9         480          11759      1.2
       SARO       44087      1.6         345          15210      1.5
       SEMI      273961      9.8         440         120543     11.8
       SELO       34280      1.2         170           5828      0.6
       SIRO       99030      3.5         250          24757      2.4
       SIBI      402388     14.4         420         169003     16.6
       SOLD      521276     18.6         470         245000     24.0
       SONO       47744      1.7         350          16710      1.6
       SOFT      360000     12.9         300         108000     10.6
       SUSI       59843      2.1         170          10173      1.0
       SULI      194882      7.0         350          68209      6.7
       SULZ      173198      6.2         380          65815      6.5
       SUSZ      120000      4.3         200          24000      2.4
       SUS2      144000      5.1         280          40320      4.0

   Total mkt.   2800430    10C.0         364        1018941    100.0


                        INFORMATION ON VODITE MARKET
                  Unit       Market      Retail       Retail     Market
      Brands     sales  U    share  %U   price  $     sales  K$  share  %$

       VEVO       31525     26.6         810          25535     30.7
       VEVU       75888     63.9         640          48568     58.4
       VOLT       11265      9.5         800           9012     10.8

   Total mkt.    118678    100.0         700          83116    100.0
```

corresponding forecasted values for the next period. The new inventory holding, sales force, and market research costs are also given.

If new brands have been introduced on the market during the simulated period, or if existing brands have been modified, the values of their physical characteristics and their recommended retail prices are given. It is easy to recognize the origins of a brand from its name, the first letter indicating the product type (Sonite or Vodite) and the second one identifying the company to which it belongs.

Information is then given on Sonite and Vodite Markets providing for each brand on the market: unit sales, market share based on units, recommended retail price, retail sales in dollars, and market share based on value.

THE DECISION FORM

A sample completed Decision Form is shown in Figure 4.6. It is the Decision Form of Firm 1 in Period 5, which resulted in the Company Report described previously. Although this discussion does not attempt to present an exhaustive list of possible ways of filling up this form, we do provide a general discussion of the type of information typically entered. A complete explanation of the possible entries is given in the context of the problems that the firm

Figure 4.6: Sample Decision Form

MARKSTRAT DECISION FORM

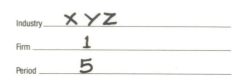

Industry __XYZ__

Firm __1__

Period __5__

PRODUCT MANAGEMENT

Brand Names	Name of R&D Project (if modification or introduction)	Production Planning (thousand units)	Advertising Budget (thousands of $)	Advertising Research (percent)	Recommended Retail Price ($)	Perceptual Objectives (−20 to +20, or 99) Axis 1	Axis 2
SAMA	PSALM	350	2000	10	270	−11	−5
SALT	—	150	1500	6	380	99	0
SALU	PSALA	150	2000	10	480	99	13
SARO	—	140	1700	10	345	99	5

SALES FORCE

Distribution Channels	1	2	3
Number of Salespersons	13	40	35

RESEARCH AND DEVELOPMENT

Project Name	Expenditures (thousands of $)	Physical Characteristics 1	2	3	4	5	6
PSARA	100	13	6	50	25	65	130

MARKET RESEARCH STUDIES

1	2	3	4	5	6	7	8	9	10	11	12	13	14	15
Y	Y	Y	Y	Y	Y	N	N	N	N	N	Y	Y	Y	Y

(For Instructor's Use)	
O	O
ec(−) ep(+)	bd(−) bi(+)

will face. Consequently, the following chapters provide a description of alternative options with a series of examples that are shown on the Decision Form.

The industry code letter, the firm number, and the number of the current period are entered at the top of the form. The industry code letter is used only when several MARKSTRAT simulations are run simultaneously, each with five different teams.

The Decision Form is then divided into four parts dealing with Product Management, Sales Force, R&D, and Market Research Studies. In the Product Management section, there may be up to five brands with their names indicated in the first column, according to the naming conventions previously described in Chapter 2. If a modification is made to the physical characteristics of an existing brand, or if a new brand is introduced, the name of the R&D project that led to the improved or new product is indicated in the second column. If no modification to the brand is made in the current period, the second column is left blank. In the sample Decision Form, the brands SAMA and SALU were modified through the R&D projects PSALM and PSALA respectively, whereas SALT and SARO are non-modified existing brands. In order to be able to modify or to introduce a brand in a given period, it is obviously required that the corresponding R&D project had been successfully completed in a previous period. A project requested from the R&D department is never available for commercialization before the beginning of the following period. The relevant R&D project name should be indicated only in the first period of a modification or of an introduction.

For each brand, the production level request, the advertising budget, the percentage of the advertising budget spent on advertising research, and the recommended retail price are indicated in the units specified at the top of the column. The production planning request is based on your expectations of sales in the coming period. The production department can adjust the quantity requested up to a limit of 20% (plus or minus) without incurring extra costs in order to respond to the real demand. So, if you had requested 100,000 units and demand could have been 130,000, production will be adjusted automatically upward to 120,000. Because of this flexibility in production, 100,000 units would be a good forecast if actual demand were to fall between 80,000 units and 120,000 units.

When trying to reposition a brand with advertising, perceptual objectives are given with numbers that correspond to the two axes of the perceptual map. These numbers should be between +20 and −20, the maximum and minimum coordinates of the axes. If the only data available for giving perceptual objectives come from semantic scales, some adjustments are required. First, the two dimensions that appear to be most important in the semantic scale study are assumed to correspond to axes 1 and 2 of the perceptual map, respectively. Second, the 1 to 7 semantic scales need to be transformed into coordinates from −20 to +20, as indicated in Figure 4.7. These will correspond to objectives in terms of the perceptual map. If no repositioning is desired or cannot be expressed in terms of the perceptual map axes because of lack of data, the number 99 should be entered, as in the case of axis 1 for SALT on the sample Decision Form. These perceptual objectives convey information primarily of a qualitative nature (for example, how much should the lightness of the product be stressed) for the design of the advertising platform and copy, as well as for the selection of media. The numeric representation of these perceptual objectives is used only for communication purposes.

Figure 4.7: Specification of Perceptual Objectives from Semantic Scales Data

The semantic scales are defined on an interval from 1 to 7, while the perceptual objectives are defined in terms of coordinates on the perceptual map and can, thus, take values between −20 and +20:

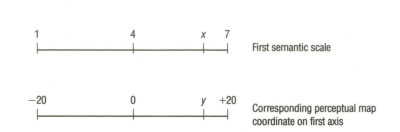

An interval of one unit on the semantic scale may be interpreted as 40/6 or 20/3 units on the axis of the perceptual map.

If only semantic scales data are available, and if value *x* on a semantic scale is set as an objective in the repositioning of a given brand, the corresponding perceptual objective expressed in terms of a coordinate *y* in the perceptual map may be computed with the following formula:

$$y = \frac{20}{3}(x - 4)$$

with *y* as the value to be used as a perceptual objective in filling in the Decision Form. This transformation is obviously crude, but the use of numbers should not hide the intrinsic qualitative nature of perceptual objectives.

Example: If a given brand is to be repositioned towards value 6 on the first semantic scale, the perceptual objective to be entered on the Decision Form for axis 1 is:

$$y = \frac{20}{3}(6 - 4) = 13.3 \text{ rounded to } 13$$

In the next section of the Decision Form, up to four R&D projects may be specified in one period. Names should be given to R&D projects according to the conventions previously described in Chapter 2. There is no need for the name of an R&D project to correspond to the name of an existing or planned brand, although all current and past R&D projects must have different names. On the sample Decision Form, Firm 1 requests one R&D project, PSARA, concerned with a Sonite product. For each project, the amount to be spent in the current period, as well as the values of physical characteristics for the desired products, should be indicated. In particular, the feasible ranges of these desired characteristics for Sonites and Vodites, as indicated in Table 2.2, should be noted.

In the last section, Market Research studies may be requested by specifying a "y" in the corresponding box on the bottom line of the Decision Form. The rectangle in the bottom right hand corner should be left blank for the instructor's use. Finally, the back of the Decision Form should contain any modifications to the standard procedure resulting from a negotiation between the firm and the MARKSTRAT administrator. These modifications may be due to the purchase of additional information, or changes of budgets based on a well defined plan. In addition, fines may be imposed on a firm for delayed decisions, espionage, or inter-firm concerted actions. Each of these modifications may be expressed in terms of an exceptional cost, a budget increase, or a budget decrease. It is essential that this document be agreed upon and signed by the MARKSTRAT administrator and a firm's representative.

THE BUDGETING FORM

The objective of the Budgeting Form represented in Figure 4.8 is to help to systematically specify the company's use of its marketing budget (extreme right-hand column) and estimate the net marketing contribution that may

Figure 4.8: Sample Budgeting Form: Part I

MARKSTRAT BUDGETING FORM—PART I
Financial Information

Industry __XYZ__

Firm __1__

Period __5__

Brand Name	SAMA	SALT	SALU	SARO		
Quantity Sold (units)	279000	123000	153000	232000		
Production (units)	280000	123000	153000	160665		
Inventory (units)	1000	0	0	0		
Retail Price ($)	270	380	480	345		
Average Selling Price ($)	166	238	299	213		
Unit Transfer Cost ($)	99	98	168	141		
Revenues (thousands of $)	46328	29212	45753	49464		
Cost of Goods Sold (thousands of $)	27621	12054	25704	32712		
Inventory Costs (thousands of $)	8	0	0	0		
Advertising (thousands of $)	2000	1500	2000	1700		7200 Advertising
Gross Marketing Contribution (thousands of $)	16699	15658	18049	15052	65458	

R&D (thousands of $) 100   100 R&D

Sales Force (thousands of $) 1964   1964 Sales Force

Market Research (thousands of $) 440   440 Market Research

Exceptional Cost or Profit (thousands of $) 2798

Net Marketing Contribution (thousands of $) 60155

Total Marketing Expenditures (thousands of $) . . . . 9704 Total Marketing Expenditures result from selected actions in the current period. The information contained in the budgeting form corresponds to the information needed to make valid decisions. It has the same structure as the first section of the Company Report and allows checking *a posteriori* for variations between a selected annual plan and the actual outcome. The MARKSTRAT software provides an automatic calculation of the numbers on this form. The crucial estimate in the budgeting process is obviously, the forecasted sales for each brand. The table on Part II of the Budgeting Form (Figure 4.9) should help formulate the production and revenue forecasts. These forecasts imply a thorough evaluation of the expected market share in each segment of each brand, as well as a prediction of the size of the market by segment for the next period. The Budgeting Form (Part II) follows the process necessary to derive the forecasts required in Part I of the Budgeting Form.

One first starts to fill out the current size (in units) of each segment in the Budgeting Form—Part II. The expected growth rate needs to be extrapolated from the history of the segment sales and from the expected behavior of firms

Figure 4.9: Sample Budgeting Form: Part II

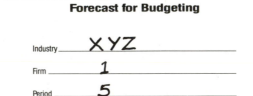

MARKSTRAT BUDGETING FORM—PART II
Forecast for Budgeting

Industry __ XYZ __

Firm __ 1 __

Period __ 5 __

	Total Sonite Market (thousands of units)			Total Vodite Market (thousands of units)			SAMA		SALT		SALU		SARO			
	Current Period	Expected Growth Rate	Forecast Next Period	Current Period	Expected Growth Rate	Forecast Next Period	Market Share	Sales	Market Share	Sales	Market Share	Sales	Market Share	Sales	Market Share	Sales
Segment 1	202	-5%	192				—	—	—	—	30%	58	—	—		
Segment 2	310	40%	433				10%	43	—	—	—	—	20%	87		
Segment 3	574	10%	632				—	—	—	—	15%	95	10%	63		
Segment 4	633	30%	823				—	—	15%	123	—	—	10%	82		
Segment 5	437	20%	524				45%	236	—	—	—	—	—	—		
Aggregate Forecasts	2156	20%	2605				10.7%	279	4.7%	123	5.9%	153	8.9%	232		
Retail Price							270		380		480		345			
Retail Sales							75330		46740		73440		80040			
Average Distributor Margin %							38.5		37.5		37.7		38.2			
Revenues							46328		29212		45753		49464			

in these respective segments. The forecast of the size of each segment for the next period can then easily be made.

The next forecast that needs to be made concerns the market share of each brand in each segment. Given the competitive nature of the market, the anticipated competitive structure and the behavior of these competitors are important determinants of these segment shares.

Once the market share of each brand in each segment has been forecasted, the sales per segment for each brand can be computed and the forecasted sales for each brand is simply the sum of the forecasts across segments. By multiplying the brand sales by the retail price, one obtains easily the forecast of retail sales (in dollars). All these computations are relatively straightforward. The computation of the revenues, and therefore of the average selling price, is slightly more difficult. In computing the average selling price for a brand, one has to take into account the recommended retail price,

Figure 4.10: Sample Planning Form: Part I

MARKSTRAT PLANNING FORM—PART I
General Performance

Industry __XYZ__

Firm __1__

		1	2	3	4	5	6	7	8	9	10
Percentage Growth	Objective					160%	20%	35%	35%	35%	
	Outcome	20%	20%	13%	18%						
Retail Sales (millions of $)	Objective					275	330	445	600	800	
	Outcome	65	78	88	104						
Revenues (millions of $)	Objective					169	200	270	360	480	
	Outcome	40	48	54	64						
Gross Marketing Contribution (millions of $)	Objective					65	85	115	155	200	
	Outcome	16	22	25	23						
Net Marketing Contribution (millions of $)	Objective					60	65	88	120	160	
	Outcome	14	19	20	20						
Sonite Market Share (based on volume)	Objective					30%	30%	30%	30%	30%	
	Outcome	18.4%	16.8%	16%	15.1%						
Sonite Market Share (based on value)	Objective					27%	27%	25%	25%	25%	
	Outcome	15%	13.3%	12.6%	12.7%						
Vodite Market Share (based on unit volume)	Objective							10%	20%	30%	
	Outcome										
Vodite Market Share (based on value)	Objective							8%	16%	25%	
	Outcome										
Total Market Share (based on value)	Objective										
	Outcome	15%	13.3%	12.2%	12.0%	25%	23%	26%	28%	30%	
	Objective										
	Outcome										
	Objective										
	Outcome										

the expected allocation of brand sales between distribution channels, and the margins practiced by each channel.

The average distribution margin is the weighted average of the distribution margins in each channel, where the weights are the proportion of the brand sales in these channels. For example, if a brand has 50% of its sales in channel 1, 20% in channel 2, and 30% in channel 3, the average distributor's margin will be, given that the margins in channels 1 through 3 are respectively 40%, 35%, and 40%:

$$\text{Average margin} = (0.5 \times 40) + (0.2 \times 35) + (0.3 \times 40) = 39\%.$$

The revenues are therefore 61% (100% minus 39%) of the retail sales. These forms are essentially internal to the Marketing Department and are not submitted to the administrator. However, given the importance of the budget in the implementation of the strategy, it is recommended that these forecasts be made each period as accurately as possible.

THE PLANNING FORM

The Planning Forms in Figures 4.10 through 4.13 are designed to formalize quantifiable objectives and to provide a basis for the appraisal of a company's performance over successive simulated years of the MARKSTRAT simulation. The Planning Form—Part I presents a set of performance criteria. Some room

Figure 4.11: Sample Planning Form: Part II

MARKSTRAT PLANNING FORM—PART II
Marketing Expenditures

Industry __XYZ__

Firm __1__

		Periods									
		1	2	3	4	5	6	7	8	9	10
Advertising (millions of $)	Objective					7.2	10	13	13	13	
	Outcome	5.2	4.3	4.5	5.5						
Sales Force (millions of $)	Objective					1.9	3	4	4	4	
	Outcome	1.5	1.5	1.5	1.9						
R&D (millions of $)	Objective					0.1	5	2	2	2	
	Outcome	0	1.0	3.4	1.4						
Market Research (millions of $)	Objective					0.4	0.8	1	1	1	
	Outcome	0.3	0.3	0.3	0.3						
Total Marketing Expenditures (millions of $)	Objective										
	Outcome	7.0	7.1	9.7	9.1	9.7	18.8	20	20	20	

is left in order to specify other items that could also be considered relevant in the evaluation of the firm's performance.

The Planning Form—Part II specifies the four major types of expenditures under the direct control of the Marketing Department. As these expenditures correspond to the realization of the intended implementation of the marketing strategy, an evaluation of their behavior over time can provide

Figure 4.12: Sample Planning Form—Part III

MARKSTRAT PLANNING FORM—PART III
Strategic Analysis Summary

Industry _____ XYZ _____

Firm _____ 1 _____

	Sonite Market	Vodite Market
Competitive Structure • Main Competitors' Advantage	Financial Resources for firms 2, 4 & 5. Strong positions in segments 2 & 3.	Company 2 has first movers' advantage.
• Main Competitors' Weaknesses	Attention of leading firms (2, 4 & 5) diverted to vodite market.	Poor product
• Threats of New Entries	Possibly in segments 4 & 5.	Companies 4 & 5 most likely to enter.
• Mobility Barriers	Distribution	Opportunity due to still low barriers to entry.
Competitive Behavior • Main Competitors' Marketing Intensity	Advertising for firms 4 & 5. Sales force for firm 5.	Advertising
• Competitive Reactions	Price pressures in segments 2 & 5.	Price cut very likely.
Economic and Environmental Dynamics	Inflation threat to margins in low price segments.	Not sensitive to economic situation.
Company Competitive Position Assessment • Strengths	SAMA and SALT in high growth segments 4 & 5.	Late entry will benefit from better technological market knowledge.
• Weaknesses	Repositioning closer to ideal points required for most products.	Need to build strong sales force before vodite entry.
Company Allocation of Resources Assessment (Current/Future) • Portfolio	Invest only in Sonite market in next 2 periods to build strong position before entering vodites.	Investment priority starting in period 6.
• Synergies		Sales Force.
• Risks	Uncertainty in brand repositioning.	

valuable information for appraising the performance of the firm. Figure 4.12 shows an example of the Planning Form—Part III, which summarizes the strategic analysis performed by Firm 1 in order to evaluate their strategic position. The concepts involved in this form are discussed in detail in Chapters 5 through 9, where many strategic situations are described along with the components of marketing strategic analysis. On the Planning Form—Part

Figure 4.13: Sample Planning Form: Part IV

MARKSTRAT PLANNING FORM—PART IV
Main Strategic Options

Industry ___XYZ___

Firm ___1___

Segmentation and positioning _Sonites: cover all segments, specialize on 2,4 and 5 by product improvements, 1 and 3 with same product._

Product and Brand Strategy _Build strength in Sonites first with advertising and sales force. No new products. Develop Vodite position through R & D._

Advertising Strategy _Increase advertising significantly for all Sonite brands and proportionally more for repositioning._

Sales Force and Distribution Strategy _Build sales force to 160 people in next 3 years with current distribution mix (15% channel 1, 45% channel 2, 40% channel 3)._

Research and Development Strategy _Sonites: marginal development for product repositioning. Vodites: major effort with objective to introduce Vodite brand in period 7._

Others _If Sonites repositioning strategy unsuccessful,_
- _reconsolidate the Sonites Portfolio_
- _postpone Vodite entry_
- _exploit opportunity in Sonites market while leading firms shift their attention to Vodites._

IV, the firm should specify the main strategic options on which the formulated plan is based as shown in Figure 4.13. This form should be analyzed and updated each period according to the company's evolution. Although these planning forms are primarily for internal use, they may be requested at any time by the MARKSTRAT administrator in his or her negotiations with the firm.

The successive plans realized in the course of the simulation will help the firm to evaluate and present its activities at the end of the simulation. Since each company starts in a different initial situation, it is not possible to directly compare the results of the five firms. It is, however, interesting to compare their different approaches in light of their specific characteristics and to evaluate their respective successes and failures. These forms offer a basis for comparing the evolution of the firms and for analyzing the elements that determined their respective strategies.

CHAPTER 4 SUMMARY

Company Reports

1. **Decisions**

2. **Messages**

3. **General Results**

    Units sold

    Production level in units

    Inventory level at end of period in units
    (previous inventory + production − units sold)

    Retail price (recommended price to be paid by consumers)

    Average selling price (retail price − distributor's margin)

    Unit transfer cost (agreed upon with production)

    Revenues (units sold × average selling price)

    Cost of goods sold (units sold × unit transfer cost)

    Inventory holding cost (inventory units × unit transfer cost
    × holding cost as a percentage of transfer cost)

    Advertising (total brand advertising expenditures)

    Gross marketing contribution (revenues − cost of goods sold
    − inventory holding cost − advertising)

    R&D (total annual expenditures for all R&D project)

    Sales force (total annual expenditures)

    Market research (total costs of all the studies purchased)

    Exceptional cost or profit

    Net marketing contribution (gross marketing contribution −
    R&D − sales force − marketing research − exceptional cost
    [or + exceptional profit])

    Budget (increases with net marketing contribution
    within minimum and maximum levels)

4. **Marketing Results**

    Market share based on units of each brand

    Number of distributors by channel for each brand

Company Reports (continued)

5. R&D

Project name

State of completion of project

Physical characteristics

Cumulative expenditures

Additional investment required

Minimum realistic unit cost

6. Cumulative Results

Brand information:
- starting period for cumulative results (period 0 or period when the brand was introduced)
- total units sold
- cumulative retail sales
- cumulative revenues
- cumulative cost of goods sold
- cumulative inventory holding costs
- cumulative advertising
- cumulative gross marketing contribution

Total cumulative R&D expenditures

Total cumulative sales force expenditures

Total cumulative market research expenditures

Total cumulative exceptional cost or profit

Total cumulative net marketing contribution

7. Newsletter

GNP growth rate during the current period

GNP growth rate estimated for the following period

Inflation rate during the current period

Inflation rate estimated for the following period

Inventory holding cost *per annum* as a percentage of transfer cost

Cost of a salesperson for the following period

Cost of firing a salesperson for the following period

Cost of training a new salesperson for the following period

Cost of each market research study for the following period

Names, characteristics, and retail price of brands introduced or modified in the current period

For each market (Sonite and Vodite), sales, market share (based on units and on value), and retail price of each brand

Decision Form

Product Management—For each brand commercialized:

- Production planning (number of units to be produced)
- Advertising budget
- Advertising research (percentage of advertising expenditures that will be used for research, as opposed to buying media space and time)
- Recommended retail price (price paid by consumers)
- Perceptual objectives (image to be communicated based on two most important dimensions used by consumers to evaluate the brands. Rating from -20 to $+20$. 99 indicates no change in perception is desired.)

Sales Force

- Number of salespersons in each channel of distribution

Research and Development—
For each project currently under development:

- Annual expenditures
- Physical characteristics to search for

Market Research Studies

- Specification of studies purchased

Internal Documents

1. BUDGETING FORM—PART I: Financial Information

2. BUDGETING FORM—PART II: Forecast for Budgeting

3. PLANNING FORM—PART I: General Performance

4. PLANNINF FORM—PART II: Marketing Expenditures

5. PLANNING FORM—PART III: Strategic Analysis Summary

6. PLANNING FORM—PART IV: Main Strategic Options

CHAPTER 5

Market Segmentation & Positioning

Each MARKSTRAT company starts with two Sonite brands. During the course of the simulation, companies may introduce new Sonite or Vodite brands, and reposition or withdraw existing ones. The maximum number of brands marketed by one company in a given period is limited to five. This constraint makes it extremely important to find optimal segmentation and positioning strategies. The positioning and repositioning of brands with respect to the specific needs of various consumer segments is a major aspect of the MARK-STRAT companies' marketing strategy.

The strategic issues surrounding market segmentation and product positioning can be summarized in three questions, which will be discussed in turn.

1. Where do we want to be positioned?

2. How do we design the product appropriate for this positioning?

3. As the environment changes, how can we reposition our existing brands?

The purpose of this chapter is to provide a framework and some methodologies to help make these decisions. The proposed approaches rest on the notions of brand perceptions and consumer preferences. Therefore we will first discuss how perceptions and preferences are assessed and the basic strategically relevant inferences that can be made from a perceptual map.

ASSESSING PERCEPTIONS AND PREFERENCES

One basis for analyzing the positioning of each competitive brand is the perceptual mapping of similarities and preferences obtained in Market Research Study 5, an example of which is shown in Figure 5.1. The example in Figure 5.1 is presented for explanatory purposes only and should not be used during the simulation, as it does not correspond to actual conditions. The study provides a two-dimensional map, as this configuration was found statistically

Figure 5.1: Perceptual Mapping of Brands Similarities and Preferences

	COORDINATES	
IDEAL POINTS	**Axis 1**	**Axis 2**
Segment 1	−4.4	15.8
Segment 2	−4.2	−1.0
Segment 3	16.3	7.5
Segment 4	15.5	4.8
Segment 5	−13.2	−11.9
BRAND PERCEPTION		
A : SAMA	−6.1	12.8
B : SALT	14.5	−5.0
C : SALK	−3.0	5.5
D : SARE	15.5	10.0
E : SEMI	11.5	4.5
F : SELF	14.2	7.5
G : SETA	−2.2	14.4
H : SIRO	−11.0	−12.8
I : SIBI	−7.7	−12.5
J : SIRU	18.6	8.1
K : SOLD	−5.7	3.5
L : SONO	−10.8	10.1
M : SONY	19.7	9.5
N : SULI	17.0	4.3
O : SUSI	−11.5	−10.5

satisfactory. The interpretation of the two dimensions shown is not reported here, although it will be in the actual study. Each axis is arbitrarily scaled from −20 to +20.

The numbers 1, 2, 3, 4, and 5 on the graph represent the positioning of the ideal points for each of the five segments. For instance, consumers from Segment 3 would globally most prefer a brand which would have coordinates at 16.3 on axis 1 and 7.5 on axis 2 of the perceptual map. Note that this point only represents the average ideal or preference of individuals in this segment. In fact each consumer has a different preference, which could be represented by a distribution around the mean preference. However, the preferences within a segment are sufficiently similar so that the ideal point represents well the overall global preference of the segment.

The letters on the graph correspond to the positioning of the competitive brands on the market at the time of the study, as indicated in the lower right corner of the figure. No significant difference was observed between the perception of the brands by various market segments. This means that although the segments prefer different ideal products, they perceive existing brands in a similar way. Thus, only one map for all segments is needed, rather than a separate map for each segment.

This map graphically summarizes a great deal of information with regard to the relative perception of the various brands. As a first step, it indicates the relative competition which may be expected between the different brands. The prime competitors for brand SEMI (E) are expected to be, in decreasing order of importance: brands SELF (F), SULI (N), SARE (D), SIRU (J), and SONY (M). These brands are indeed perceived as being positioned closer to each other by consumers. The decreasing order of importance is determined by the straight-line distance between SEMI and the other brands' positions.

On the other hand, little competition should be expected between brands SEMI (E) and SIRO (H), which are positioned far apart and should accordingly satisfy different needs. Cannibalization may also appear if a company's brands are positioned too close together; as, for instance, SIRO (H) and SIBI (I), which are both marketed by company 3. The relative preference of a segment for different brands may also be inferred from the distance between the segment's ideal point and the positions of the brands. In our example, SIRO (H), SIBI (I), and SUSI (O) are principal competitors for Segment 5. SETA (G) is in a privileged situation with Segment 1, while there are no brands positioned close to Segments 2's ideal point.

The semantic scale ratings provided in Market Research Study 4 also give perceptual and preference information for Sonites. The semantic scale results are less accurate than those obtained through perceptual mapping because of the cruder methodology used, but they are substantially less expensive to purchase. For Vodites, only the semantic scale ratings are available (Market Research Study 10).

In order to obtain the values on the semantic scales, the set of relevant attributes is determined *a priori*, contrary to MDS (multidimensional scaling) methodology. The range of the scale (1 to 7) has fewer points as well, so that the precision of the ratings is not as high. In particular, when relating perceptions of the degree to which a given brand possesses an attribute with the actual physical value of the brand on a characteristic, the reduced range might prohibit the discovery of complex non-linear relationships. However, the ease of gathering data on semantic scales enables the use of a large sample size, which results in very reliable values of the semantic scales.

OPTIMAL BRAND POSITION

Key objectives of segmentation and positioning strategies are (i) to anticipate the needs of consumers, (ii) to target attractive market segments, and (iii) to position brands for segment dominance. These objectives can be reached by the choice of an appropriate segmentation and positioning strategy that will recognize the attractiveness of various market segments (in terms of profit potential and potential for long term dominating positions) and the synergies among businesses or segments.

The issues concerning synergies among segments and risks associated with uncertainties will be discusssed in detail in the chapter on allocation of resources. Here, we will concentrate on major questions leading to the positioning that would be appropriate for a given brand. From a strategic standpoint, one possibility is to position the product so as to satisfy as best as possible the need of one specific segment. The other alternative consists of positioning the brand so as to reach several segments and possibly achieve greater economies of scale and greater experience through larger volume, leading to lower costs.

This second positioning strategy is illustrated in Figure 5.2. Brand SELT is shown equidistant from the ideal points of segments 1 and 2. In general, this strategy is not appropriate for the long term, as this position is difficult to

Figure 5.2: Example of Positioning for Multiple Market Segments

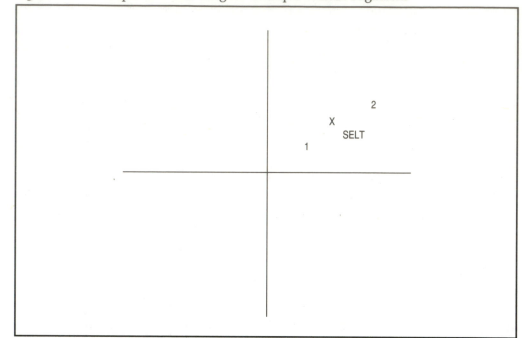

defend. A competitor might enter and better satisfy the need of a segment by specializing in that segment. This leads to the difficult position of being "stuck in the middle." However, there are conditions which might make this strategy feasible. These issues will be discussed in greater detail in the chapter on competitive strategies. Briefly, this positioning strategy might be appropriate in cases where the segments are too small for a single segment dominance position to be profitable or if the brand "stuck in the middle" can establish barriers to entry, for example, through large advertising expenditures.

The exact position to search for depends on our expectations of future needs for the segment or segments involved and on the demand for the brand for a given position. Once the "optimal position" has been found, we will consider the issue of finding the physical product attributes that correspond best to that positioning. Then we will discuss the repositioning alternative.

In order to determine the best position for a brand, the marketing strategist must analyze the dynamics of demand preference to anticipate the needs and preferences of the relevant segments. The demand by each of the segments should be forecasted as well as the market share for the brand in question, given its position and given the positions that competitive brands are expected to hold. Costs must then be evaluated to derive the profitability of different positioning strategies. The optimal brand position question can, therefore, be analyzed in a three-step process:

1. Prediction of ideal points
2. Forecasting of brand demand, which involves
   (a) forecasting of segment demand
   (b) forecasting of brand market share
3. Forecasting of brand transfer cost.

Prediction of Ideal Points

Ideal points or preferences reflect the needs of the consumers within a given segment. These needs gradually change as the consumers' values and behavior evolve over time. These changes typically are due to changes in the environment, which in turn does not change drastically from one period to the next. Therefore, changes in preferences are due for the most part to multiperiod environmental trends. These trends are not necessarily external to the industry. Indeed, the actions of the competitors in the industry can have a significant impact on these trends.

Marketing decisions of the firms in the industry impact the segments' evolution in terms of their size, the importance of the dimensions characterizing the brands in the consumers' perceptual space, and consumers' preferences in terms of the degree to which they desire the product to possess given attributes. One type of analysis appropriate for evaluating the trends consists of tracking the evolution of the ideal points over time. If the patterns over time are stable enough, it is then possible to predict the position of an ideal point as a function of time. In Figure 5.3, for example, the preference for the dimension represented on the graph decreases over time. The trend line can be drawn on the graph or a regression equation can be estimated to predict the position several periods ahead.

Forecasting Brand Demand

As indicated above, forecasting brand demand involves the forecast of sales for each segment relevant for the brand, as well as the forecast of the market

Figure 5.3: Evolution of Ideal Points Over Time

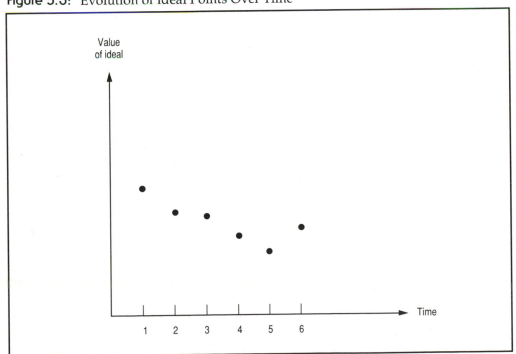

Figure 5.4: Time Series Analysis of Demand for a Segment

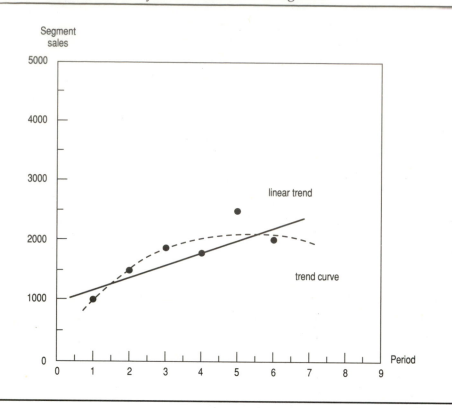

share of the brand in each segment, given a certain positioning. Then the expected sales of the brand can be computed.

Forecasting Segment Sales. Several alternatives are possible to forecast demand for a given segment. The simplest method is a trend analysis. However, this implies that the environment will evolve in a constant manner. Even though trend is an important element of the segment's sales, a saturation level might occur when enough potential customers have purchased the product. This would suggest the use of a diffusion model that would take saturation into account. Although the trend probably represents the major environmental forces impacting demand, the decisions of the firm also have a significant impact, as indicated earlier. Therefore, a third possibility is to analyze the relationship between competitive actions and segment demand.

Figure 5.4 represents the evolution of sales of a segment over six periods. The trend line can be used to forecast demand at periods 7 and 8. However, the trend is not necessarily a linear function of time. Therefore, the curve that best fits past points might give a better forecast than a straight line trend. A curve is also represented in Figure 5.4.

This curve indicates a decline in the growth rate of the segment. This could be due to the potential market becoming saturated. More complex diffusion models can sometimes be used to represent such an evolution process.*

*See, for instance, Gary L. Lilien and Philip Kotler, *Marketing Decision Making*, New York, Harper & Row, 1983.

The sales (in units) at a given period can be regressed on (1) the cumulative sales up to the previous period and (2) the square of the cumulative sales up to the previous period, using time series observations. The estimated coefficients can then be used for prediction purposes, since at each period the cumulative previous sales are known.

Instead of using the diffusion model approach, it could be observed that the deviations from the trend curve in periods 4 and 5 are due to a decrease in period 4 of advertising expenditures for this segment, followed by an increase in period 5. It is then possible to add advertising expenditures for the brands competing in that segment as an independent variable in a regression, in addition to a trend factor.

Any of these three methods (and possibly some combination) can be used to forecast the sales of the market segments.

Forecasting Market Share. Market share in the long term should be equivalent to purchase intentions, as the product should be available through appropriate distribution to those consumers who wish to buy it. Purchase intentions are determined by two main factors: brand awareness and brand positioning. Although the exact relationships are difficult to assess, information given in study one for the current position of the brand with the current awareness level can be used in a first step. These would be accurate if brand awareness and brand positioning, the factors indicated above that determine purchase intentions, are stable.

If changes in positioning can be anticipated, in particular for the firm's own brands, the impact of these changes should be assessed, as they would affect purchase intentions. In particular, if other brands are expected to be positioned close to the brand for which the forecast is being made, cannibalization is likely to occur. The degree of cannibalization in terms of purchase intentions would, therefore, need to be assessed.

Expected Brand Demand. Expected brand sales can now be computed by adding the brand sales of each segment. Figure 5.5 provides an example of the computations involved. The sales level of the brand originating from a given segment is the product of the segment's expected size and the expected purchase intentions for the brand within that segment. The total expected brand sales level is the sum of the brand sales over the relevant segments.

Forecasting Brand Transfer Cost

In order to compute the expected profitability of a brand position, the costs of reaching that position need to be assessed, as well as the cost advantages due to increased sales obtained from a better position. The evaluation of the costs of reaching a given position needs to take into account R&D, advertising and sales force expenditures as discussed in the Budgeting and Planning sections. At this point, we will concentrate on the impact of production volume on unit transfer costs.

As indicated earlier, physical characteristic #6 is the average cost for a total production of 100,000 units. This transfer cost, used between the produc-

Figure 5.5: Computing Expected Brand Sales

Segment	Segment Expected Size (in units)	Expected Purchase Intent of Brand SAND	Expected Brand Sales
1	133	0.35	18
2	916	0.035	32
3	333	0.028	9
4	1111	0.429	477
5	1521	0.005	08
		Total Expected Brand Sales:	544

tion department and the marketing department, follows the gains in productivity obtained through production experience as per a contractual internal agreement between the two departments.

The Experience Curve. The origin of the experience curve is the learning curve. The learning curve resulted from the observation that productivity of repeated human labor tasks increases as the number of times the task is performed increases. Thus learning effect generally follows a specific pattern: every time the number of times the task is performed doubles, productivity increases by a constant percentage. This finding, therefore, indicates decreasing returns to task repetition.

The Boston Consulting Group (BCG) observed similar patterns of cost reduction every time that cumulative production of a product doubled across a broad range of industries.* The phenomenon that BCG observed is more general than the learning curve, as it goes beyond labor costs. In fact, the "experience effect" can result from a variety of sources in addition to labor productivity, for example: substitution of cheaper or more efficient raw material or components, production standardization, improved efficiency of production equipment, or new production processes.

Another source of cost reduction is the introduction, resulting from research and development programs, of new products that are more efficient. In MARKSTRAT, this last source is separated from the other sources of cost reduction listed above. Indeed, the first set of sources of experience effects is beyond the management of the marketing department. While cost reductions due to any of these reasons do not occur automatically, in MARKSTRAT the production departments have the motivation to achieve these cost reductions. As for the cost reductions due to development of new (efficient) products, it is the responsibility of the marketing department to make such requests, as the marketing department controls the R&D budget. We will therefore refer to the experience curve here in MARKSTRAT as the experience effect, which is automatically generated by production management.

---

*See, for instance, G. S. Day and D. B. Montgomery, "Diagnosing the Experience Curve," *Journal of Marketing*, Vol. 47, Spring 1983.

This cost reduction which is distinct from cost reduction obtained from Research and Development is very regular in MARKSTRAT and applies to any new product being produced. Consequently, for a given product, every time cumulative production doubles, transfer costs from the production department to the marketing department fall by a constant percentage. The curve can be represented as in Figure 5.6. In this example, it is an 85% experience curve meaning that every time cumulative production doubles, unit transfer cost decreases by 15%. A property of this constant rate of decrease in cost is that when plotted on log-log paper as in Figure 5.7, the experience curve appears as a straight line. The axes are now expressed as the logarithm of cumulative production and the logarithm of unit transfer cost for the horizontal and vertical axes, respectively. The advantage of this property becomes evident when estimating the experience rate and forecasting future transfer costs.

In order to forecast the average transfer cost for a given expected level of cumulative production, a six-step procedure is now presented. Although this method is based on only two points, it has the advantage of being simple. The reader may easily extend it to multiple observations with the use of regression techniques.

Six-Step Forecasting Procedure. The six steps of the procedure are now described.

1. The first step consists of obtaining the transfer cost at an early period with the corresponding cumulative production of units at that time.

Figure 5.6: A Typical Experience Curve (85%)

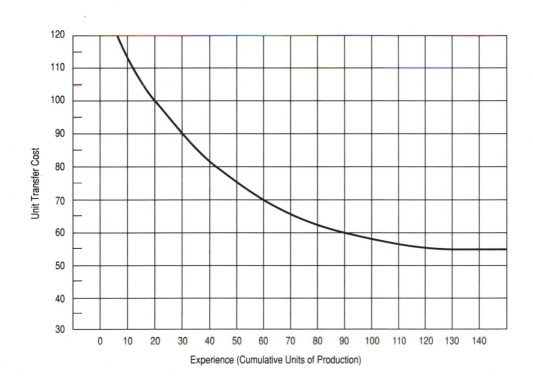

Unit Transfer Cost

Experience (Cumulative Units of Production)

Figure 5.7: The Experience Curve with Transformed Axes

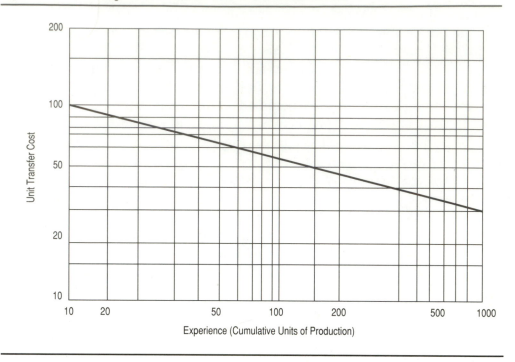

The transfer cost is easily read from the company report in the general results section. The cumulative production at that time is the cumulative sales shown in the cumulative results section of the report for the same period. To this should be added the inventory of the brand at the end of the period.

2. In step 2, the same procedure is followed for a later period. For that period, both the cumulative production and the new transfer cost should be obtained.

3. The transfer cost needs to be adjusted for inflation, however, to correspond to the same monetary value as in the period of reference used as in step 1. Inflation rates that should be used to adjust cost are given in the newsletter section of the company report.

4. The shape of the experience curve, as discussed above, becomes a straight line when drawn on log-log paper. Therefore, the two points should be plotted on log-log paper with the cumulative volume on the horizontal axes and cost on the vertical axis. Then the line between the two points can be drawn.

5. The cost can be obtained for a new cumulative volume by drawing a vertical line from the value of the new cumulative volume on the horizontal axis up to the curve. A horizontal line can then be drawn from the intersection point to the vertical axis to derive the new cost.

6. The actual transfer cost is obtained by adjusting the cost obtained above for inflation corresponding to the period used as the base in step 1 until the period for which the projection is being made. Expected inflation rates need to be used for future periods.

Example of Transfer Cost Forecasting. An example of this procedure now follows.

> ***Step 1:*** In the relevant section of a company's report in period 3, the cumulative sales at the end of period 3 of brand SARA are 396,000 units. This is also the amount of cumulative production if there is no inventory. The current unit transfer cost is $155.

> ***Step 2:*** At the end of the next period, period 4, cumulative sales of SARA are 796,000 units. There is, in addition, an inventory of 44,000 units for this same brand. Cumulative production of SARA at the end of period 4 is thus 840,000 units. The transfer cost for period 4 was $144.

> ***Step 3:*** The inflation rate during period 4 can be found in the news-letter section of the company report and was 11%. Therefore the cost, adjusted for inflation, in period 3 monetary units is $129.73 ($144/1.11).

> ***Step 4:*** using the two points obtained in steps 1 and 3, the experience curve can be drawn on log-log paper as illustrated in Figure 5.8.

> ***Step 5:*** Assuming that the requested production for the next period is 500,000 units, the cumulative production would then be 1,340,000 units for period 5 (840,000 units plus the period 5 production of 500,000 units). The cost corresponding to that level of cumulative production can be indexed from the graph in Figure 5.8. A vertical line starting on the horizontal axis at a cumulative production level of 1,340,000 units is drawn until it reaches the experience curve line. Then a horizontal line is drawn to the left until it reaches the vertical axis. The cost can be read at this point on the vertical axis in Figure 5.8, a point which shows a cost of $125.

Figure 5.8: Drawing the Experience Curve on Log Log Paper

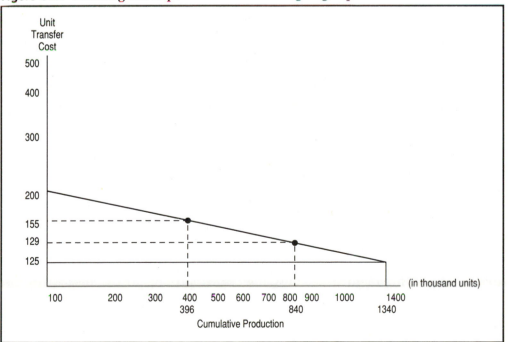

Step 6: The final step consists of adjusting the cost for period 4 inflation (11%) and expected inflation for period 5, which is indicated in the newsletter. Assuming this expected inflation rate is 13%, the final cost expected for period 5 is therefore $125 \times 1.11 \times 1.13 = \$156.8$.

Matching Product Attribute with Position

So far, the desirable position to attain in the perceptual space has been derived considering demand and cost trends. In this section, the objective is to find the physical characteristics of the product that would correspond to such a position. Therefore, at this point, the team managing a company knows the coordinates where the product should be positioned, either in the perceptual space derived from the multidimensional scaling study (study 5) or from the semantic scales of study 4 for the Sonites and of study 10 for the Vodite market.

In the semantic scale studies, the brands are evaluated by consumers on scales measuring the perception of consumers corresponding to the characteristics of the product. Only the three most important characteristics are reported in the study. In the multidimensional scaling study, the two dimension solution fits the data. The dimensions are interpreted as the perceptions of the physical characteristic of the product that correlates most highly with the dimension. Therefore, in both cases, whether management uses semantic scales or multidimensional scaling, it is possible to relate the perceptual dimension or scale to an actual physical characteristic of the product (one of the first five characteristics or price). Consequently, in order to find the physical characteristic levels that correspond to a given perception, the strategic analyst must investigate the relationship between the actual physical attribute of a product or a brand and the consumers' perceptions of that attribute.

A simple way to summarize the information that a team possesses about that relationship is to plot the perceptions versus the actual characteristics. Figure 5.9 illustrates such a plot. The horizontal axis corresponds to the perceptions about the price of the various brands and the vertical axis shows the actual recommended retail price. Each brand is a data point that can give information about this relationship. Consumers' perceptual distortions which appear are due to the natural psycho-physical property of a given physical attribute, to past experience with existing products, and to advertising effects.

In the MARKSTRAT market, although consumers cannot know precisely the value of a brand on a physical characteristic, they cannot be duped, and the plots of the type described above (as in Figure 5.9) should describe the nature of perceptions relatively well. The relationship can be summarized as in Figure 5.9 by drawing the curve that fits the data. A straight line can be used as a first approximation. In Figure 5.9, the deviations around the line are relatively small, indicating that the relationship can be summarized relatively well by a straight line. The line corresponding to the best fit to the data can be found by regressing actual price on perceived price. Then, by projecting the positioning objective on the line, the actual physical value for

Figure 5.9: Relationship Between Perceived Price and Actual Price
              (Semantic Scale Data)

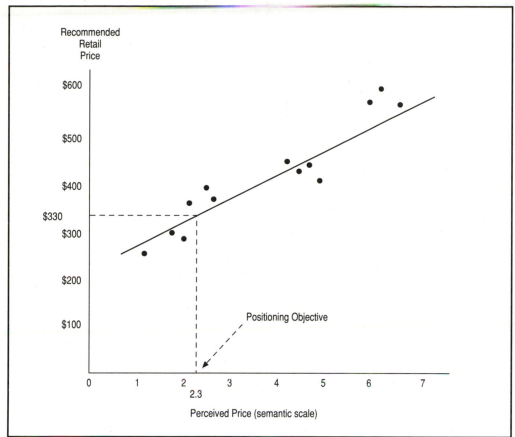

the corresponding characterisitic can be found easily. On Figure 5.9 the retail price corresponding to a perception of 2.3 on the semantic scale can be found to be approximately $330.

Figure 5.10 provides the same information as given by Figure 5.9. However, the scale from the multidimensional scaling is used on the horizontal axis. As indicated earlier in this chapter, these scales are more precise, as they provide a continuous scale from −20 to +20 instead of the seven-point scale used with the semantic scales. The direct consequence of that greater range and scale refinement is that the information about the relationship between perceptions and actual characteristics might be more precise. In particular, if the relationship is not linear, as in the illustration discussed above, the MDS scale should provide better information. However, sampling errors should not be ignored, as they could hide more complex relationships. The curve that best fits the data should be used.

This analysis assumed that there were data available, with enough data around the region corresponding to the perceptual objectives. If there is no brand in the market (such as occurs before the first entry in the Vodite market), the only information available concerns some perceptual measure of an ideal product. It is very difficult, however, to restate these perceptions as a physical characteristic, as consumers might not even comprehend the

Figure 5.10: Relationship Between Perceived Characteristic and
Physical Characteristic Value (MDS Scale)

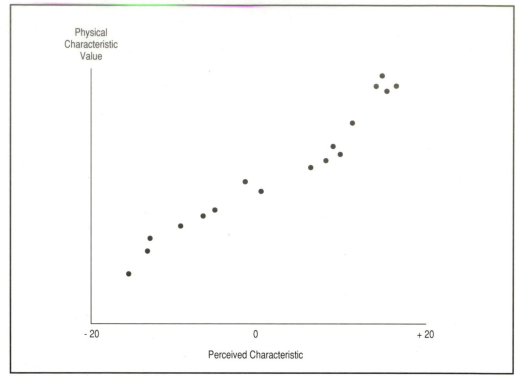

physical attributes, due to the lack of reference that occurs with a completely new product.

These difficulties, typical of completely new products, are probably best resolved by test marketing the product. Consequently, a pioneer who does not need fast market penetration, due to lack of competitive threat, might develop one or several products, produced in small quantities, in order to learn how they are perceived in the market. This approach, however, provides that same information to competitors!

When few data points are available, it could be preferable simply to determine the range of physical characteristics from the closest brands available in the market without fitting the curve to the entire range of products. Figure 5.11 shows that, in terms of design, brands A and E are the closest brands on each side of where the new brand should be positioned. The closest brand on the design dimension is brand E, which has a perceived design of 4.5 on the semantic scale. Information available on the physical characteristics of brand E indicate that the actual design index of this product has a value of 6. This brand is perceived a little too low compared to where the new brand should be positioned. The closest brand higher than the objective is brand A, with a perceived design of 6 and an actual design index of 8. Consequently, the new brand should be between 6 and 8. If the distance between these two neighbors is not too large, a linear interpolation can be done between the two points. In the example discussed, the design index specification would be: $6 + (8 - 6)(5 - 4.5)/(6 - 4.5) = 6.7$, rounded to 7.

Figure 5.11: Determination of Physical Attribute Range (From Semantic Scales)

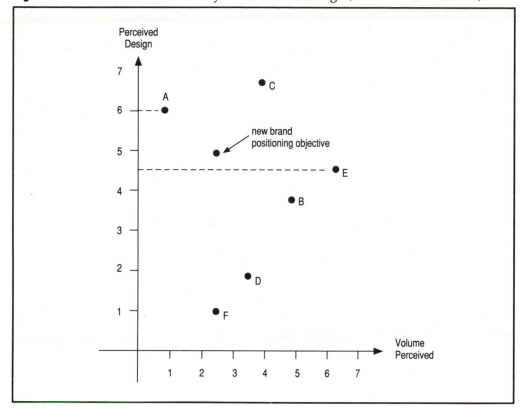

In summary, several methods can be used in order to specify the physical characteristics of a product once the desired perceptions are known. The choice depends on the availability of data. All of these methods, although they ignore multiple factors, offer approximations which should become more accurate as more data becomes available over time.

_____ **REPOSITIONING STRATEGIES**

Once a brand has been sold in the market, consumers have a certain idea about the brand, which is represented by its position in a perceptual space. Over time, demand and competitive dynamics affect what should be the optimal positioning of a brand. In MARKSTRAT, brands may be repositioned to adapt to new environmental conditions.

Repositioning can be achieved by advertising or by research and development. Using advertising to reposition a product requires three types of decisions:

1. Specifying perceptual objectives for the brand. For instance, if one wants to reposition SEMI (E) closer to the ideal point of segment 4 in Figure 5.1, one could specify perceptual objectives of 15 on axis 1 and 5 on axis 2. This would serve as a guideline for the design of appropriate advertising platforms, copy, or media plans.

2. Allocating an advertising budget for the brand. The higher this budget, the further one may expect to be able to reposition the brand.

3. Allocating an advertising research budget is necessary for copy testing and media selection. The higher the advertising research budget, the more accurate one may expect the repositioning to be in terms of reaching the perceptual objectives.

These decisions are entered in the product management section of the decision form. An example, discussed now, is presented in Figure 5.12. SARI and SAND are existing brands, but SAND is being modified using the characteristics used in R&D project PSAND (issues dealing with R&D, including the treatment of obsolete inventory, are discussed in the next chapter). The perceptual objectives, as communicated to the advertising agency, are specified in the last two columns of the product management section of the decision form. Axis 1 corresponds to the most important dimension as perceived by consumers, and axis 2 corresponds to the next most important dimension. These dimensions are therefore different for the Sonite and Vodite brands: different dimensions are important for different markets. It should be first noted that a brand might not need to be repositioned on both dimensions. Indeed, if the perceptions on one dimension correspond to what consumers want, there is no reason to use advertising to change that perceptual value. Instead, changes in perceptions should be concentrated on only one dimension and the advertising copy should be designed so that the other dimension remains unaffected. The code 99 serves that purpose. It indicates to the advertising agency that the perception on the dimension for which the code 99 was entered should not change.

If the brand's position were satisfactory on both axes, the code 99 would be entered on both columns for that brand. In that case, the advertising objective is purely to improve the brand awareness with persuasive arguments which reinforce the current perceptions held by the consumers.

Here, the firm wishes to reposition the brand SARI on the most important dimension. The objective given to the advertising agency is a perception of −15 on a scale from −20 to +20. The firm appears to be satisfied with the current positioning of SARI on axis 2 and does not want to modify it. This is indicated by the code number 99. If the positioning of SARI had been satisfactory for both axes, then the code number 99 would have been entered on both columns. For brand SAND, which is being repositioned, the perceptual objectives are 13 and 5 for axes 1 and 2 respectively. Given that it is a product modification with new physical characteristics and that both dimensions are to be advertised, a larger budget ($5,000,000) is spent on SAND than on SARI. Also, the amount of that budget to be used on research is higher (10% versus 5%) because more copy testing is needed to insure correct comprehension of the message and to generate the highest quality creative work possible. This means that 10% of the $5,000,000 budget will be used to improve the efficiency of the repositioning, as well as the efficiency of each dollar spent. The remaining $4,500,000 will be used to buy media space and time.

Brand repositioning by advertising is limited, however, by the actual physical characteristics, and consumers' perceptions of these character-

Figure 5.12: Decisions for Repositioning a Brand

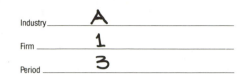

MARKSTRAT DECISION FORM

Industry _____ A _____

Firm _____ 1 _____

Period _____ 3 _____

PRODUCT MANAGEMENT

Brand Names	Name of R&D Project (if modification or introduction)	Production Planning (thousand units)	Advertising Budget (thousands of $)	Advertising Research (percent)	Recommended Retail Price ($)	Perceptual Objectives (−20 to +20, or 99)	
						Axis 1	Axis 2
SARI		300	3000	5	200	-15	99
SAND	PSAND	200	5000	10	500	13	5

SALES FORCE

Distribution Channels	1	2	3
Number of Salespersons			

RESEARCH AND DEVELOPMENT

Project Name	Expenditures (thousands of $)	Physical Characteristics					
		1	2	3	4	5	6

MARKET RESEARCH STUDIES

1	2	3	4	5	6	7	8	9	10	11	12	13	14	15

(For Instructor's Use)	

ec(−)   ep(+)   bd(−)   bi(+)

istics may be shifted only within a certain range by advertising. At some point, it becomes more profitable to reposition a brand by changing its physical characteristics than by advertising alone. This requires the successful completion of an R&D project, which results in a product with the desired new characteristics.

Issues concerning the development of new products will be discussed in the next chapter. However, it is important to point out that the choice of repositioning through an advertising strategy versus a new product development strategy depends on the extent to which repositioning is desired and is a function of the current level of brand awareness. It also depends, of course, on the ability of the firm to complete R&D projects with the physical characteristics of the products that correspond to the market needs.

As described above, the perceptual mapping of similarities and preferences is an important tool for the design of positioning and repositioning strategies. It may, however, lead to inadequate decisions if used without taking other factors into account. One should note that various brands have different awareness levels. One brand may be positioned close to a segment's ideal point but draw few purchases from the consumers if it is unknown. In addition, it can be expected that the higher the awareness level of a brand, the more difficult it will be to reposition the brand because consumers have become knowledgeable about the brand. The five segments represent different volumes of potential sales and are at different stages of their development. Their needs evolve over time and so, too, do their ideal points. Although the perceptual map reproduces brand similarities and preferences satisfactorily, as expressed by a sample of individuals, it is certainly incomplete; other dimensions may enter into consumers' perceptions.

CHAPTER 5 SUMMARY

Assessing Perceptions and Preferences

- Consumers' perceptions of products affect their purchasing decisions.

- Competition is more intense between products which are perceived to be more similar by consumers.

- Consumers have a higher preference for brands which they perceive to be closer to their ideal combination of benefits (ideal point).

Optimal Brand Position

- *Multi-segment positioning strategy:* attracting consumers from several segments.

- *Mono-segment positioning strategy:* concentrating on a targeted segment.

- *Prediction of ideal points:* anticipating the evolution of consumers' needs.

- *Forecasting brand demand:* anticipating the growth of each market segment and the market share obtainable in each market segment.

- *Forecasting brand transfer cost:* using the experience curve concept to project the evolution of unit transfer cost according to cumulative production.

- *Matching product attribute with position:* translating desired product positions from market research studies (semantic scales or perceptual maps) into specification of physical characteristics and price levels.

CHAPTER 6

The Marketing and R&D Interface

This chapter discusses issues involved in implementing a marketing strategy as it relates to interaction with the Research and Development Department. After assessing a situation and developing a marketing strategy which anticipates the needs of the market, the strategy must be implemented. One of the most important aspects of implementation is specifying the characteristics of the product that will be offered to consumers. Given the uncertainty about the evolution of the market, it is probable that you will need to develop a portfolio of products in order to be ready to implement contingency plans and strategies. Therefore, in this chapter we introduce the methods by which the marketing department and the R&D department communicate with each other. Then the relationship between the specific R&D strategy and the implementation of the marketing strategy will be discussed.

Figure 6.1 summarizes the marketing–R&D interface. Marketing requests a project from the R&D department by specifying a project name, a budget, and the physical characteristics of the desired product. The Company Report for the following period will indicate whether the project has been successfully completed or not. If the desired product has not been found, the marketing department may ask R&D to pursue the project. In this case, it will have to invest additional funds in the project, without changing its name or characteristics. Alternatively, the project may be dropped, in which case the investment previously made is lost. Or, if one of the characteristics (except cost) of the desired product is changed, then a new project with a different name must be launched—without benefit from the investment previously made. Only the cost characteristic of an ongoing project may be changed, particularly if inflation is to be taken into account.

If the R&D project has successfully been completed, the marketing department may use the newly developed product to modify an existing brand or to introduce a new brand. The name of the project does not in any sense restrict the application of the new product. For instance, a new product developed through the R&D project "PSARO" may be used to modify the

Figure 6.1: The Marketing–R&D Interface

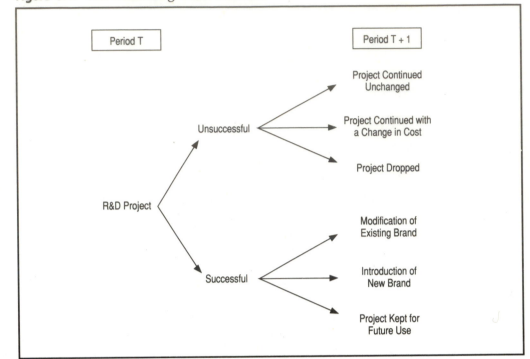

existing brand "SALT" or to launch a new brand named "SAFE." Alternatively, the firm may choose not to exploit the new product immediately, in which case it still remains available for use in future years. The product is then always available at the cost at which it was completed, adjusted for inflation.

It is important to note that it takes a minimum of one period, and sometimes several periods, between the launching of an R&D project and its possible use in the market place. Thus, the marketing-R&D interface requires particularly careful planning.

COMMUNICATION WITH THE R&D DEPARTMENT

Project Code Names

The R&D department is composed of research teams working on specific projects. Projects are identified by code names. These code names have nothing to do with the use of the project, once completed, by the marketing department. The codes are simply used so that the marketing department can ask an R&D team for some information about the progress of the corresponding R&D work over time. The code names are chosen by the marketing department. These names follow the conventions already presented in chapter 2. The first letter must be a "P" to indicate that we are dealing with a project rather than an actual brand. The second letter follows the convention that an S indicates that the research will be executed as a Sonite product and a V indicates a Vodite. The last three characters of the project code name are chosen by the teams as they wish.

Once a project name has been completed, the code name remains forever associated with the product resulting from the R&D project. Therefore, the project with its associated product characteristics is filed under that code name. Consequently, no new project should use the same code name, as it would in reality create confusion. The name of a completed project cannot be reused for a different project, even if the new project is only to search for a minor modification of the product. For example, each firm has two completed R&D projects at the beginning of the simulation. These two projects are used to launch the two brands each firm has commercialized. For example, firm 3 markets two brands, SIRO and SIBI. The R&D projects corresponding to these brands are respectively PSIRO and PSIBI. Therefore, no new R&D project can use these names, as the projects have been completed in the past and are registered in the files of the firm under these two code names.

A project, however, is not necessarily completed by the R&D department within the year in which the request is made by the marketing department. In fact, in many cases, the budget given to the R&D department will be insufficient and/or the average cost of the first 100,000 units (characteristic #6) will be infeasible. In these cases, the project can be continued the next year until completion, unless the marketing department decides to abandon the project. If the firm decides to continue the project, its specifications have not changed (except possibly characteristic number 6, the unit cost) and the same code name should be used. Therefore, a project code name is associated with the search for a product with specific physical attributes defined by the values of characteristics one through five.

If the marketing department realizes that one (or several) of the first five characteristics requested is not right for the market, this implies that a new project code needs to be issued. This also means that the budget invested in the abandoned project is a sunk cost which will not be used towards the completion of the new project. This situation is illustrated with the following example, for which the decisions are summarized in Figure 6.2.

In period 3, project PSILK was requested with a budget of $1 million. This budget proved to be insufficient, and an additional budget of $1.5 million was requested by the R&D department to complete the project. In period 4, the same project code, PSILK, is used with the same characteristics and an additional budget of $1.5 million is provided. The targeted unit cost (characteristic 6) is also increased from 200 to 204 to take into account the 2% inflation in the last period.

Eventually the marketing department realizes that because of changes in preference in the market, a volume (characteristic 3) of 50 is too high and 45 dm^3 is more appropriate. Thus, a new R&D project with a new code name, PSILI, should be started. The budget spent for PSILK in period 3 would be lost, since the project was canceled. If, on the other hand, the first five characteristics remain unchanged, but cost (characteristic 6) needs to be adjusted to reflect more realistic expectations, the project code is still valid, as the same

Figure 6.2: Continuation of an R&D Project

Period 3 Request

Project Name	Budget	Physical Characteristics					Cost
		1	2	3	4	5	
PSILK	1000	15	8	50	10	50	200
PVIVA	3000	80	15	80	7	60	200

Period 4 Request

Project Name	Budget	Physical Characteristics					Cost
		1	2	3	4	5	
PSILK	1500	15	8	50	10	50	204
PSILI	2000	15	8	45	10	50	200
PVIVA	1000	80	15	80	7	60	350

R&D team continues working on the same product, as determined by the first five characteristics. Therefore, in the case of PVIVA, shown in Figure 6.2, the minimum realistic cost being $350, the cost is adjusted from $200 in the period 3 request to $350 in the period 4 request. The other five characteristics remain unchanged and the project code remains PVIVA.

Product Characteristic Requests

The characteristics of the Sonite and Vodite products have been described in Chapter 2. In particular, the range feasible for each characteristic is reported in Table 2.2 and is also summarized at the end of this chapter. A product specification may consist of any combination of these characteristics as long as each is an integer number and remains within its respective range.

This does not indicate whether a higher level on one characteristic is better or not for consumers, as illustrated in the previous chapter. Neither can one assume that it is easier (requires a lower budget) to "downgrade" a product on one characteristic than to "upgrade" a product. In other words, it is quite possible that it would take a $1 million budget to complete a project for a product which would have a power of 50 watts and $2 million to complete a project for a product with 30 watts. Similarly, it should not necessarily be expected that a lower frequency product will cost less to manufacture than a higher frequency product. The transfer cost of a product clearly depends on the characteristics of the product. However, the transfer cost also depends on the specific experience of a firm for similar products, thereby creating a source of competitive advantage and possibly a barrier to entry in a given market.

The product characteristics to be requested for a given project follow directly from the analyses described in chapter 5. However, the cost characteristic is more complex, as the R&D departments in MARKSTRAT do not necessarily indicate whether a product could have a lower cost than the cost requested. The R&D department can provide information about the minimum cost that they are willing to guarantee. This information can be requested in a feasibility study or will be reported if the cost requested is infeasible because of its low value. However, the fact that this information is not automatically provided suggests different strategies with regard to the R&D department.

One simple way to specify a cost in an R&D project is to start at the price that consumers are willing to pay for that product. Given an objective of returns or margins, the maximum cost possible to realize that objective can be computed. This might not be the lowest cost achievable, but it provides a basis above which the strategy would not be attractive.

For example, if the market is not willing to pay more than $300, this implies the following calculations. The distributors' margins should be subtracted from the price to obtain revenues at manufacturer's selling price. Given the distribution channel's expected share for the product (for instance, 15%, 40%, and 45% respectively for channels 1, 2, and 3), and given that the three channels of distribution have margins of 40%, 35%, and 40% respectively, the average distributor's margin is the weighted average of the three margin rates, where the weights are the channel shares.

Therefore, in this example, the average distribution margin is (40% × 0.15) + (35% × 0.40) + (40% × 0.45) = 38%. Consequently, the manufacturer's selling price is the retail price minus the margin, which is $114 (i.e., $300 × 0.38), or a price of $186. If the objective of the firm on gross margins is 40%, the maximum cost that would satisfy this objective is $112 [i.e., 186 − (186 × 0.4)]. A request can then be made to the R&D department to research a product with such a cost. After completion, new R&D projects can be started to reduce this cost.

An alternative method for determining the cost characteristic is by doing many feasibility studies, as the R&D department would provide information as to the lower cost that they are willing to guarantee. This will be discussed in the next section.

Budget

The last decision to make when requesting an R&D project is how much should be spent on the project. This question is particularly important given the nature of the interaction with the R&D department. When making a project request, the marketing department determines the size of the investment to be made on a yearly basis. If the budget is insufficient, additional funds can be provided in subsequent years.

However, the R&D department operates, like the marketing department, as a profit center. Consequently, profits are made by accepting more than would be required to complete a project if the marketing department is willing to pay more than necessary. This would result from marketing department ignorance of the efficiency of the firm's R&D department. Therefore, an important task of the marketing department vis-à-vis its interaction with R&D is to develop a good understanding of the cost structure of the products and of the efficiency of the R&D department. Again, this calls for requesting R&D product feasibility studies.

A feasibility study is requested like any other product except that the budget invested is relatively small. The minimum budget below which the R&D department does not guarantee that it will provide information is $100,000 for both Sonite and Vodite products.

More generally, the budget required to complete a project depends on both the characteristics specified and the experience of the firm with similar products, in particular the experience of the R&D department in completing similar projects in the past. The budget depends also on the cost request for characteristic number 6. If a firm has already benefited from the experience curve, it becomes less expensive for that firm to reduce the cost through R&D than it is for a firm with fewer cumulative production units. In summary, it can be expected that the more similar a project is to one that has been completed, the lower will be the budget required to complete this new project. Also, if a transfer cost has been lowered because of production experience, this will facilitate a project with a lower cost.

Not all characteristics are similar in terms of the difficulty of completing a project with a given set of characteristics. It could be cheaper, for example, to improve volume than to improve weight. Therefore, the marketing department might have to trade off certain characteristic specifications for the cost characteristic and for the budget required to complete the project.

As in any research enterprise, the completion of the project depends in part on uncertainty. Although the performance of the R&D department is far from being random, for a given budget there is always a probability of not completing the project. It is, however, the case that the completion probability increases with the R&D budget.

Given all these influencing factors, it is difficult to indicate a general order of magnitude for R&D budgets. However, as indicated in Chapter 2, industry experts estimate that an adequate budget in period 1 to hope to complete a Sonite project ranges from $100,000 to $1,000,000. This range would apply for products similar to those currently available in the market. For a Vodite project, it has been estimated that $2,000,000 is a minimum budget to expect project completion. Again, the budget depends on the specification of characteristics.

R&D DEPARTMENT RESPONSES

The R&D department schedules its work by assigning projects to R&D teams. These teams will work during the year on the many requests they have from the entire firm, including from other divisions. Consequently, it takes a period of one year to obtain any response from the R&D department. For the marketing department, the result of this scheduling is that it becomes critical to plan ahead. Lack of long term planning penalizes the efficiency of the marketing department, as opportunities could be missed and costs might be higher.

Given that the product has feasible characteristics, that is, features that fall within the range of feasible characteristics summarized in Table 2.2, the R&D department responds to the marketing department in any of three ways.

Project Completed Message

The R&D department indicates that a project is successfully completed in the R&D section of the company report. An example is given in Figure 6.3. A completed project can be used the following period or any future period, as discussed in the next section on the utilization of completed R&D projects. Therefore, in the example in Figure 6.3, project PSEAS and PSENS are now available.

Insufficient Budget

As shown in Figure 6.3 for project PSEXS, what is needed to complete such a project is an additional budget of $300,000. If the team decides to continue the project next period, the same first five characteristics need to be entered under the same project code.

Figure 6.3: Example of R&D Section of Company Report

Period 4

Project Name	Available	Physical Characteristics						Cumulative Expenditures (K$)	Additional Investment Required (K$)	Minimum Realistic Unit Cost ($)
		1	2	3	4	5	6			
PSEXS	No	10	7	50	25	37	124	100	300	
PSENZ	No	15	8	50	20	80	161	1200	100	240
PSEAS	YES	16	7	50	25	30	156	100		
PSENS	YES	17	7	50	30	87	172	500		

However, the sixth characteristic, cost, behaves somewhat differently. In fact, given that there is a certain level of inflation in this MARKSTRAT environment, by keeping the cost unchanged, a request for a real cost lower than the request at the previous period is in effect being made. The R&D department does not guarantee such a lower cost. Therefore, in order to keep the same project request, the cost (characteristic #6) should be adjusted for inflation. The expected inflation rate for the future period is indicated in the newsletter and the information provided by the R&D department updates automatically the unit cost of a project based on this expected inflation rate.

This is illustrated in the R&D decision shown in Figure 6.4. Project PSEXS is continued in period 5 with the additional budget of $300,000, as discussed above. The first five characteristics remain unchanged from the project PSEXS requested in period 4 (see Figure 6.3). However, the cost request, which was $120 in period 4, has been adjusted in Figure 6.3 by the R&D department for a 2% expected inflation rate next period. Therefore a cost of $124 is now requested to be guaranteed to complete the project in period 5. It should be noted that the information provided by the R&D department in the R&D section of the Company Report updates numbers for inflation. For example, in Figure 6.3, the cost shown for PSEXS in the research and development section of the period 4 report is $124 instead of $120, which was the cost requested at period 3.

Under these specified conditions of cost and additional budget, the R&D department guarantees that the project will be completed next period. Clearly, the additional funds necessary to obtain a guarantee from the R&D department can be perceived as a high price to pay for such a guarantee. Indeed, the marketing department might decide not to invest as much and take a chance of completing the project with a certain probability that is subject to chance.

Unrealistic Cost

The last response possible by the R&D department indicates that the cost requested as characteristic 6 is too low to be feasible, given the other characteristics. Then the minimum realistic cost is indicated as illustrated in Figure 6.3 for project PSENZ.

The additional funds required by the R&D department to guarantee the completion of the project at this cost are then specified. Again, all that is needed to complete the project is, using the same project code, to change the cost characteristic to the minimum realistic cost and provide the additional funds. An example is provided the R&D decision shown in Figure 6.4. Project PSENZ is being completed with certainty, as the requested additional budget of $100,000 is transferred to the R&D department and the cost has been changed to $240, the minimum realistic cost.

It should be noted that in both cases—insufficient funds or unrealistic cost—the additional budget required to guarantee completion does not need to be invested in the next period. The guarantee applies to any future period, provided that the amounts (*both additional budget and cost*) are adjusted for inflation occurring during the waiting period.

UTILIZATION OF COMPLETED R&D PROJECTS

An R&D project, once completed, makes the corresponding product available for production. The marketing department might not choose to use that availability in the next period: it might keep the product in reserve for future use. But if the team does decide to use the new product opportunity, two options are available. Either the product is entered on the market as a new brand, or an existing brand is re-formulated with the physical characteristics corresponding to the project.

Figure 6.4: Decisions to Complete R&D Projects—Period 5

MARKSTRAT DECISION FORM

Industry _____ **A** _____

Firm _____ **2** _____

Period _____ **5** _____

PRODUCT MANAGEMENT

Brand Names	Name of R&D Project (if modification or introduction)	Production Planning (thousand units)	Advertising Budget (thousands of $)	Advertising Research (percent)	Recommended Retail Price ($)	Perceptual Objectives (−20 to +20, or 99)	
						Axis 1	Axis 2

SALES FORCE

Distribution Channels	1	2	3
Number of Salespersons			

RESEARCH AND DEVELOPMENT

Project Name	Expenditures (thousands of $)	Physical Characteristics					
		1	2	3	4	5	6
PSEXS	300	10	7	50	25	37	124
PSENZ	100	15	8	50	20	80	240

MARKET RESEARCH STUDIES

1	2	3	4	5	6	7	8	9	10	11	12	13	14	15

(For Instructor's Use)

ec(−)   ep(+)   bd(−)   bi(+)

Brand Introduction

A brand is introduced in the market by entering a brand name which has not been used in the past in the first column of the product management section of the decision form. This brand name is completely independent of the code used for the R&D project. This R&D project code, however, needs to be specified in order for the production department to know the product specification. This is indicated in the second column of the product management section of the decision form, next to the brand name. This needs to be indicated only during the period of introduction. In the following periods, the production department remembers which product specifications to use.

Figure 6.5 provides an example. Product SARA is being introduced in the market using the product with the specification corresponding to the R&D project PSAXI. Given that the brand is just being introduced, advertising must be spent in order to develop consumers' awareness of the brand. Brand SARA is being introduced with a small advertising budget and without perceptual objectives, probably to provide information to management as to how the brand is being perceived. If the positioning is satisfactory, a greater advertising investment will be scheduled in the next period. If, however, the perceptions need adjustment, advertising can still be used to reposition the brand. In the case where a high advertising budget had created a high level of brand awareness, it would have been difficult to adjust perceptions through advertising. This example illustrates a safer but slower approach, which might only be appropriate under conditions of low levels of competition.

Brand Modification

In the decision form shown in Figure 6.5, brand SAMA, which is one of the original brands marketed by company 1, is being modified using the physical characteristics corresponding to project PSARA. Again, the code name of the R&D project has no impact on what the project can be used for. The only difference in entering these decisions on the decision form is that brand SAMA was on the market before.

There are several consequences of this decision. First of all, the production department is now producing units of SAMA with the new product characteristics. The inventories corresponding to the obsolete products have to be sold outside the MARKSTRAT world, as the consumers in MARKSTRAT would not accept an old version of the product. This occurs even for product modifications of cost only, as the new model appears to be different as a result of material substitution and different production processes. In such a case, inventories are automatically sold to a trading company that buys the obsolete product at a price corresponding to 90% of the transfer cost. As the units are still in the possession of the product department, which charges the marketing department when units are sold, the obsolete units must then be purchased from the production department and paid for. Consequently, a loss of 10% of transfer cost is taken on the obsolete inventory. This loss will appear as an extraordinary cost in the next period company results.

To illustrate this process, let's consider that firm 2 has an inventory of 56,118 units of brand SEMI at the end of period 2. The transfer cost of SEMI at this time is $107 per unit. In the next period, period 3, the brand SEMI is being modified with the specification of a new R&D project, PSELY. Consequently, the inventory of 56,118 units evaluated at a transfer cost of $107 per

Figure 6.5: Example of Brand Modification and Brand Introduction

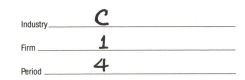

MARKSTRAT DECISION FORM

Industry _____ *C* _____

Firm _____ *1* _____

Period _____ *4* _____

PRODUCT MANAGEMENT

Brand Names	Name of R&D Project (if modification or introduction)	Production Planning (thousand units)	Advertising Budget (thousands of $)	Advertising Research (percent)	Recommended Retail Price ($)	Perceptual Objectives (−20 to +20, or 99) Axis 1	Axis 2
SAMA	PSARA	200	2000	5	400	-5	99
SARA	PSAXI	100	1500	8	450	99	99
SAVA	PSARA	150	3000	8	600	10	99

SALES FORCE

Distribution Channels	1	2	3
Number of Salespersons			

RESEARCH AND DEVELOPMENT

Project Name	Expenditures (thousands of $)	Physical Characteristics 1	2	3	4	5	6

MARKET RESEARCH STUDIES

1	2	3	4	5	6	7	8	9	10	11	12	13	14	15

(For Instructor's Use)

ec(−)   ep(+)   bd(−)   bi(+)

unit will be sold to the trading company at 90% of that cost, or $5,404,160. The loss of $600,463 (10% × 56,118 units × $107 transfer cost) will be shown as an extraordinary cost in in the Company Report of firm 3 in period 3. Note that some differences may occur between the loss reported and the computations due to the rounding of the unit transfer cost reported on the output. These differences are, however, small.

The second consequence of a brand modification concerns the perception by consumers. Both Sonites and Vodites are product categories that consumers buy after a fair amount of information processing. Therefore, when a brand is modified, the changes in the physical characteristics of the product are perceived as soon as the modified product is available in the market. The usual perceptual distortions and biases apply, but the changes are reflected immediately in the new positioning of the brand in the perceptual space.

Since the brand name has not changed, however, the awareness level associated with that brand is conserved. This presents a clear advantage compared to the introduction of a new brand, as lower funds are necessary to establish the brand in its new position, and therefore to gain market share. Due to the ineffectiveness of advertising in repositioning a brand with a high level of awareness, modifying the physical characteristics of a well established brand will usually be necessary to reposition it effectively.

Keep for Future Use

The newly completed R&D project does not need to be used in the period following its completion. In fact, a company planning ahead would have products available in advance. Also, given the uncertainties in demand and in competitors' strategies, the development of contingency plans is important. In order to be ready to implement these plans, products should be readily available. Once an R&D project is completed, the company can put it into reserve and bring it to the market whenever desired. The characteristics of the project remain unchanged, except the transfer cost, which is increased by inflation every period.

Multiple Brands with Same Characteristics

Once a project is completed, it indicates that manufacturing has been found feasible and production can start. What decisions are made on the marketing side about how to market the product is an independent issue. Consequently, the same product can be marketed under different names. This could occur in competitive situations where the presence of multiple brands could build barriers to the entry of new brands by competitors. This situation could also occur when the same basic products would be distributed to different segments which may be willing to pay different prices.

This situation is illustrated by the introduction of brand SAVA in Figure 6.5 using the same product (corresponding to R&D project PSARA) that was used to modify brand SAMA. Notice, however, that the prices charged are $600 and $400, respectively. Therefore, two brands with the same basic physical characteristics are available in the market. This is made possible by differentiating the brands through different packaging and differences in the product that are not perceived by consumers and that are not essential. Hence, these differences are implicit and, therefore, ignored in the MARKSTRAT simulation.

The implication of these differences in the non-basic physical characteristics of the product concerns the production line. The two products need to be produced on different production lines. Consequently, there are no shared costs between the two products. In particular, each product follows its own experience curve and the production of one product does not benefit the other product in terms of its cost.

R&D STRATEGIES

Most R&D projects concern new products with a specific combination of physical characteristics which differs from those designed by the firm in the past. However, in this section, we will first discuss a different kind of R&D, designed not to modify physical characteristics of the product but to reduce the cost of production (transfer cost). Special issues in developing the R&D strategy are also discussed. The role and procedures of feasibility R&D studies are described, as are the implications of the accumulation of know how on the strategies of R&D actions over time. Finally, the issues involved and the procedures to follow for developing the R&D plan are discussed.

Cost Reduction Projects

Although the experience effect contributes to declining costs over time, experience alone is an insufficient force for maintaining margins in competitive industries. Consequently, firms must turn to the Research and Development department for finding new processes, substituting materials, and/or changing the technology in order to reduce costs of production, and therefore transfer cost.

Such projects can be requested by the marketing department of MARK-STRAT firms from their R&D departments. All they need to specify is a project code which satisfies the requirements mentioned earlier in this chapter (the project code has nothing to do with the current brand or R&D project for which the cost is being reduced). The first five characteristics of the project correspond to the existing product for which the cost is being reduced. Then the cost characteristic is the cost set as the objective of the cost reduction project. The marketing department does not indicate or get involved with the suggestions about how to decrease cost. The R&D team in charge of this project searches for a way to lower cost without affecting the value of the first five characteristics.* The R&D team will first check past projects and the brands currently marketed, so that past completed projects with the same physical attributes and their current costs are used as the base upon which the R&D team will try to improve. The budget required to complete such a cost reduction project varies by firm and depending on the amount of R&D experience developed over time by each firm.

---

*Of course, the first five characteristics of a product can be changed to lower the cost as well.

Apart from the budget to allocate to that project, the only other decision to make concerning that project is the cost (characteristic #6) to request. Of course, as for the other characteristics, requesting a very low cost enables the marketing department to obtain information from the R&D department for the next period about the minimum cost that the R&D department is willing to guarantee. If the cost returned by the R&D department is higher than the cost of the first 100,000 units of the current product, this is to be interpreted as a sign that the lowest cost possible has already been achieved.

However, this does not mean that the cost to be specified should necessarily be under the current cost. Clearly, if the cost of the first 100,000 units can be lower than the current cost, so much the better. It will certainly occur, however, that the cost which the R&D department can provide is lower than the average cost for the first 100,000 units of the current product but is higher than the current cost. This new project can, however, lead to costs lower than the current product's cost. This is due to the fact that after the product modification, production starts a new experience curve. By the time the brand is known in the market, sales could be substantial and cumulative production could double extremely fast, possibly within the first year of production. Consequently, while the older product might have been in the part of the experience curve where gains in productivity were minimal (the flat portion of the curve), the new product starts on a new experience curve and therefore benefits from high levels of productivity gains.

This is illustrated in Figure 6.6. The current product had an average base cost for the first 100,000 units (characteristic #6) of $170. Currently, the cumulative production has doubled and the current cost is $110. By request-

Figure 6.6: Cost Reduction R&D

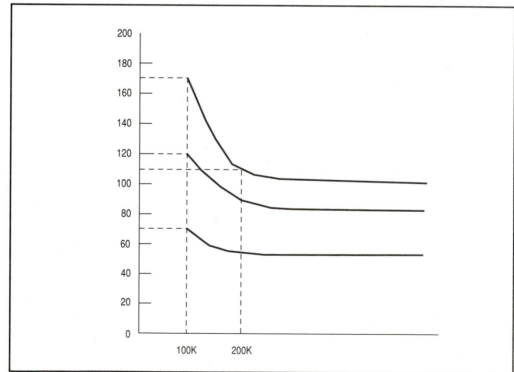

ing a new base cost of $70, the objective would be achieved. However, this would correspond to a drastic cost reduction, which might not always be possible. A base cost of $120, although higher than the current cost of $110, is shown on the figure to yield a cost which within a brief time will be lower than the current product cost. In fact, it can be seen that this would occur between 100,000 and 200,000 cumulative production units.

This has just demonstrated that the cost of a research and development cost reduction project does not need to be lower than the current cost. But what should be the actual cost requested for characteristic 6?

There are basically two methods of deciding. The first one, briefly mentioned earlier, consists of specifying a very low cost with a low budget (as a feasibility study) and waiting for the R&D department to indicate what is the lowest cost they can achieve. This will be efficient when time has low value, i.e., when planning for R&D is done well ahead of time.

Although it is clearly an indication of good strategic management, responses to the marketplace have to be rapid in many circumstances. The second approach can then be used. Part of the strategic plan consists of profitability objectives which require a certain level of margin. Given that the marketing department knows the price at which the brand can be sold, the distribution margin of the distributor, and the required company margin, the maximum cost possible to enable that margin level can be computed. This will be the cost objective for the product. However, it is not yet the cost to be specified as characteristic #6, as cost reduction will be achieved through experience.

Let us assume that the retail price needs to be $400 and that the average distribution margins for the product with the projected distribution in the various channels is 38%. The manufacturer's selling price is therefore $248 [i.e., $400(1 − 0.38)]. If the objective for the gross margin is 40%, the cost should be $148.80 [i.e., $248(1 − 0.4)]. However, it is expected that 400,000 units will be sold and therefore produced during that period. The cost of $148.80 is therefore the cost after benefitting from production experience.

Figure 6.7 illustrates this point by showing the cost of $148.80 on the experience curve at the location corresponding to a level of cumulative production of 400,000 units. In order to find the cost corresponding to the first 100,000 units (the cost to specify in the R&D project), it is sufficient to move back along the experience curve to the level of cumulative production of 100,000 units. The cost is shown to be $200 in Figure 6.7. This assumes that the experience curve rate has been estimated as discussed earlier.

Feasibility Studies

As noted in several occasions, it is particularly important to learn as much as possible about the feasibility of products and the funds necessary in order to complete research and development projects. Although feasibility studies require time, since the information is not available before the end of the period during which it has been requested, feasibility studies are part of the implementation of the long term strategy. Consequently, if the R&D program is established well ahead of time, a more systematic approach can be used. The

Figure 6.7: Cost Specification of an R&D Project

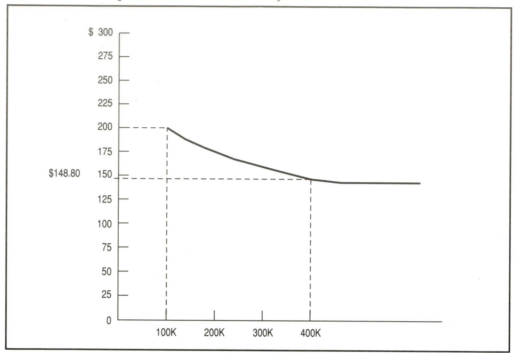

lack of strategy and planning indeed results in short term reactions which have not been anticipated. As a consequence, the R&D activity is not planned and the firm might not have the opportunity to request feasibility studies. Greater inefficiencies will result.

The product is the most important marketing mix variable to implement a strategy, as without a product, there can be no strategy at all. Therefore, R&D activity is crucial to the implementation of a marketing strategy. Feasibility studies can be ordered for a minimal budget of $100,000 for either the Sonite or Vodite market. All opportunities for investigating R&D possibilities should therefore be used, as they provide the necessary information to (1) complete a project efficiently, (2) investigate cost structures and physical characteristic combinations that will provide maximum margins, (3) implement contingency plans rapidly.

Sequential R&D Projects

As indicated before, the R&D department does not start a project each time from scratch. In fact, the R&D teams work by marginally improving upon the most similar products corresponding to projects that have been completed. This has a direct effect on the order in which projects should be investigated for greatest efficiency. Instead of requesting R&D on similar projects in the same time period and moving to different product characteristics at the next period, it will be more efficient to work sequentially and improve on existing products. At one period, R&D might be working on a product with a maximum frequency of 30 Hz and a volume of 60 dm^3. Only after this project has been completed will the company search for a high maximum frequency product of 40 Hz, all other characteristics remaining unchanged.

Planning R&D Activities

Product policy is, although not sufficient in itself, the most critical aspect of the implementation of a strategy. It determines the businesses in which the firm will be competing. This in turn determines the allocation of resources to the various businesses. Consequently, R&D activities should be viewed as a means to achieve a given strategy. The strategy must, therefore, be well laid out before even starting a research and development program, just as is the case for advertising or sales force expenditures. Given this view of the role of R&D as a key component of the implementation of the marketing strategy, and given the delays involved in completing R&D projects, this activity needs to be carefully planned for the entire period covered in the strategic plan. A three step planning process can be found valuable:

Step 1: Define overall marketing strategy and contingency strategies,

Step 2: Define R&D objectives,

Step 3: Define the R&D program.

We now discuss the content of each of these steps and in particular develop the last stage of the R&D program specification.

Define overall marketing strategy and contingency strategies. As indicated above, this step is a *sine qua non*, as no coherent R&D program can be elaborated without knowing where the firm is going. Therefore, the strategy of the firm should clearly be stated in terms of the businesses (products) in which the firm plans to compete and the particular positions that the firm wants to achieve in each market in the future. The timing is particularly important, as it takes a fair number of products to implement the strategy.

The contingency strategies should also be defined with the same concerns and the same degree of elaboration. Given that these strategies would be quickly implemented in case of the occurrence of environmental and competitive factors that *a priori* are considered less likely to occur, the basic ingredients, such as the products, should be ready in order to avoid any delay in the implementation of the new strategy.

Define R&D objectives. Once the strategy and the contingency strategies are developed, the objectives of R&D need to be described. More specifically, these objectives concern the number of R&D projects to be started, corresponding to each business, and the priorities involved in these projects. The priorities in terms of cost reduction projects vis a vis product development with new physical characteristics need to be established.

Define the R&D program. Now the positions corresponding to the businesses in which the firm wants to compete are already stated and the general characteristics of the R&D program (R&D objectives) have been established over time. However, the R&D program is only defined after the actual physical characteristics to develop have been decided. Only then can the R&D budget be determined, since the physical characteristics determine what funds will be necessary to invest to complete the projects. Finally, the timing of R&D should cover the design of feasibility studies that will provide information to improve the efficiency of the R&D department.

(i) *Determine physical characteristics of products corresponding to positioning desired in the future.*

We assume here that the positioning to be reached in the perceptual space is known. Let us emphasize, however, that given the time necessary to complete R&D projects and the long term nature of strategy, these positions should not be based on the current preferences but on the expectations of where the product/brand should be positioned in the future. The future might very well concern periods three, four, or five years from now. The specific characteristics of a product corresponding to a future position should therefore be specified. This specification can only be done efficiently by knowing the relationship between actual product characteristics and the perceptions on the corresponding dimensions, as discussed in Chapter 5.

Such a relationship is illustrated in Figure 6.8. The horizontal axis shows the semantic scale value of design and the actual ratings are indicated on the

Figure 6.8: Relationship Between Physical Characteristics and Perceptions on Corresponding Dimensions

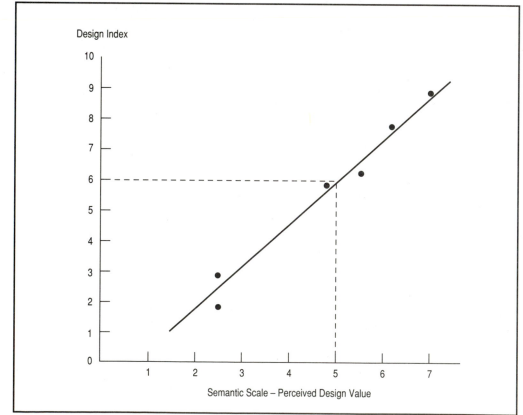

vertical axis. Given this relationship, the design index (physical attribute) which would be perceived on the semantic scale as a 5 is an index of 6. This number is obtained by a vertical projection onto the line representing the relationship and then by a horizontal projection to the vertical axis. A complete discussion of this procedure was presented in the previous chapter.

(ii) *Estimate funds (R&D budget) necessary to complete R&D projects.*

One of the elements of the strategic plan deals with financial considerations involving expected returns and investments necessary to obtain specified objectives. The investments in R&D represent a large part of the budget. Consequently, these funds have to be planned carefully. In particular, the proposed plan should establish the feasibility of a strategy in terms of providing over time the resources necessary to implement the strategy.

A prerequisite for evaluating the funds that will be necessary for R&D is knowledge about what type of research can be expected from the R&D department and with what budget. Therefore it is critical to learn as much as possible about the effectiveness of the R&D department. This suggests intensive interaction between the marketing department and the R&D department. Communication is established through R&D project requests that take the form of feasibility studies.

(iii) *Request feasibility studies for improving the efficiency of the R&D department.*

A feasibility study is basically identical to any R&D project request. The only difference is the size of the budget given the R&D department to study the feasibility of the product. The R&D department provides feedback in terms of the budget required to complete the project and minimum realistic costs for a budget of $100,000. Any additional budget will be used towards the completion of the project.

However, given the uncertainties associated with such projects, it is more efficient to gather as much information as possible by requesting multiple feasibility studies rather than spending more on one project that might have to be abandoned. Figure 6.9 presents four R&D projects that provide information about the budget required to complete a project at two levels of characteristic 3 (50 and 45) and at different costs. A low cost feasibility study, PSURE, will probably provide the minimum realistic cost as well.

CONCLUSION

In this chapter we have provided information as to the key basic components of the implementation of a strategy: the product design via research and development. The R&D projects that are requested by the marketing department do not deal with fundamental research, which would not be under the control of the marketing department. On the contrary, these R&D projects are basic ingredients for the implementation of the firm's marketing strategy, as they concern production feasibility and processes for specific product

Figure 6.9: Feasibility Studies

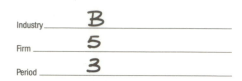

MARKSTRAT DECISION FORM

Industry ___ *B* ___

Firm ___ *5* ___

Period ___ *3* ___

PRODUCT MANAGEMENT

Brand Names	Name of R&D Project (if modification or introduction)	Production Planning (thousand units)	Advertising Budget (thousands of $)	Advertising Research (percent)	Recommended Retail Price ($)	Perceptual Objectives (−20 to +20, or 99)	
						Axis 1	Axis 2

SALES FORCE

Distribution Channels	1	2	3
Number of Salespersons			

RESEARCH AND DEVELOPMENT

Project Name	Expenditures (thousands of $)	Physical Characteristics					
		1	2	3	4	5	6
PSUVA	100	15	8	50	10	50	200
PSUMA	100	15	8	45	10	50	180
PSULL	100	15	8	50	10	50	150
PSURE	100	15	8	50	10	50	100

MARKET RESEARCH STUDIES

1	2	3	4	5	6	7	8	9	10	11	12	13	14	15

(For Instructor's Use)	

ec(−)   ep(+)   bd(−)   bi(+)

features. This chapter has provided information that will help the MARKSTRAT teams to implement their strategies. It also provides them with a discussion of issues involved in the management of R&D over time.

This chapter and the preceding one, chapter 5, offer the indispensable basic tools for developing and implementing the marketing strategy. The next chapter covers additional types of analyses that should improve the evaluation of alternative strategies and the efficiency of their implementation.

CHAPTER 6 SUMMARY

R&D Project Name Conventions

- R&D project names consist of five letters

- The first letter is always "P"

- The second letter identifies the type of product that is being searched for ("S" for Sonites and "V" for Vodites)

- The last three letters may be freely chosen by a company, as long as its projects (current and past) have different names

- The R&D project name bears no relationship to the commercialized brand name. Thus, "PSUZZ" may be used to improve existing brand "SULI" or to create a new brand "SUZI"

An R&D project name should be structured as follows:

P				

"P" for Project	Product Type: S = Sonite V = Vodite	Freely chosen alphabetical letters or numbers to identify the project		

Example:

P	V	O	X	3

This R&D project is a Vodite. The last three characters identify the project and consequently the letter following the product type (letter "O" in this example) does not mean that this project is developed by firm 4.

Feasible Ranges of the Physical Characteristics Values for Sonites and Vodites

	Physical Characteristics	*Feasible Range*
Sonites:	Weight (*Kg*)	10 – 20
	Design (*index*)	3 – 10
	Volume (*dm*^{3})	20 – 100
	Maximum Frequency (1000 *Hz*)	5 – 50
	Power (*W*)	5 – 100

	Physical Characteristics	*Feasible Range*
Vodites:	Autonomy (*m*)	5 – 100
	Maximum Frequency (1000 *Hz*)	5 – 20
	Diameter (*mm*)	10 – 100
	Design (*index*)	3 – 10
	Weight (*g*)	10 – 100

Key Rules about Communication with R&D Department

- Communications with the R&D department are made through the R&D part of the decision form. The answers from the R&D department come in the R&D section of the output. Therefore, the R&D department response time is a one-year period.

- The name of a project that has been completed cannot be re-used for a new project, even if it is a cost reduction project (each team has two completed projects at period 0: PSAMA, PSALT, PSEMI, PSELF, PSIRO, PSIBI, PSONO, PSOLD, PSUSI, PSULI, according to the firm vowel).

- Once a project has been started under a given name, the only modification of the uncompleted project that can be requested under the same project name is the base unit cost (characteristic 6).

- All messages sent by the R&D department concerning costs and budgets required to be certain to complete the project requested by the Marketing department during the period are adjusted for inflation. Note that if a project is not completed, the R&D department changes automatically the base unit cost (characteristic 6) for the next period to take inflation into account. Maintaining the same cost as the previous period would correspond to a request for a lower real cost. The R&D department could not guarantee the completion of such a requested project.

- Each product, whether marketed under an existing brand name (brand modification) or under a new brand name (introduction), starts a new experience curve upon introduction. Consequently, in the case of a product modification due to a cost reduction, costs go down the new experience curve faster than before the modification. This needs to be taken into account for requesting the base unit cost (characteristic 6) of the new product. In particular, although a project with very low cost might be impossible to complete, a somewhat higher cost than the current cost could result very fast in a lower cost than could ever be realized without a new R&D project.

- If a product is modified and marketed under an existing brand name, the new characteristics will be perceived by consumers immediately.

- New products are different from existing products, even if they share the first five characteristics (but at a different cost). Consequently, a brand modification due to a cost reduced product results in unusable inventory. Disposing of this inventory results in an exceptional cost equal to 10% of transfer cost.

Planning R&D Activities

1. Define overall marketing strategy and contingency strategies.

2. Define R&D objectives.

3. Define the R&D program.

   For each time period covered in the strategic plan:

   (i) Determine physical characteristics of products corresponding to positioning desired in the future.

   (ii) Estimate funds (R&D budget) necessary to complete R&D projects.

   (iii) Request feasibility studies for improving the efficiency of the R&D activity.

Competitive Strategies

The design of a marketing strategy is based in large part on the assessment of competition. Therefore, competitive analysis constitutes a basic preliminary investigation upon which the strategic plan rests. The first section of this chapter covers briefly the main elements of a competitive analysis. These elements affect the marketing strategy of a firm and should be considered in developing a strategic marketing plan in the MARKSTRAT simulation. The second section of the chapter discusses alternative competitive strategies open to the MARKSTRAT firms. The conditions when each of these generic marketing strategies might be appropriate are also discussed. The last two sections of this chapter concern specific strategic issues arising when introducing a new brand in an existing or a new market and when defending the firm's position under attack from a new or existing competitor.

COMPETITIVE ANALYSIS

The notion of industry and competitor analysis has been particularly exposed by Porter.[*] This line of work has established a checklist of conditions affecting the level of competition in an industry. Although it has been the predominant perspective in strategy, its economic emphasis has restrained its view mostly to the analysis of competitive structure. The marketing orientation of strategy leads to considering additional factors that help address the fundamental questions needed for guiding the marketing strategy of a firm.

The questions that need answers for marketing strategic purposes have been stated by Weitz:[†]

1. Who are the firm/brand's competitors?
2. How intense is the competition in a market?

---

[*]Porter, Michael E. (1980), *Competitive Strategy*, New York, NY: The Free Press. Porter, Michael E. (1985), *Competitive Advantage*, New York, NY: The Free Press.

[†]Weitz, Barton A. (1985), "Introduction to Special Issue on Competition," *Journal of Marketing Research*, 22 (August).

3. How does competition affect market evolution and structure?

4. How do competitive actions affect the firm's marketing decisions?

5. How do firms achieve and maintain a competitive advantage?

Clearly, question number 5 encompasses all aspects of a strategy and therefore is covered by all the chapters of this manual. The rules, principles and generalizations that concern the design of a marketing strategy as discussed in the manual have for objective this long term sustainable competitive advantage. The answer to the first question is a condition for being able to answer any of the others. We will discuss this issue related to the definition of market boundaries first. However, the emphasis of this section will be on assessing the intensity of competition in a market as it impacts the choice of markets to compete in. We will also discuss the effects of competition on the market and consequently on the firm's marketing decisions.

Defining the Set of Relevant Competitors

Competitors are potentially the five firms in a MARKSTRAT industry. However, in terms of brands, the competition is usually within a market segment. Consequently, one issue concerns the definition of the brands competing in a market segment. The product market analysis or methodologies used in marketing research can provide an important input in assessing that question. However, the product market analysis provides only a snapshot of a competitive situation at a point in time. In fact, when dealing with strategic planning, the long term perspective forces the analyst to consider the factors that would change the competitive situation in the years ahead.

Marketing has offered the market product perspective with such methodologies as the multidimensional scaling analysis provided in MARKSTRAT as a research study. Porter has supplied a broader perspective with the notion of strategic group, or more recently, of industry segment.* The firms in a strategic group face the same environment and compete with similar strategies. This typically implies that the firms in the same strategic group compete in the same market segment. However, this condition is not necessary, nor is it sufficient. A firm could compete in a segment but with a different strategy, and therefore would not belong to the same strategic group. Also, a firm might not compete in a given segment but might have a generally similar strategy, which would make this company a likely new entrant into the segment in which we are competing.

For example, from Figure 7.1, brands A, B and C compete in segment 1 and brand D satisfies the demand by itself in segment 2. Let us assume that the horizontal axis represents perceived price and the vertical axis represents a product quality dimension. In a typical analysis, the relevant market, and therefore competitors for segment 1, would be brands A, B and C. The firm marketing brand D might not be part of the set of competitors. In fact, the firm marketing brand D is able to produce a brand with the same level of quality as brands A, B and C, but charges a lower price, which could mean

---

*Porter (1980), *op. cit.*

Figure 7.1: Competitive Industry Segment Analysis

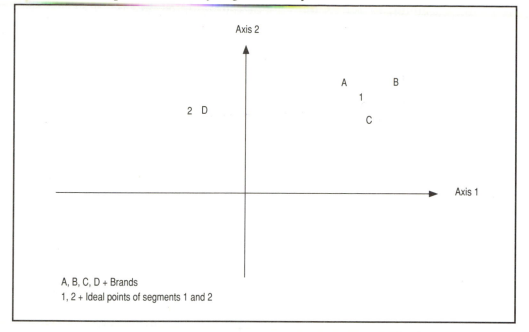

A, B, C, D + Brands
1, 2 + Ideal points of segments 1 and 2

that brand D is produced at a lower cost. Consequently, that firm could enter segment 1 and enjoy higher margins, which in the long term will give this company a competitive advantage. That threat of entry has to be considered, and, from a strategic standpoint, brand D should be part of the competitive analysis of the firms present in segment 1.

Therefore, the strategic group notion gives a somewhat different perspective from the product market approach. The two approaches, however, provide complementary views. Porter's notion of industry segment reflects this complementarity. The basic analysis of perceptions (competitive positions) and preferences (segmentation) provides the major quantitative assessment of competitive analysis at a given time. However, the more qualitative evaluations of industry structure and of competitors' strategies allow a longer term view, which enables a better assessment of who the competitors really are for marketing strategy purposes. Therefore, the analysis of perceptions and preferences is crucial for competitive analysis, but should be complemented by an industry type of analysis.

Assessing the Intensity of Competition

Structural factors. In addition to direct competition between existing firms offering similar products, Porter identifies four structural forces of an industry that influence the intensity with which firms will compete in an industry: the degree of threat of entry, the power of suppliers, the power of customers or buyers, and the threat of substitutes. Two of these factors, the power of suppliers and of customers, are not relevant in MARKSTRAT, as each segment and market (Sonite and Vodite) face the same supply characteristics and are marketed through the same channels to individual consumers. Consequently, differences across markets or segments cannot be attributable to various degrees of suppliers' power or buyers' power. However, the threat of entry and the threat of substitutes are clearly important concerns for the marketing strategists in MARKSTRAT, since these threats are different in different markets or segments.

Each firm is different in terms of its past experience in different markets and segments. Consequently, the competitive advantages of each firm are different as well. Some firms are better able (e.g., at lower costs) to satisfy the needs of some markets than their competitors. Consequently, some markets will be easier to enter by some firms than others. Apart from the number and size of the competitors present in a given market segment, the various segments and markets have different levels of barriers to entry associated with them. This may be due to the nature of the needs to satisfy, as indicated above. Or it may be because the existing competitors have been able to erect barriers to entry. The following are examples of barriers to entry in the MARKSTRAT world.

- The capital required to satisfy the needs of a given market segment varies by market segment. This is particularly clear for an innovation for which many uncertainties exist, in particular in terms of predicting what consumers want. Therefore, the risks associated with entering the Vodite market and consequently, for example, the expected expenses to develop the "right" product, might act as a barrier to entry. For firms which can afford entering the market, this might provide a first mover's advantage. The extent of the barriers depends, of course, on the capital necessary to enter and maintain a position in that market. The key questions are: (1) what level of investment is necessary to enter the market and to maintain a position in a market, and (2) what capabilities, in particular in terms of R&D, are required?

- The degree with which existing firms satisfy the need of a market segment act also as a barrier to entry. If existing competitors provide consumers with products that are perceived as corresponding to their preferences, there is little room for a new entrant in this market. However, as is typical in the early stage of a product life cycle, if needs are difficult to assess and the offerings of the market do not correspond to what consumers want, the door is open for new entries. Important marketing investments, in particular in communications, make consumers better aware of the existence of a product and may persuade them of its superiority. In addition, important marketing investments make those of competitors less visible and less effective. Thus, marketing intensity acts also as a barrier to entry. The questions to ask here are: (1) how well are the needs of the market segments served and (2) what level of marketing investment do existing competitors make in this market segment? For example, Figure 7.2 represents a competitive situation where seg-

Figure 7.2: An example of a barrier to entry established by ideal product positioning

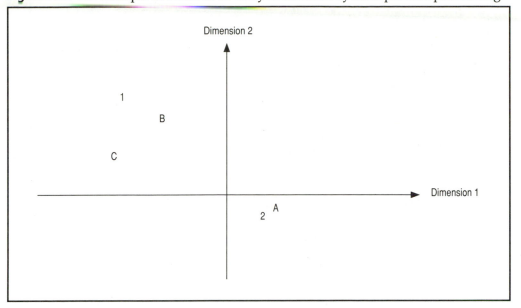

ment 2's needs are very well satisfied by brand A, as brand A is positioned next to the ideal preference for that segment. Even though there are more brands directed at segment 1, it will be more difficult to enter segment 2 with a new brand than segment 1, assuming similar marketing investments made by the firms currently present in these segments.

■ The degree to which existing competitors control the distribution channels are also indicators of the height of barriers to entry. If existing competitors cover extensively the key channels of distribution used by consumers in a market segment, it will be more costly to enter that segment. The distribution channel plays an important strategic role, for it has a considerable impact on the sales of the brand. This impact is typically of long term duration. The relevant questions are: (1) what are the crucial channels for the market segment and (2) what level of effort is expended by the sales force of existing competitors in these channels.

■ Finally, an important barrier is economies of scale and cost declines through experience. Cost reductions which are possible to achieve in some market segments due to the size of these markets might not be realizable in other market segments. It is critical to have low costs to generate profits which are greater than competition in order to re-invest and possibly create higher barriers to entry. Hence, competition in a market must be assessed in cost terms. The questions to ask are: (1) what is the size of this market, now and in the future and (2) how fast can costs decline for the type of products in this market (through basic learning and through R&D)?

All these structural factors are certainly key to understanding competition in the MARKSTRAT environment. The questions that they raise help in developing a broader strategic perspective. However, these structural factors do not indicate how we can expect firms to behave in each market segment. Marketers are interested in evaluating what is happening within an industry and what will happen in that industry. Consequently, it is important for the design of a marketing strategy to also assess the *behavior* of competitors.

Competitive Behavior. Marketing researchers assessing the effectiveness of the marketing mix variables have realized the importance of considering competition as part of the marketing system to be modelled. Indeed, if competitors in a market make their marketing mix decisions as a function of what other firms are doing or are expected to be doing based on their past behavior, the level of resources invested in that market is likely to follow a cyclical pattern. This pattern can very easily be observed by considering the evolution of expenditures and prices in the market, separately for each competitor or at the aggregate industry level. In a very competitive market, advertising expenditures and sales force expenditures would increase over time. In a less competitive market, these marketing investments may have a tendency to decrease. This is illustrated in Figure 7.3 where advertising expenditures are plotted over time for two market segments. Segment 2 is shown to be more competitive that segment 5 as expenditures arise more steeply over time. The plot of sales force expenditures by channel also indicates that more competition occurs in channel 1 than in channel 2. An essential part of competitive response concerns the product itself. Therefore, one would expect R&D expenditures to increase as well in competitive markets. However, one phenomenon that often arises in very highly competitive markets is that the resources are diverted from long term objectives—of which new product development is a crucial part—to short term reactions to and in anticipation of competitive moves. This is partly due to the lack of budget to cover all fronts, short term and long term, and also to the over-emphasis on defending short term performance. Consequently, while expenditures on existing products/brands might increase over time in competitive intense markets, R&D expenditures might not follow the same pattern. In fact they might rather increase first but as the competition becomes more and more intense, resources are depleted and R&D expenditures might decrease.

This pattern of reaction is therefore essential to understand the type and extent of competition in a market. These reaction patterns should therefore be determined as part of the competitive analysis task. Competitive reaction is specifically taken into account in a model of the firms' marketing decisions. Marketing mix decisions are expressed as a function of the current values of the competitors' marketing mix and as a function of their past decisions. These functions allow the estimation of reaction elasticities. A reaction elasticity is the percentage change in the value of a marketing mix variable (say advertising) of a brand when the other brand changes the same or another marketing mix variable by one percent. Therefore, the reaction elasticity represents the behavior of one brand in reaction to another brand. These reactions are simple if one firm (a brand) reacts with the same marketing instrument it is reacting to (for example, reacting to an advertising increase by a competitor

Figure 7.3: Marketing Expenditure Trends

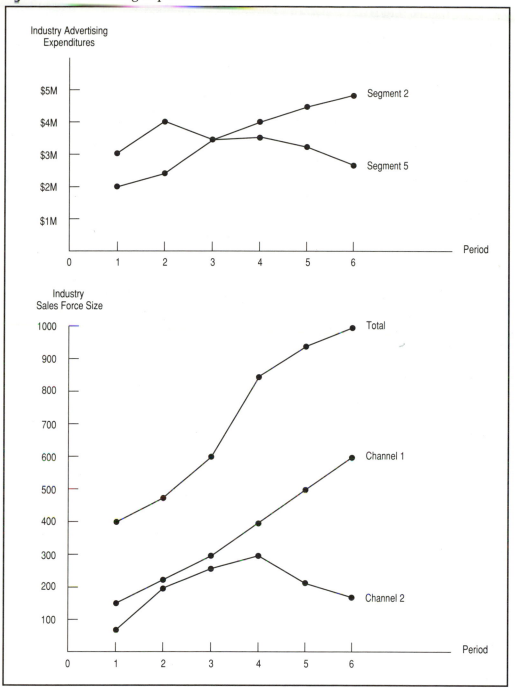

by increasing your own advertising expenditures). It is a complex reaction if the firm reacts with a different marketing mix variable, for example decreasing price when the competitor increases advertising expenditures.

In general, positive reaction indicates the presence of active competitive behavior. Then, the greater the reaction, the more competitive the pair of firms is. The reaction elasticities can also be negative, indicating a lack of competition, even showing evidence of competition avoidance. For example, when one firm increases its advertising, the other pulls back. Therefore, there is a continuum of competitive reactivity, varying from competitive avoidance to strong rivalry. Although these approaches have limitations (e.g., stability over time), they offer quantitative measures which are relatively easy to estimate using simple regression analysis on time series data about the marketing activities of each competitor. These data can be obtained in MARKSTRAT to assess the intensity of competition in each market segment. The competitivity of a market has direct implications on the attractiveness of this market, as a competitive market will require greater resource commitment. Consequently, the number of brands competing, the way the existing brands compete and the degree to which new brands are likely to enter the market are important strategic factors to be analyzed when deciding whether to enter a market or not. It is also an important part of the analysis necessary to decide how to enter a market. The size of the initial commitment and the speed with which one would enter the market depends on these factors. For example, the decision to build awareness fast or, instead, to cautiously ensure an adequate positioning for the new brand is clearly dependent on these factors. In a highly competitive market, speed is required as existing competitors would respond quickly to a weakness of an entrant. If, on the other hand, the market is not very competitive, working slowly on the brand positioning before awareness is too high would be recommended.

The analysis of competition can also provide crucial information as to the competitive strategy to adopt. The long term competitive advantage of one firm can only be assessed by understanding the competition. Industry structure as well as the nature of competitive reactions and behavior enables the marketing strategist to assess what the strengths and weaknesses of the various competitors, including their own firm, are. This assessment will drive the competitive strategy to adopt. However, several basic competitive strategies often compete. The next section of this chapter intends to present general or "generic" bases of competitive advantage. The conditions under which each generic basis is more appropriate for designing the marketing strategy are then discussed.

COMPETITIVE STRATEGIES

Competitive strategies are based on the objectives of developing and maintaining a long term sustainable competitive advantage. In this section, we will discuss two generic bases of competitive advantage. The bases of competitive advantage which can be used are first defined. Then, the characteristics of the environment which determine which strategy is more appropriate are discussed.

Basis of Competitive Advantage

According to Porter a generic marketing strategy can be represented along two main dimensions: the scope of the targeted market and the basis of the competitive advantage. The scope of the targeted market corresponds directly to the segmentation strategy discussed in chapter 5. The basic conclusion of that chapter was that each segment must be evaluated separately and, in most situations, each segment that the firm decides to serve should be reached with a differentiated strategy. Therefore the segment is the level of focus that should serve as the basic level of analysis. Because of mobility barriers between segments, however, a more global view is necessary as well. These issues conclude this chapter

Two broad classes of competitive advantages have been identified in the strategy literature: cost advantage and product differentiation advantage. In a given segment, the firm must attain at least one of these competitive advantages to be effective in the long run. For that, the firm must have (1) an advantage over competition (2) on an attribute that the consumer will perceive as important. For example an advantage over competition on the ability to manufacture a high frequency product better (higher levels and/or at lower costs) is not a competitive advantage if consumers do not care about the attribute frequency. Similarly, a cost advantage where the differential profits cannot be used to better satisfy demand (in quality or quantity) will not be a competitive advantage. Therefore, in such a case of costs lower than competition, the firm must be able to lower its price if the market is price elastic or spend the additional profits for example on advertising if and only if it pays to advertise. Let us consider in turn these bases of competitive advantage and then we will discuss when one may be more appropriate than the other.

Cost Leadership. Cost leadership can be achieved in MARKSTRAT through experience (the experience curve) and/or Research and Development. Because of the gains in costs due to the experience curve which applies to transfer prices, everything else being equal, a firm can achieve a cost lower than competitors. Although production levels can be inflated (relative to sales of the brand) in earlier periods of the brand introduction to lower the costs, in the long term this strategy assumes market dominance in terms of market share. Otherwise, inventory holding costs would counter the gains obtained through higher levels of production. Market share is therefore an important objective for such a strategy. The basis for gaining share and the cost of attaining market dominance are discussed below. Briefly, however, market share can be gained by appealing to the consumers' needs either for low prices or for a "better" product (i.e., perceived closer to their ideal preference) or both.

Competitors, however, can challenge this cost leadership through cost gains obtained from their R&D. Consequently, cost leadership cannot in general be solely attained from market dominance. Such a strategy requires an appropriate research and development program as discussed in chapter 6. It should be pointed out here from a competitive strategy standpoint that different firms have different positions vis-à-vis their costs and the likelihood of being successful in their cost reduction R&D activities. This type of competitive advantage is, however, not predetermined by exogenous factors. Indeed, the nature and extent of past R&D activities of each firm contributes the most significant part of their ability to become a cost leader. Although some firms might have this advantage in the earlier periods of the simulation, this leadership or potential leadership can be challenged by other firms during the simulation.

Cost reduction through R&D can be obtained through projects operating solely on costs of material and manufacturing processes but keeping the key characteristics on a product unchanged. Another way to achieve cost reduction is through product re-design. Some physical product characteristics are more expensive to produce than others. One might be willing to trade off some level of physical attribute for a cost reduction, as long as it affects consumers' perceptions in a small way. For some characteristics which do not appear important to the consumers, preferences would be practically unaffected. Therefore, the objective should be to design the product with the level of that product characteristic which provides the lowest cost. This approach must be considered even though the strategy of the firm might not be based on cost leadership. In both cases, the R&D expenditures for reducing the cost of the product might not be justified.

Other sources of cost advantages can consist of synergies with other products. These synergies are minimal in MARKSTRAT because each brand is marketed under a different brand name without umbrella branding or advertising. Each brand is also produced independently in different plants. Even if two brands share the same R&D project but are differentiated by their prices, they each follow a separate experience curve using different packaging and production facilities. However, synergies do exist in terms of R&D and distribution. For R&D synergies, we refer the MARKSTRAT participant to chapter 6. As for distribution synergies, they are due to the fact that the sales force carries all the brands marketed during a period. Therefore, selling multiple brands demanded by consumers shopping in similar distribution outlets decreases the cost of selling these brands.

Production cost can be a very important factor of success in some competitive environments, in particular because lower costs provide better margins than competition; these margins can then be reinvested in marketing activities for which other firms do not have the resources to respond. In general, but more especially for the firm adopting a cost leadership strategy, it will be crucial to investigate the three sources of cost reduction discussed above: experience curve effects, R&D cost reduction programs and product synergies. Ignoring one of these sources can give an opportunity to competition to challenge this cost leadership. In addition, cost leadership does not mean that the product features can be worse than competition. At least parity on the product itself might be required to implement a successful cost leadership strategy.

Product Differentiation. Product differentiation in MARKSTRAT concerns the decisions that enable the firm to position a brand at a given location in the consumers' perceptual map. These decisions are discussed in chapter 5. Product differentiation can be attained through R&D or advertising. Product positioning and, therefore, product differentiation play a central role in MARKSTRAT. More specifically, each firm can evaluate the sensitivity of demand to the position of a product. Therefore, given the importance of having a correct positioning and given the difficulty to maintain a position in a segment due to demand and competitive dynamics, the implementation of a product differentiation strategy can present a real challenge.

As indicated earlier, consumers in MARKSTRAT have preferences in terms of the product attributes that they desire. The brand that is perceived closest to the ideal of a consumer segment should have the highest market share, given that the consumers are aware of the brand and given that the brand is available in the proper distribution outlets. Consequently, it is essential that a brand be perceived as corresponding to consumers' preferences for a given segment, at least from a market share perspective. From a profitability point of view, a "perfect" position might not necessarily be worth the cost of achieving such a position. However, a brand which is not positioned close to an ideal point offers opportunity to competitors to move in and establish a position in this segment. Therefore, a proper position is crucial for the product differentiation strategy as a basis of a sustainable competitive advantage.

It is not guaranteed, however, that such an advantage is sustainable in the long term. The ability to sustain a competitive advantage through positioning depends on multiple factors. One factor is the stability of consumer preferences. In some segments, for example, consumers' needs and preferences are changing only very slowly, if they are changing at all. Other segments keep up with the latest technologies and modify their product requirements over time. Another factor is the existence of barriers to entry or mobility barriers that prevent other brands to be repositioned so as to displace the current leader. Competitors might not have the technology and/or expertise to bring a new brand into the market that would be better positioned. For example, different companies have different abilities to complete R&D projects with specific characteristics. Some companies can bring to term products with high power with a reasonably low budget; others can find it easier to have a better design. Even imitation can be harder for some characteristics than others. If imitation is possible, other firms could have a cost disadvantage. Also, competitors might not be able to change the perception of their existing brands in a market because of the high level of awareness of these brands or because of the lack of funds necessary to reposition a brand through advertising. Some of these barriers can be created or heightened by the segment leader.

Generally, however, it is difficult to sustain a differentiated advantage in MARKSTRAT, although it is not impossible. Competitors have each relative advantages that they develop. However, they all have opportunities to compete in most segments. Consequently, the bases of competitive advantages are not determined once and for all. Indeed, the ability to sustain an advantage depends on the decisions of the players over time and depends on their ability to plan for protecting their competitive advantages.

Choice of Basis of Competitive Advantage

An essential part of the marketing plan is therefore to establish which of the two broadly defined bases of competitive advantage is appropriate and to design a consistent plan over time to sustain that advantage. This choice of the bases of competitive advantage depends on a number of factors related to the firm itself and related to demand characteristics. However, these two bases of competitive advantage are not mutually exclusive. In many cases, they are actually operating as complements. This complementarity does not eliminate the need for choosing one as the main basis of the initial strategy. A final element for making this strategic choice of the basis for competing is the cost involved in maintaining that competitive advantage.

- *Firm characteristics.* The firm characteristics concern the relative comparative ability of one firm to perform a particular function. For example, a MARKSTRAT firm might be able to improve a Sonite brand on the power characteristic with a minor cost differential. Other firms might complete the same project with a cost characteristic substantially higher than this firm's cost. These differential abilities are basic to the choice of the basis of competitive advantage on which to develop a marketing strategy. Differential cost advantages exist not only for R&D, as discussed above, but also in terms of the firm performance in positioning and re-positioning their brands in the market, the efficiency in advertising and in obtaining distributors for the brand. For choosing the cost basis of competitive advantage, the firm must be able to maintain a dominant position in the market, as discussed earlier.

- *Price elasticity of demand.* Demand for a brand is said to be price elastic if it increases significantly when price is decreased. In this case, cost becomes a crucial element of competition as any competitor with a lower cost can reduce its price and gain a substantial market share. Consequently, in price elastic segments or markets, cost leadership will be a necessary requirement to maintain the brand market share position. This might not be the only requirement, however.

- *Complementarity of bases of competitive advantage.* In fact, in order to sustain a cost advantage, whether demand is price elastic or not, a high market share is often required because of the gains in productivity due to experience. The value of market share is particularly important when each firm has exhausted the possibilities of reducing cost through technological progress. Therefore, when the market matures and Research and Development produce marginal cost reducing innovations, the experience curve becomes the main source of competitive advantage on costs. An important question is how can this market share dominance be obtained. When the market is price elastic, cutting price will increase market share. Depending on the competitive situation, though, this impact can be only temporary. Indeed, it can be anticipated that competitors in the same segment will react by cutting their prices as well, starting a price war. A product differentiation strategy can also achieve a gain in market share which will result in lower costs. This indirect way of obtaining lower costs might avoid direct confrontation with competitors. It might be harder for competitors to react on product attributes, or at least their reactions might take longer as the process of product differentiation through R&D or advertising can take longer to implement than a price cut. Consequently, product differentiation might be in some cases the only way to also achieve a cost competitive advantage.

■ *Costs for achieving a competitive advantage.* The costs for Research and Development programs are a substantial part of the MARKSTRAT firms' budgets. All firms gather information about the feasibility of specific R&D projects and about the budgets required to complete them. It is important to estimate the R&D budgets spent by other firms as well. In MARKSTRAT, different firms can complete the same R&D projects with different budget levels because of their differences in past R&D experience. This means that the cost of maintaining a position in a market segment is different for different competitors. The handicap due to these different budget requirements can prevent completely a firm from maintaining a position in a market segment due to their budget size limitation or to their R&D experience. The cost of repositioning through advertising can be prohibitive as well for some companies as their high brand awareness might prevent them from adjusting consumers' perceptions through advertising. Also, if competitors spend large budgets in advertising, the feasible share of voice of a firm with a limited budget could be too insignificant to show any impact. Finally, the costs of maintaining cost leadership are not only due to the R&D Budgets and to expenses necessary to dominate a market. In fact the most significant impact on profits might be pricing, as a decrease in price reduces margins which might not be compensated for by a gain in sales. None of these costs should be ignored because the choice of the basis for competing with other firms depends as much on their costs for maintaining an advantage as it does on the current position of the firm vis-à-vis its competitors.

ENTRY STRATEGIES

When a firm intends to market a new product or a new brand, a series of marketing decisions must be made about when to enter, with what mix of marketing variables and how aggressive the introduction should be. The following decisions are, therefore, analyzed in this section: (1) the timing of the entry in terms of pioneering advantages, (2) the signaling of the entry to the competitors, (3) the brand introduction marketing mix allocation and (4) the scale of the entry.

Pioneer Advantage

The empirical literature offers evidence of a general advantage of being first in a market (Urban *et al.* 1986, Biggadike 1979, Whitten 1979, Bond and Lean 1977).* We will review the arguments advanced for that inherent advantage. However, there are also risks associated with pioneering which will be discussed next.

Monopolistic Profits. Being first means that there is no other competitors in the market. Consequently, in theory, the single firm can realize monopolistic profits. The danger, however, is that the high profitability attracts new entries unless some types of barriers have been erected. In MARKSTRAT, a brand positioned by itself close to a segment can indeed be in that position because that brand satisfies the needs of that segment and it could be difficult for competitors to develop a product at least as good. This implies, however, that the pioneer has taken advantage of the best opportunity for brand positioning. If instead, the brand had been positioned further from the ideal points, a new brand could enter in a better position on the perceptual map and the advantages of the lack of early competition would disappear immediately. Nevertheless, depending on the extent of awareness established in the market, a residual advantage might remain. The first mover needs, however, to possess a high awareness level and needs to spend advertising dollars to increase the later entrants' costs of gaining awareness and a position in the consumers perceptual maps.

Distribution Support. In addition, and possibly a more sustainable advantage can be derived from having an established distribution support system. If the pioneer brand sells and is supported by an appropriate advertising program, distributors might not have an incentive to carry the brand of later entrants. This is achieved in MARKSTRAT by coordinating the marketing mix program, thinking about the long-term impact of sales force allocation to the distribution channels.

Production Experience. Finally, the first mover benefits from a greater accumulation of experience in production which gives cost advantages over competition. This would suggest, therefore, the largest scale of production possible to achieve the fastest learning effect possible.

These advantages are not, however, without risk. Indeed, going after a new market such as the Vodite market necessitates making decisions with limited information. Consumers have difficulty expressing their needs when

---

*Urban, Glen L., Theresa Carter, Steven Gaskin and Zofia Mucha (1986), "Market Share Rewards to Pioneering Brands: An Empirical Analysis and Strategic Implications," *Management Science*, 32 (June), 645–659. Biggadike, Ralph E. (1977), Entering New Markets: Strategies and Performance," Report No. 77-108, Marketing Science Institute, Cambridge, MA. Whitten, Ira (1979), "Brand Performance in the Cigarette Industry and the Advantage to Early Entry, 1913–1974," Federal Trade Commission, Bureau of Economics, June. Bond, R. S. and D. F. Lean (1977), "Sales Promotion and Product Differentiation in Two Prescription Drug Markets," *Economic Report*, Federal Trade Commission, February.

the product is not available yet. This is particularly the case for a completely new product (radical innovation), but occurs as well for a segment of an existing market where there is no competitor. It is difficult to translate feasible physical characteristics of potential new products into preferences, and to evaluate the relative impact of alternative strategies. This situation reflects the risks of innovating because of the limited information available to make decisions. A possibility is to introduce a new product with limited marketing resources to investigate the market reaction to a given entry strategy. This is similar to performing a market test. It reduces the risk of engaging important resources for a given strategy but gives time for competition to react more effectively.

Entry Signaling

The signaling of the entry can impact the long term profitability of the intro-duction because it provides information (correct or sometimes misleading) to competitors, to distributors and to consumers. In MARKSTRAT, consumers react to the product offerings and are not influenced beyond the marketing mix variables. Distributors behave also according to industry practices that are not influenced by the behavior of an individual firm. Nevertheless, the simulation does take into consideration the dynamics of market share, sales growth and advertising support on the behavior of distributors. This issue is addressed in chapter 9. Signaling in MARKSTRAT is the result of the behavior of competitors and occurs only through the decisions of each firm. Each firm tries to interpret the decisions of each competitor to anticipate their strategies. Any information provided through the marketing mix decisions is likely to influence the other competitors' decisions. For example, heavy allocation of resources on a segment might be interpreted by competitors as an intention to focus on that segment and might give time to the firm to develop an R&D project directed at another segment. Launching an early Vodite could indicate an intention to allocate major resources to that market. This could deter smaller firms from entering the Vodite market.

Marketing Mix

New brands can be successfully marketed even though they are not first in a market. They need, however, to provide a differential advantage to the con-sumers. In addition, late entries not only need to catch up on the existing competitors' awareness level, but they also need to communicate the product benefits with heavy advertising expenditures, possibly beyond the existing competitive brands' advertising levels. This large allocation of resources to advertising for late brand introductions is reinforced by the necessity to spend more advertising to position the new brand effectively. The advertising message, and therefore, the perceptual objectives and advertising research, play a particularly more important role for late entrants than for the pioneer.

The size and the allocation of the sales force need not necessarily change when a new brand is introduced. These decisions depend on the distribution synergies of the new brand with the existing portfolio of the firm. If the markets or market segments corresponding to the new brand have similar shopping behaviors than the segments already served by the firm, no reallocation might be necessary. Costs can therefore be saved by sharing the sales force and distribution costs.

Scale of Entry

A large scale brand introduction is necessary because of cost gains due to experience when the competition sells similar products. If potential entries by other firms are a threat, large scale gives the entrant a cost advantage that will deter new brand introductions by competitors. Even without considering experience curve effects or the threat of further brand introductions, a large scale entry can signal to existing competitors commitment to the brand and the expectation of a strong reaction if the introduction of the brand is challenged. A large scale entry, therefore, can be used as a signal to competitors to stay away.

The entry can, however, cause a strong reaction from the existing competitors if they feel really threatened. In such a circumstance, profits will be lowered by this increased rivalry. If these reactions are expected, it is a better entry strategy to build the level of sales slowly and introduce the brand at a smaller scale level which will not draw as much attention from the competitors and will not cause a strong reaction.

Another reason for a small scale entry is the uncertainty about a new market. In a segment where there is no product offering or in a new market such as in the Vodite market, it may be more prudent to introduce a brand with a small scale to test the market and learn from the first periods of introduction instead of committing resources that could be wasted if consumers do not respond as anticipated to the new brand. Similarly, competitors' reactions are difficult to predict in some cases. Then, a market test (small introduction) should be performed to evaluate how competitors are going to adapt to the new competitive environment.

DEFENSIVE STRATEGIES

In this section, we first review the decision variables that the firm can use to defend its position. Then we discuss the factors that determine the effectiveness of defense strategies. These strategies can be caused by a competitive entry or an aggressive existing competitor.

Elements of Defensive Strategy

The decisions that need to be made when reacting to a competitor threatening the firm's positions are: (1) the direction of the reaction (e.g., attack versus retrenchment), (2) the marketing mix variables which will change as part of the defense strategy, (3) the degree or size of the reaction and (4) the market or market segment(s) in which the firm should react.

Directions of Reactions. The reactions can be categorized according to four types: (1) retaliate, (2) accommodate, (3) ignore and (4) abandon. Retaliation corresponds to a declaration of war, wherein the firm wants to signal its intention to fight back. A decision to accommodate indicates instead that there is room for all players and that each might be better off if they would cooperate. This strategy can be implemented by cutting back on the marketing effort. The decision to ignore means that the firm does not change its marketing mix strategy, at least until more is learned about the strategy of the competitors and its impact on the firm sales, market share and profits. Finally, the decision to abandon corresponds to an exit of that brand that reflects its lack of competitive advantage in that market. Indeed, it might be more costly to fight back or stay in than to abandon and concentrate on more attractive brands and markets.

Marketing Mix Variables. The marketing mix variables are all the decision variables of a brand offered in MARKSTRAT, for example, price, advertising, sales force, repositioning, new brand introduction, etc. An interesting issue concerns which marketing variable mix to react with. Should the firm react with the same marketing instrument as the attacking firm, or should it use a different marketing mix, reflecting the use of a different strategy than the attacker.

Size of Reaction. A large early reaction can deter the aggressor and reduce its expectations in this market. Each firm should evaluate what it will take to convince the aggressor to slow down on its attack. This might depend on the size of the reacting firm. A small reaction could be sufficient for a large firm to send a warning signal to the aggressor.

Domain of Reaction. In some cases, the strongest signal can be send in a different market or market segment than the one where the aggressor attacked. This is the case for example, if the defender can hurt seriously the attacker in another market and not on the market of the aggression.

Determinants of Choice of Defensive Strategy

In this section, we discuss which combination of the reaction decisions described above is most effective under a given situation facing the defending firm. Four sets of characteristics influence the reacting defensive strategy to adopt: the strategy of the entrant, the expected behavior of all the competitors, demand factors and characteristics of the defending firm.

Entrant Strategy. Typically, when a new competitor enters the market, prices can be expected to go down to reflect the increased competition. This, however, assumes price elastic markets. Correspondingly, this behavior can be expected only in some of the MARKSTRAT segments. If the new brand or an existing brand competes on price, it might become more profitable to reposition and compete in a different market segment with a differentiated product where the brand feature is a competitive advantage. Advertising can then be increased relative to its level before the aggression to represent the additional repositioning task. A large entry should generate a strong response with all effective marketing instruments to make the aggression unsuccessful if it is a likely outcome. If there is little chance to reduce the impact of the aggression, it might be better to abandon right away an already questionable weak position.

Expected Behavior of Competitors. It is clear that the success of a defensive strategy, like any strategy, depends on how competitors are going to react to it. Therefore, knowledge of competitors is extremely important to design the proper defensive strategy. Given the difficulty of anticipating competitors' behavior in response to the firm's defensive strategy, which is in most cases idiosyncratic to the specific situation, it is particularly worthy to evaluate the impact of several types of competitive reactions on the effectiveness of the defensive strategy of the firm. Contingency plans can then be developed as certain behaviors emerge from the competition.

Demand Factors. Price retaliation has been recommended when the preferences in a given market are homogeneous. This is likely to occur when a market is newly created so that consumers have not yet established strong preferences and the market is not yet fragmented. This could be the case also in the maturity stage of the product life cycle when the competing products are similar, commodity like, and when competition is based solely on price due to the high price sensitivity of these markets. Accommodation in terms of decreasing the marketing effort (advertising, sales force, etc.) is a more profitable strategy in a mature market where competitive activity does not affect primary demand levels.

Firm Characteristics. Small brands are in a worse position in MARKSTRAT because of the experience curve effects on costs. Therefore, when market growth starts to slow down (and *a fortiori* when it becomes negative), competitive intensity typically increases. In these environments, smaller brands will become unprofitable first. Consequently, they should exit that market (segment) while they are still generating some cash.

CONCLUSION

In this chapter, competitive strategies have been discussed. First, we have developed key elements of competitive analysis that help design a marketing strategy in MARKSTRAT. Then we discussed the basis of competitive advantages and under which environment each basis of advantage is most sustainable. Finally, we discussed the determinants of a strategy to introduce a new brand and to defend the position of a brand under attack. For each of these two situations, we have discussed the factors to assess in a particular simulation of MARKSTRAT in order to design the most effective strategy.

CHAPTER 7 SUMMARY

Competitive Analysis

Defining the Set of Relevant Competitors

- Product Market Analysis of Perceptions and Preferences
- Industry Segment Analysis

Assessing the Intensity of Competition

- Structural Factors
    - Degree of threat of entry
    - Threat of substitutes
    - Barriers to entry in MARKSTRAT can be:
        Capital required
        Degree to which existing firms satisfy consumers' needs
        Marketing investment levels
        Coverage of key distribution channels
        Economies of scale/experience

- Competitive Behavior
    - Marketing expenditure trends
    - Reaction functions and reaction elasticities

Competitive Strategies

Bases of Competitive Advantages

- Cost leadership
  - Experience/Cumulative production
  - R&D Experience
  - Synergies with other products

- Product Differentiation
  - Positioning of each competitive brand
  - Stability of consumer preferences
  - Mobility barriers

- Choice of Bases of Competitive Advantage
  - Firm characteristics
  - Price elasticity of demand
  - Complementarity of bases of competitive advantage
  - Cost of achieving and maintaining basis of competitive advantage

Entry Strategies

Pioneer Advantages

- Monopolistic profits
- Distribution support
- Production experience

Entry Signaling

- Competitors' decisions in key segments
- Signals to be read from these decisions

Marketing Mix

- Allocation of resources to brands, segments and marketing mix variables before the new brand introduction
- Marketing synergies between new brand and existing brands

Scale of Entry

- Large scale brand introduction as a deterent for new competitive introductions
- Expected reactions from competitors to large and small scale brand introductions

Defensive Strategies

Determinants of Choice of Defensive Strategy

- Entrant strategy
- Expected behavior of competitors
- Demand factors
- Firm characteristics

Elements of Defensive Strategy

- Direction of reaction
- Marketing mix variables
- Size of reaction
- Domain of reaction

CHAPTER 8

Allocation of Resources

Marketing strategy concerns the allocation of resources to businesses that the firm wants to be in and the allocation of resources to the marketing mix variables for each brand across businesses. In this chapter, we will discuss methods for evaluating alternative strategies (1) in terms of the choice of markets/segments in which the firm can do business and (2) in terms of the amount of resources to provide for each of these markets/segments. The next chapter approaches the issue of allocation of resources to the marketing mix variables in terms of what constitutes the "functional" marketing strategies.

This chapter is divided into three sections which correspond to three steps in the analysis that leads to the allocation of resources decisions. The first section discusses how businesses or product/markets fit together in the concept of a "balanced" portfolio for the firm. The second section discusses the specific issue of evaluating new businesses in terms of their potential and their fit within the firm's strategy. Finally, the last section presents a list of determinants for guiding allocation of resources within the portfolio.

EVALUATION OF PRODUCT-MARKET PORTFOLIO

One approach to the analysis of product/market portfolios consists in representing the various businesses in which the firm operates in a two dimensional map. This map offers diagnostic information as to the position of the firm and as to how the various businesses in which the firm is involved fit together.

To summarize this diagnostic information, each of the two dimensions is divided into a number of ranges so that each business belongs to a cell. The product/market portfolio matrix analysis consists in evaluating the businesses based on the set of cells in which the firm operates. In this section we discuss briefly two types of matrix approaches to product/market portfolio analysis, standardized and individualized,* and show how they can be used in MARKSTRAT. We also point out the limitations of these methodologies and illustrate them in the context of MARKSTRAT.

A Standardized Approach: The Growth/Share Matrix

The Boston Consulting Group[†] has proposed to consider two dimensions to represent a portfolio of products: market growth and relative market share. We shall first discuss the rationale for choosing the two dimensions. Then we will discuss the specific selection of the relative market share and market growth variables. Next we discuss the selection of the unit of analysis. We also give examples of portfolios in MARKSTRAT. Finally, we present some of the issues that are raised when using this methodology.

Rationale for Matrix Dimensions. The motivation of the original portfolio analysis is financial in nature. Basically, cash generation and cash usage are the two key elements of evaluation of a business, and of a set of businesses. Therefore, a business can be simply evaluated by how much cash it generates (or is expected to generate) and by how much cash investment is necessary. Under the assumption that capital can only be generated internally from within the firm, it is clear that some long term equilibrium of businesses that generate cash and of businesses that require capital investments should be attained. In MARKSTRAT, although additional budgets can be negotiated with the administrator under certain conditions determined by the game administrator, this assumption is correct. Budgets are some function of the net marketing contribution and investments are only permitted within the constraint of the budget limit.

Figure 8.1 represents four businesses corresponding to four extreme cases in terms of these cash usage and cash generation dimensions. The horizontal axis represents the level of cash generated and the vertical axis represents the level of investment required. Business A does not generate a high level of cash, but does not require much cash either. From a financial point of view, it is not clear what the use of this business is for the company. Therefore, from a purely financial perspective, this business should be eliminated. However, this business could have other purposes. It could enable the company, because of its sales volume, to achieve greater economies of scale and/or benefit from a greater experience (from an experience curve point of view). Consequently, this business could reduce the cost of other businesses which can be made even more attractive from this financial point of view. It could be also that this business contributes to the image of the firm or to its competitive position. The first example concerns the interactions between businesses in terms of costs, or cost synergies. These cost synergies, in MARK-

---

*Yoram Wind and Vijay Mahajan (1981), "Designing Product and Business Portfolios," *Harvard Business Review*, January–February, 155–165.

[†]Bruce D. Henderson (1970), "The Product Portfolio," *Perspectives*, Boston Consulting Group.

Figure 8.1: The Cash Basis of Portfolio Analysis

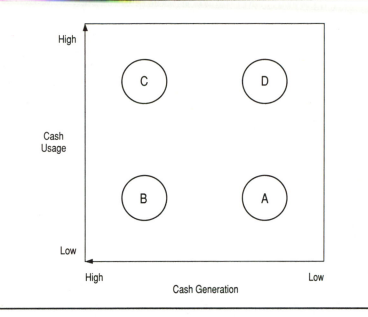

STRAT, do not concern economies of scale in production or experience effects on production costs. This is because each brand is manufactured on different production lines and each follows a different experience curve. However, marketing cost synergies can exist in terms of sales force and distribution, for example.

The second type of synergies between businesses is on the demand side. However, there is little pure demand synergy in MARKSTRAT due to the fact that each brand competes independently. Nevertheless, because of competition, a brand may play a role as part of the competitive strategy of the firm. By staying present in a market, a firm can prevent another firm from generating the cash that could be used by this competitor later in another market or business.

These examples illustrate some limitations of the purely financial view of a portfolio. Nevertheless, as indicated earlier, given that firms in MARKSTRAT must thrive to grow with their own resources, MARKSTRAT firms must plan with keeping in mind that they must generate their own resources for implementing their strategies in the long run.

Specific Variable Selection. The rationale for portfolio analysis described above is difficult to use because of the difficulty of measuring the cash generation potential of a business as well as the capital investment levels for these businesses. Therefore, correlates of cash generation and cash usage are typically used to derive a portfolio map in terms of the cash dimensions underlying the financial portfolio rationale. The Boston Consulting Group has suggested that market growth is closely related to cash usage and relative market share is a "good" indicator of cash generation. Low growth markets, it has been argued, are typically mature markets where little cash is required

Figure 8.2: A Typical Portfolio Representation

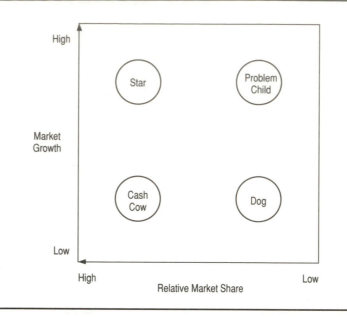

while high growth markets necessitate high investments to develop the market and to fight increasing competition which becomes attracted by these markets. On the other dimension, relative market share has been used as an indicator of the ability of a business to generate cash. This relative market share is usually computed as the market share of a product divided by the market share of its largest competitor. The argument used for justifying the relative market share variable (or market share in general, although different classifications result depending on the definitions),* is that a business with a higher share enjoys a greater experience in terms of cumulative production than its competitors. This enables that business to produce at a lower cost and to generate higher margins. The rationale for the value of relative market share rests, therefore, in the existence of an experience effect. When the experience effect exists, as in MARKSTRAT, it is clear that, other things being equal, a relationship between relative market share and profitability should exist.

Therefore these two variables, market growth and relative market share, have been typically substituted for cash usage and cash generation in the portfolio analysis, as indicated in Figure 8.2. The typical growth/share matrix defines two levels (low and high) for each variable (market growth and relative market share) to develop the four well known cells of *cash cow* (high relative market share in low growth market), *star* (high relative market share in high growth market), *dog* (low relative market share in low growth market) and *problem child* (low relative market share in high growth market). The ideal portfolio, replicating the rationale of cash equilibrium explained above, suggests that a firm should not have any business in a low growth market with a small relative market share. Instead, a firm should use the cash generated by businesses in the low growth markets with high relative market

---

*Yoram Wind, Vijay Mahajan and Donald J. Swire (1983), "An Empirical Comparison of Standardized Portfolio Models," *Journal of Marketing*, 47, 2 (Spring), 89–99.

shares (the cash cows) to reinvest in the problem children, the stars being self sufficient. The assumption is that this investment and therefore allocation of resources across businesses will enable businesses in high growth markets to build their share and become stars. As the market matures and the growth rate slows down, the stars become automatically cash cows. Therefore the "ideal" portfolio creates a dynamic process which is self perpetuating as long as there are new problem children to take over in the cycle and replace the once cash generating products.

It should be pointed out at this point that the relationships between market growth and cash usage and between relative market share and cash generation are not without controversy. Indeed, it is not clear that low growth markets generate cash, even when the business is in a high relative market share position. Low growth markets are typically markets at the maturity stage of the product life cycle. These markets are often fragmented with multiple market segments of different value in terms of size and margins. They are also characterized by a high level of competition. The number of competitors that have entered these markets is high, and even though some might exit when growth slows down (as occurs with a shakedown of the industry structure), competitors might engage in escalation of marketing expenditures due to competitive reactions to each others' marketing decisions. While such competitive behavior can help expand the market in the early stages of the product life cycle, the only outcome at such a late stage is a cut in margins.

In high growth markets, it is assumed in the rationale used for selecting market growth as an indicator of cash usage, that cash is necessary to fight new competitors which enter the market and to develop the market. It is often the case, however, that some competitors might benefit from the investments of other competitors (such as the pioneer's). Cash consumption does not need to be high in such cases.

A similar problem occurs with the market share variable. The experience curve is not the only factor to consider, because other bases of competitive advantage can be more profitable and more sustainable in the long term. In addition, market share is only an outcome variable which is not under the control of the firm. Indeed, the more important question would be "What are the determinants of profitability?" There is no doubt that market share has a double role to play, one from the cost side if there are economies of scale and experience effects, and one on the demand side because of the larger volume of sales generated. The main determinants of market share is the marketing mix strategy. Therefore, beyond cost issues, market share is not generating in a causal sense greater cash per se. The issue is one of the relationship between the marketing mix variables and market share or the costs involved in gaining the share, which can be represented by the marketing mix elasticities.

The typical portfolio analysis assumes that it is easier (requires less investment) to gain share in a high growth market because competitors' sales might still increase, even though their share decreases. This assumes that competitors are somewhat complacent, which is sometimes observed in some high growth industries. However, all competitors who strive for market share

are unlikely to be complacent at a stage where they believe that they can maintain and even improve their position because of different bases of competitive advantage which might be sustainable in the long run. It is therefore likely that they are not going to give up easily and abandon territory while they still have a chance. Therefore, it can also be quite costly to gain market share in high growth markets. This is an area where the competitive notions developed in chapter 7 can be used to evaluate the difficulty of gaining share and the extent to which high growth markets are really preferable.

So far, we have assumed that the four cells in the matrix had been identified. The problem of assigning the cut-offs delimiting the low and high levels of each variable (market growth and relative market share) is therefore posed. There are several definitions of relative market share. One which is frequently used consists in computing the business market share divided by the industry leader's market share if the business analyzed is not the leader, and if it is, the business leader's share is divided by the next closest competitors with the next highest share. In that case, a natural cut-off is the level of relative market share of 1.0. However, this is rather constraining because only one competitor per industry will be in a cash cow or star position. Some companies consequently prefer to use lower cut-off points at 0.7 or 0.8. Opposed to this, other firms want to give a product a cash cow or star position only if it has a significantly dominant position and use higher cut-off points at 1.2 or even 1.5.

For market growth, the cut-off point is usually determined on the basis of the average growth of the mix of markets in which the firm is present. One can, however, decide on a higher level to develop a more aggressive approach in the search for new market opportunities, or a lower level to emphasize the possibility to grow with established products,

In fact, the cut-offs for both variables are rather subjective. Therefore the portfolio analysis should consider this issue and find a justification for the value selected in a given application and compare different definitions.*

Unit of Analysis. Another issue that arises in developing a portfolio analysis concerns the unit of analysis. What does constitute a business? In MARK-STRAT, two alternatives are possible. It is possible to consider the Sonite and the Vodite markets in the aggregate. Each firm has a given market share in each of these markets. This, however aggregates all the segments as if they were homogeneous. Instead, each market segment has its own peculiarity in terms of market size, stage of development, competition, etc. Consequently, it is in general more appropriate for the MARKSTRAT firms to evaluate their portfolio using each brand in each segment as the unit of analysis. Given that a brand can sell in multiple segments, even though it is positioned for a given segment, it could be appropriate to represent the same brand in different locations in the portfolio to correspond to each segment in which the brand is sold. However, these sales outside the segment for which the brand is positioned are usually relatively small. Consequently, the main segment for each brand might be sufficient to represent the firm's portfolio.

---

*Wind, Mahajan and Swire (1983), *op. cit.*

Figure 8.3: An Unbalanced Portfolio

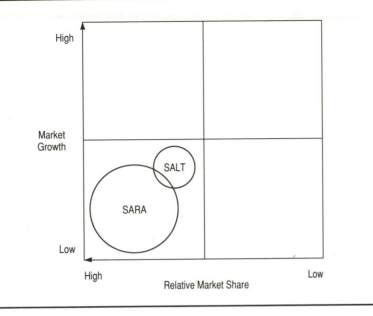

Examples of MARKSTRAT Portfolios. In spite of the limitations of the growth/share matrix pointed out above, diagnostic insights (in particular in terms of source of financing) can be gained by such a matrix representation. The main objective to keep in mind is the maintenance of the cash balance over time. Therefore, a portfolio where some cells would be empty should be carefully analyzed to check whether the firm is heading into financial difficulties in the future. For example, Figure 8.3 presents a portfolio which must be very profitable currently, as evidenced by two products in a leadership position in low growth markets (with large sales volume as indicated by the diameter of the circles around each brand). However, the future is compromised by the absence of new products to maintain sales and profitability in the long term. After the markets for SALT and SARA decline, there is no product to maintain the firm's position. This portfolio is typical of shortsighted profit maximization objectives.

Figure 8.4 presents another case of a problematic portfolio. While the firm has been successful with the SULI and SUFA brands, three brands are not positioned properly. Given their lack of clear competitive advantage in their respective market resulting in a low share, these brands should probably have been pruned from the portfolio. These brands do require some resources which would probably be better used in other markets. Therefore, even though these three brands might still generate some level of profitability, the portfolio representation should bring the team's attention to the fact that the resources used for these brands might be used more efficiently in other markets. Consequently, a re-allocation of resources should be considered.

The example above is not always leading to a conclusion of exit from the market as proposed above. In fact, Figure 8.5 shows a different portfolio where it can be necessary to maintain the brand in a "dog" position. This firm markets two brands that are in growing segments and one in a low growth

Figure 8.4: A Portfolio Representative of Inability to Prune Poor Performers

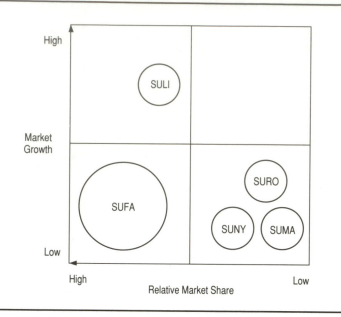

Figure 8.5: A Necessary "Dog" Brand

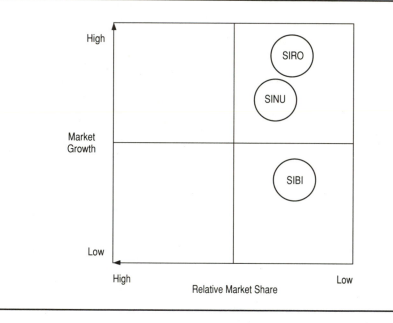

segment. None of these brands dominates its respective segment as they all have a small relative market share. This is relatively representative of a smaller firm with limited resources. In that case, the SIBI brand, if profitable, should be maintained as it does provide some profits which can be used to develop new products for the future. This strategy can be very effective in particular when the competition in the low growth segment is weak.

Issues with the Growth/Share Matrix. We have pointed out a number of issues with the usage of the growth/share matrix. The discussion above does not exhaust the list of limitations of this methodology, although those described above are particularly appropriate in the MARKSTRAT simulation. There are nevertheless two major issues that are basic to that method and which are worth mentioning: the use of a single variable each for use and generation of cash, and the normative implications of the portfolio assessment.

It is clear that each of the financial dimensions is not appropriately represented by a single indicator. Therefore errors are introduced if all the determinants of cash usage and market share are not used. This issue is partially remedied in the discussion below of individualized portfolios.

Even more basic is the problem of the implications of the portfolio assessment. The growth/share matrix provides a potentially useful diagnostic tool. It summarizes simply where the firm stands in terms of its relative market share position and in terms of the segment growth in which it conducts business. It can even present some elements of the financial equilibrium situation of the firm. However, this type of portfolio analysis provides little information as to how to re-allocate resources across the brand/segments. This is due to the lack of information contained in this analysis about the opportunities of gaining share and about the costs of gaining this share. These opportunities and cost differ for different alternatives, even among those in the problem child cell. This issue is valid for individualized portfolio as well. Consequently, this issue will be discussed after the section on the individualized approach.

An Individualized Approach: The Attractiveness/Position Matrix

In this approach, the market growth variable is replaced with a more complicated construct of the attractiveness of an industry/market/segment. The portfolio that is derived loses, therefore, its financial interpretation. Indeed, an attractive market does not necessarily uses more or less funds than an unattractive market. However, if a market is attractive, it must be worth some level of investment. Therefore resources should be allocated to markets that are attractive. In addition, the better the competitive position (or potential position), the greater the competitive advantage and therefore the greater the resources that the firm should be willing to devote to maintain this position or to build that position.* Therefore, this attractiveness/position matrix indicates the positions of each of the businesses of the firm and indicates which are worth investing for maintenance of position or to build a position.

Figure 8.6 shows an example of such a matrix. The SEMI and SECU brands should not receive resources as the market segments they are in are not believed to be attractive. On the other hand, SELF and SELL are in attractive markets. The allocation of the resources between these two brands depends on the costs involved in order to maintain SELL's position and on the costs involved to move SELF from a weak to a strong position, if at all possible. It depends also on the relative benefits as represented by the

---

*Note, however, that this does not necessarily imply that greater resources are needed. However, if needed, the opportunity justifies the allocating of the resources.

Figure 8.6: An Example of the Attractiveness/Position Matrix

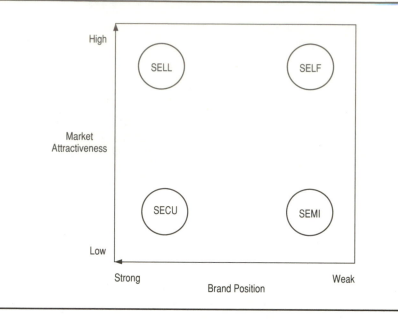

attractiveness dimension. However, in the specific case of SELF and SELL in Figure 8.6, given the same level of attractiveness, only the costs to achieve and maintain strong positions are relevant to the allocation of resources questions. Unfortunately, the portfolio matrix does not provide explicitly the information necessary to answer that question. The costs can be, however, indirectly represented in the attractiveness dimension.

This issue illustrates the first aspect of the development of this approach: What are the components of these two dimensions? We now discuss the process that one must go through to develop the individualized matrix. The process is parallel for the attractiveness and the position dimensions. However, they each have some peculiarities. We therefore discuss the process that leads to an attractiveness/position matrix by first discussing the attractiveness dimension, and then the position dimension.* Once each brand/segment is located on each of these dimensions, we conclude this section by pointing out the main factors that are missing when using these portfolio analyses as an allocation of resources device.

Assessment of the Attractiveness of a Market. The attractiveness of a business can be assessed using a four step process, as outlined below:

Step 1: Determine the relevant list of factors contributing to the attractiveness of businesses for the firm.

Step 2: Determine the direction and form of the relationship between each factor and the attractiveness measure, and assess the value of each business on each contributing factor developed in step 1.

---

*These sections follow closely the procedure proposed by Derek F. Abell and John S. Hammond (1979), *Strategic Market Planning: Problems and Analytical Approaches*, Englewood Cliffs, NJ: Prentice Hall.

Step 3: Determine the weight by which each factor contributes to the attractiveness measure.

Step 4: Compute the value of each business on the attractiveness measure.

We now illustrate this procedure as it can be used by MARKSTRAT firms. In particular, we provide a list of factors that are particularly relevant in MARKSTRAT.

Step 1: The following factors can *potentially* influence the attractiveness of a market:

MARKET FACTORS

- Market/Segment size in units
- Market/Segment growth rate
- Market/Segment primary demand elasticity to price
- Advertising elasticity (primary market/segment demand)
- Shopping habits of consumers in market/segment
- Demand elasticity to product features
- Forecasting accuracy of market/segment size
- Forecasting accuracy of market shares

COMPETITION

- Number of brands competing in market/segment
- Size of competitors (their available resources)
- Marketing mix strategy of competitors
- Reactivity of competitors in market/segment
- Positioning of competing brands
- Threat of new brand introductions in market/segments
- Extent of barriers for each competitor not yet in market/segment

FINANCIAL FACTORS

- Contribution margins
- Experience effects

Step 2: After the relevant factors from the list above have been selected, the firm must determine for each factor whether a high value of that factor leads to a greater attractiveness or not, and by how much. This can be done by defining categorical levels for each factor. For example, it can be assessed that a market size below 1,000,000 units per year is a low level of attractiveness (to which a value of, for example, 0 is assigned). A value of 1.0 can be assigned for the high level of attractiveness which might be judged to be for a market size above 5,000,000 units per year. Between 1,000,000 and 5,000,000 units, a value of 0.5 can be assigned for a medium level of attractiveness.

This step must be performed for each factor selected in step 1. This could result in the following data, assuming these factors below were selected in step 1:

	Score
■ Market/Segment size in units	0.5
■ Market/Segment growth rate	0
■ Number of brands competing in market/segment	1.0
■ Reactivity of competitors in market/segment	1.0
■ Contribution margins	0.5

Step 3: In this step, each factor selected in step 1 must be assigned a weight such that the total across all factors sums to one. The example below illustrates how the weights can be assigned.

	Weight
■ Market/Segment size in units	0.15
■ Market/Segment growth rate	0.15
■ Number of brands competing in market/segment	0.30
■ Reactivity of competitors in market/segment	0.15
■ Contribution margins	0.25
	1.00

In this example, the number of brands already competing is the most important factor that determines the segment's attractiveness. This could be due to the fact that it is difficult to perform well both from a marketing and financial perspective in a market with many brands. This factor is also twice as important as the segment size or growth rate. This weighting scheme is clearly subjective and should represent the best judgments of the managers of the firm. It should be kept in mind, however, that these assessments are approximate and a sensitivity analysis could be appropriate to check to what extent the final evaluations would change when the weights vary.

Step 4: In this last step, we compute the level of attractiveness of the market for which the factors have been assessed. The level of attractiveness is the weighted average of all the factor ratings as computed below.

	Score	Weight	Value
■ Market/Segment size in units	0.5	0.15	0.075
■ Market/Segment growth rate	0	0.15	0
■ Number of brands competing in market/segment	1.0	0.30	0.3
■ Reactivity of competitors in market/segment	1.0	0.15	0.15
■ Contribution margins	0.5	0.25	0.125
		1.00	0.65

This value of attractiveness, 0.65, is therefore assigned to this market segment.

Assessment of the Position of a Business. The procedure to follow for the position dimension is similar to the process of assessing the attractiveness of a market/segment:

Step 1: Determine the relevant list of factors contributing to the position of businesses for the firm in their respective market/segment.

Step 2: Determine the direction and form of the relationship between each factor and the position measure, and assess the value of each business on each contributing factor developed in step 1.

Step 3: Determine the weight by which each factor contributes to the position measure.

Step 4: Compute the position of each business on the position measure.

Step 1: The following factors might contribute to the position of a business in a market/segment.

MARKET FACTORS
- Market/Segment share based on units sold
- Market/Segment share based on value
- Sales volume of brand in units
- Sales volume of brand in value
- Growth rate of market shares (based on units and value)
- Growth rate of sales (based on units and value)
- Brand price elasticity
- Brand advertising elasticity
- Brand sales force elasticity
- Influence of brand on market/segment size

COMPETITION
- Competitive advantage
- Price elasticity of competitive brands
- Advertising elasticity of competitive brands
- Sales force elasticity of competitive brands
- Cross-elasticities for each marketing mix variable

FINANCIAL FACTORS
- Brand margin
- Cumulative production versus the competitive brands'

Step 2: After the relevant factors from the list above have been selected, the firm must determine for each factor whether a high value of that factor leads to a better position of a brand or not, and by how much. This can be done by defining categorical levels for each factor. For example, it can be assessed that a market share below 0.20 is a weak position (to which a value of, for example, 0 is assigned). A value of 1.0 can be assigned for the very good position which might be judged to be for a market share above 0.70. Between 0.20 and 0.70 market shares, a value of 0.5 can be assigned for an average position.

This step must be performed for each factor selected in step 1. This could result in the following data, assuming these factors below were selected in step 1.

	Score
■ Market/Segment share	0
■ Brand price elasticity	0.5
■ Competitive advantage	0.5
■ Brand margin	0.5
■ Cumulative Production	1.0

Step 3: In this step, each factor selected in step 1 must be assigned a weight such that the total across all factors sums to one. The example below illustrates how the weights are assigned.

	Score
■ Market/Segment share	0.3
■ Brand price elasticity	0.2
■ Competitive advantage	0.3
■ Brand margin	0.05
■ Cumulative Production	0.15
	1.00

In this example, the market share and the competitive advantage are the most important factors that determine the brand's position. Price elasticity is also relatively highly weighted. This weighting could represent the fact that cost leadership is extremely important. Consequently, the market share and cumulative production reflect the position of the brand. At the same time, the brand price elasticity enables a gain in volume by lowering the price which contributes to lower costs. These lower prices could, however, affect the margins, which are not very important in this case.

Again, this weighting scheme is clearly subjective and should represent the best judgments of the managers of the firm. Therefore, a sensitivity analysis could be appropriate to check to what extent the final evaluations of the brands' positions would change when the weights vary.

Step 4: In this last step, we compute the strength of the position of the brand for which the factors have been assessed above. The level of strength of the position of the brand is the weighted average of all the factor ratings as computed below.

	Score	Weight	Value
■ Market/Segment share	0	0.3	0
■ Brand price elasticity	0.5	0.2	0.10
■ Competitive advantage	0.5	0.3	0.15
■ Brand margin	0.5	0.05	0.025
■ Cumulative Production	1.0	0.15	0.15
		1.00	0.425

This value of the strength of the position .425 is therefore assigned to this brand segment. This reflects a below average position. Now that the market attractiveness and the strength of the position have been computed, given that the values range between zero and one, it is easy to plot this business on a two dimensional map. Figure 8.7 gives an example of such a map, including the point for which we computed the values above.

Figure 8.7: The Attractiveness/Position Map

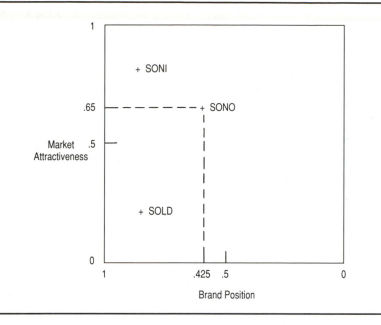

Factors Affecting the Allocation of Resources

In the example above, the portfolio of this firm is relatively eclectic. The SONI brand is well positioned. SOLD has a strong position, but in a not so attractive market. SONO is in an attractive market but with a relatively weak position. The position of SONI should be maintained and resources should be devoted to that objective. At the same time, it might be possible to improve the position of SONO, because with a strong position, SONO would improve the portfolio. Therefore, resources should be re-allocated from SOLD to SONI and SONO. This approach is more complete than the growth/share matrix as it considers many more factors, including possibly synergies, uncertainty of predicting demand and marketing mix variable elasticities. However, these qualitative evaluations are insufficient to determine the level and the nature of resources required to build a business or maintain a business in a desirable location in the attractiveness/position individualized matrix. Therefore, a better link between market share or sales and the level of the marketing mix activities is required to determine how much to invest in each marketing mix variable.

Before we discuss these issues in greater detail, we devote the next section to the assessment of a specific business: a new business in which the firm does not operate yet.

EVALUATION OF NEW BUSINESS OPPORTUNITIES

Is the evaluation of a new business different from the assessment of a business in which the firm operates already? Clearly, the attractiveness of a market can be assessed independently of whether the firm is or not in this market. The only question in respect to that point is that the evaluation of one factor of market attractiveness could depend on the characteristics of the firm with respect to that business. For example, a highly price elastic market is attractive only if the firm possesses a cost advantage. This point illustrates the fact that the assessment of market attractiveness and business position can be very complex as they are not always fully independent factors. Furthermore, for a new business, the issue of assessing market attractiveness is made more difficult because the firm does not have any market position yet. Consequently, the analysis must rely on the managers evaluations of the potential position of the firm in that business. This can be partly answered by analyzing the factors discussed above that contribute to the business position. However, many factors can only be evaluated in terms of expectations. These expectations, in turn, depend on marketing decisions. Therefore, the major issue in this case of new businesses is in terms of evaluating the strategy (nature and extent of resources) necessary to build a competitive position in these markets. This issue is indeed similar to the conclusion we have drawn from our discussion of portfolio analysis.

Therefore, an analysis of a new business is concerned about whether the market is worth investing in and if it is, how much is necessary to invest. Analyzing the attractiveness of the market as suggested before and comparing it with the attractiveness of markets currently in the portfolio can provide the answer to the first question. The answer to the second question requires the knowledge of two key factors: (1) the ability to gain a strong position and earn profits in this business and (2) the ability to establish barriers to protect a competitive advantage and consequently, the long term profitability of that business.

The second factor was discussed at length in the chapter on competitive strategies (chapter 7). The first factor, the ability to gain a strong position rests on the opportunity and the costs involved to achieve this position. Given that the opportunity must exist because this business was judged attractive, one must establish the extent of the costs, i.e. of resources necessary to establish a strong position in this market. This raises the basic question which is missing from typical portfolio analysis: How much investment is necessary to achieve a strong, sustainable position in this market? The complexity of this question is compounded by the inherent uncertainties in new market entry situations. While uncertainty is also a factor for allocating resources to existing businesses, as discussed above briefly, uncertainties about new businesses is particularly crucial. Indeed, there are typically greater uncertainties associated with new businesses. The demand is more difficult to predict (in particular if the market is at the introduction stage of the product life cycle). Also competitive reactions are difficult to forecast. These uncertainties should be critical to a risk averse manager. However, maybe more important is the risk of not investing while the firm can, a risk which has been called "missing the boat" risk.* This risk for new business is probably more important than the traditional risk of "sinking the boat" because, not only the opportunity

---

*Dickson, Peter R. and Joseph J. Giglierano (1987), "Missing the Boat and Sinking the Boat: A Conceptual Model of Entrepreneurial Risk," *Journal of Marketing*, 50 (July), 58–70.

for profitability might be costly in terms of opportunity cost, but also a competitor might take advantage of that opportunity which in the long term can affect the profitability of the businesses in which the firm which missed the boat operates. The importance of this risk depends on the length of the window of opportunity or the strategic window facing the firm.

DETERMINANTS OF ALLOCATION OF RESOURCES

The level of investment necessary to obtain a sustainable position in a market is not independent of the other markets and the level of investment in other businesses. In addition, the allocation of resources decision is affected by the ability to gain share or sales, which differs across markets and which depend on the relative effectiveness of the various marketing mix variables which also differ across businesses. Therefore, the allocation of resources decision depends on the relationship between the marketing mix variables and market share or sales. In addition, it depends on the margins of each product. As indicated earlier, synergies between businesses are the main aspects why the firm would desire to maintain a portfolio. These synergies are both on the demand side in terms of the ability of affecting demand in one business with the marketing activities in other businesses, and on the cost side by economies of scale, experience or economies of scope. Finally, uncertainty surrounding the ability to relate market share or sales to the marketing mix effort levels must affect the allocation of resources decision. These factors are discussed now in turn.

The Effectiveness of Marketing Mix Variables

More resources should be devoted to brands that exhibit a greater response to the marketing instruments because that investment will be more effective than for brands exhibiting a lower level of sensitivity to the marketing instruments. This is the case for advertising and sales force expenditures. The price decision is not an expenditure but follows the same rationale, although it is a particularly important variable which affects the margin level. Therefore, the higher the demand elasticity to the brand's price, the lower the price should be (and consequently the margins), everything else being equal. It is, therefore, essential for strategic decisions concerning the allocation of resources between multiple businesses to measure the effectiveness of the marketing mix variables. Without going into detailed measurement models, the next chapter provides a conceptual framework for specifying such models.

Product positioning is clearly a strong determinant of market share and sales because it is related to the degree with which the product is perceived to deliver key benefits and therefore the degree to which the product is satisfying the needs of the consumers. However, although positioning effects on sales or market share can be assessed, the costs associated with achieving that position are more difficult to evaluate. Indeed, we have discussed two approaches to repositioning a brand in MARKSTRAT. Research and Development in particular is a long term endeavor which is difficult to relate to product positioning. Nevertheless, the effort required to reposition a brand (through advertising or R&D) should be related to the extent with which that repositioning will affect sales or market share. This extent should vary across market segments and firms, as the product requirements, R&D capabilities and competitive activity differ across segments and firms.

Demand Synergies

As indicated earlier, demand synergies refer to the extent that the marketing variable of one brand affects positively the demand of other brands in the portfolio. Therefore, more resources should be devoted to brands that highly influence the sales of other brands. In particular, if these cross elasticities are particularly high for some marketing mix variables, greater emphasis should be placed on these variables. It is clear, however, that this cross elastic or synergistic effect should be balanced with the regular elasticity effects on the allocation of resources decision. For example, if a brand (e.g., SARA) has a low advertising elasticity, but is affected greatly in a positive way (i.e., causing an increase in sales) by the advertising of another brand in the portfolio (e.g., SALE), more advertising should be spend on SALE than would be allocated if it were not for the cross elasticity effect. However, had SARA shown a greater response to its own elasticity, less advertising should be allocated to SALE then, than in the first case.

Cost Synergies

Cost synergies could result from different phenomena. Cost synergies can be achieved in MARKSTRAT from economies of scope in marketing activities. Cost synergies can also be due to the economies of scale and experience due to cross elasticities of demand. Both of these sources of cost synergies are particularly important as they affect directly the unit margins. It is therefore important to be able to exploit them efficiently.

Cost synergies from marketing activities exist due to the fact that advertising one brand can expand the primary demand of a market segment. Consequently, achieving sales objectives for two brands in the same market segments can be less costly in terms of advertising expenditures than if there were no synergy. More importantly, synergies can be achieved in terms of the sales force. Because all sales people carry all the brands marketed by the firm, additional sales force might not be required to sell a brand buying from the same channel of distribution.

The unit transfer cost can be lower due to experience curve effects when cross elasticities occur. Therefore more effort should be expended to market brands for which the marketing instruments affect the level of sales of other products for which cost per unit and experience is important.

Uncertainty and Risk

Finally, uncertainty in predicting demand, in particular the degree with which the marketing mix strategy predicts performance, should be a strong indicator of the degree of investment provided for that brand. The greater the uncertainty, the smaller amount of resources a risk averse manager would allocate to that brand. This allocation rule should recognize, however, that behind this inaccuracy of prediction there might also be an opportunity for a high level of sales or market share generated by a given marketing mix strategy. Consequently, opportunities and risk aversion should be balanced by the firm managers in considering uncertainty.

CONCLUSION

In this chapter, the factors to consider when allocating resources to the various brands and market segments have been discussed. Several approaches such as the matrix type of portfolio analysis or individualized portfolio evaluation approaches were discussed and evaluated. In particular, we pointed out the benefits as well as the limitations of such approaches and we illustrated their application in the particular context of MARKSTRAT. Finally, we have discussed additional factors to consider when making allocation of resources decisions for marketing strategy purposes. These include the explicit recognition of the relative effectiveness of the marketing mix variables for each brand or market segment combination, the evaluation of demand as well as cost synergies between product/markets, and the formal assessment of uncertainties and risk associated with each market.

CHAPTER 8 SUMMARY _____

Evaluation of Product-Market Portfolio _____

■ **The Growth/Share Matrix**

Premises

- High market share generates cash revenues
- High market growth uses more cash resources

Guide for the Growth/Share Matrix in MARKSTRAT

- Unit of analysis: brand/segment combination
- Use multiple definitions of market share
- Market segment growth rate cut-off depends on market segments in which the firm has products.

Issues with the Growth/Share Matrix Approach

- Market growth is not the only factor related to cash usage
- Market growth is not necessarily related to cash usage
- Market share is not necessarily related to cash generation (it ignores the cost of gaining share and could over value the effect of the experience curve)
- There are multiple factors leading to profitability
- Cash is not the only consideration in evaluating a portfolio
- Internal cash balance is not always desirable
- Cut-off values are arbitrary
- Unit of analysis depends on level of analysis

■ **The Attractiveness/Position Matrix**

Market Attractiveness (*see* next box)

Business Position (*see* box on page 146)

Market Attractiveness

■ **Assessment of Market Attractiveness:**

Step 1: Determine the relevant list of factors contributing to the attractiveness of businesses for the firm.

Step 2: Determine the direction and form of the relationship between each factor and the attractiveness measure, and assess the value of each business on each contributing factor developed in step 1.

Step 3: Determine the weight by which each factor contributes to the attractiveness measure.

Step 4: Compute the value of each business on the attractiveness measure.

■ **Factors Leading to Market Attractiveness:**

MARKET FACTORS

- Market/Segment size in units
- Market/Segment growth rate
- Market/Segment primary demand elasticity to price
- Advertising elasticity (primary market/segment demand)
- Shopping habits of consumers in market/segment
- Demand elasticity to product features
- Forecasting accuracy of market/segment size
- Forecasting accuracy of market shares

COMPETITION

- Number of brands competing in market/segment
- Size of competitors (their available resources)
- Marketing mix strategy of competitors
- Reactivity of competitors in market/segment
- Positioning of competing brands
- Threat of new brand introductions in market/segments
- Extent of barriers for each competitor not yet in market/segment

FINANCIAL FACTORS

- Contribution margins
- Experience effects

Business Position

- **Assessment of Business Position:**

    Step 1: Determine the relevant list of factors contributing to the position of businesses for the firm in their respective market/segment.

    Step 2: Determine the direction and form of the relationship between each factor and the position measure, and assess the value of each business on each contributing factor developed in step 1.

    Step 3: Determine the weight by which each factor contributes to the position measure.

    Step 4: Compute the position of each business on the position measure.

- **Factors Contributing to Business Position:**

    MARKET FACTORS

    - Market/Segment share based on units sold
    - Market/Segment share based on value
    - Sales volume of brand in units
    - Sales volume of brand in value
    - Growth rate of market shares (based on units and value)
    - Growth rate of sales (based on units and value)
    - Brand price elasticity
    - Brand advertising elasticity
    - Brand sales force elasticity
    - Influence of brand on market/segment size

    COMPETITION

    - Competitive advantage
    - Price elasticity of competitive brands
    - Advertising elasticity of competitive brands
    - Sales force elasticity of competitive brands
    - Cross-elasticities for each marketing mix variable

    FINANCIAL FACTORS

    - Brand margin
    - Cumulative production versus the competitive brands'

Important Factors Influencing Resource Allocation That Need to Be Explicitly Recognized

- Effectiveness of marketing mix variables

- Demand synergies

- Cost synergies

- Uncertainties and risk

CHAPTER 9

Functional Strategies

MARKSTRAT involves multiple decisions that enable the MARKSTRAT firms to implement their marketing strategy. The marketing mix variables are represented by a set of possible decisions (rather than just expenditures). In addition, firms must forecast specific demand for each brand in order to ensure the availability of the product in the market place. These decisions enable the firms to implement their marketing strategy in detail. In this chapter, we discuss how these decisions can be made with the full information which will enable the teams to implement properly their strategy and, therefore, to achieve their goals. First we discuss how the decision variables are related to marketing objectives (market share or profitability, for example). Then we discuss in greater details each of the main relationships. The objective is to enable the MARKSTRAT teams to understand how consumers respond to their decisions.

KEY EFFECTS OF MARKSTRAT STRATEGIC DECISIONS

The mains effects of the decision variables in MARKSTRAT are represented graphically in Figure 9.1. These factors are interrelated to arrive at market share and profits.

A necessary condition for buying a given brand is that consumers are aware of the product and its attribute values. Purchase intentions are determined by the consumers' perceptions of the various brands relative to the ideal brand or preference of the segment. Market share is determined by these intentions to purchase, given that the product is available and that the competitive products are available in sufficient quantities to satisfy the demand of consumers who prefer them. This availability is, from a marketing point of view, determined by the distribution network, which is a function of the sales force size in the appropriate channels of distribution (although

Figure 9.1: The Main Effects of Marketing Decisions

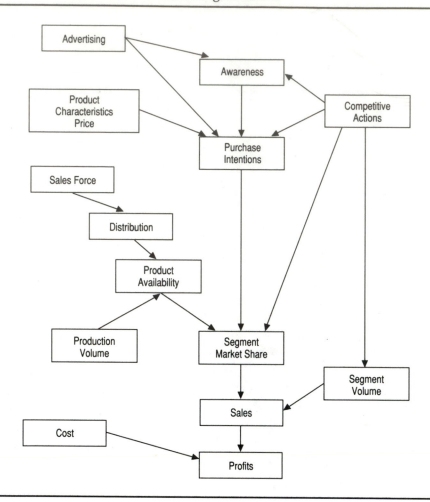

other factors influence distributors as well, as discussed below). This availability also assumes that the brands have been manufactured in sufficient quantity. Purchase intentions are, therefore, a key element of market share. They are affected by a number of marketing variables. As indicated, awareness is a strong determinant of behavioral intentions. As advertising is the main source for building awareness in MARKSTRAT, advertising impacts purchase intentions through the awareness level. However, the perceptions of each brand, which are determined by the physical characteristics of the brands, including price, are also affected by any advertising which aims to persuade or reposition the brands. Therefore, market share is a function of the marketing mix variables, as explained by this set of relationships.

Competitive actions in terms of the marketing mix variables are clearly represented through the purchase intentions variable, which is relative to all the brands in the market. Competition is also modeled through the marketing variables themselves, as it is the share of voice which counts in advertising rather than an absolute budget effect. Similarly, the pressure created by the sales force on distributors is a relative factor which depends on the sales forces of all competitors. The marketing variables affect market share as described above, but firms' decisions also impact primary demand segment by segment. Therefore, the marketing mix strategies of the firms determine not just market share but the market's evolution. The segment sales volumes and the brand market shares completely determine the sales of each brand. The gross profits of the brand follow after taking the costs into account, costs which vary as a function of past cumulative sales due to the experience effect. Within this basic structure, we now proceed to describe some of the main characteristics of the basic functional relationships.

FUNCTIONAL RELATIONSHIPS

All the relationships between the decision variables and the intermediary consumer responses as well as market share are non-linear in form. Following the view that, most of the time, a threshold exists before effects can start and that, after a point, decreasing returns to scale occur, most relationships in MARKSTRAT, whether they deal with advertising effects or sales force effects, can be expected to be accurately represented by an S-shaped functional form. In addition, competitors' decisions interacting on consumer response as well, the response functions to marketing mix variables are very complex. A strategic implication is that this creates asymmetries in response functions across brands, as well as the possibility of establishing mobility barriers. This possibility is further reinforced by some inertia in the market. Indeed, the awareness function considers both learning (through the advertising effects described above) and forgetting (through a lagged awareness effect on current awareness). Similarly, opportunities in repositioning through advertising are a function of the existing positions, moderated by the awareness level of the brand: a brand with high brand awareness has much greater difficulty in changing its perceptions through advertising than a brand with a low awareness. However, this does not mean that purchase intentions are stable over time. In fact, new entries in the market and successful repositioning strategies (either through advertising or R&D) can alter the market share structure substantially from one period to another. The implication is that the markets in MARKSTRAT are fluid and very competitive. Although firms may develop advantages over time, the competitive structure remains unstable. Hence, it might be difficult to protect a given position without a proactive marketing strategy.

Preferences

Preferences of a market segment are an inverse function of the distance of a brand from the segment's ideal point in a multi-dimensional perceptual map. This distance is, however, weighted so that everything else being equal, the more important dimensions have a larger weight. This distance for a brand is relative to the other brand distances to the ideal point. Preferences or purchase intentions are also affected by the awareness level of the brand. Therefore, the awareness level of a brand and its distance to the ideal point of a segment determine the attractiveness of the brand. Purchase intentions represent the relative attractiveness of a brand for a segment.

The perceptual map is an essential part of the MARKSTRAT model, as it contributes greatly to the competitiveness of the markets. Indeed, if we assume a new brand can achieve an awareness level comparable to that of existing brands, the ability to position the new brand close to the ideal point determines the extent of the market share for the new brand and the loss in share of existing brands, *ceteris paribus*. Also, a brand better positioned on the most important dimension will ensure a greater share.

Consequently, positioning is a central part of marketing strategy. The ideal point model reflected in the market research studies indicates that there is an optimal level of each attribute desired by consumers. This is particularly important in MARKSTRAT, as perceived price is one of the dimensions in the perceptual space. Consequently, price elasticities are relatively complex to estimate. In general, because the purchase intent function (and consequently the market share function) is highly non-linear, the parameters representing the contribution of each determinant are not easily estimated. This complexity contributes to the challenges of implementing a marketing strategy, as decisions cannot simply be based on a few estimated (or guessed) parameters.

Market Share

Market share is determined relatively straightforwardly based on purchase intentions. The only additional factor to consider to understand market share behavior is the availability of the brands on the market. This availability depends on the willingness of distributors to carry the brand. Willingness of the distributors is in turn a function of several factors, such as the sales force, advertising levels, and the trends in the brand sales. Again, this function is not linear, and the interactions between marketing mix variables explain why the marketing mix strategy must be coordinated for maximum efficiency.

Primary Demand

Primary demand by segment is partly evolving according to the different stages of the product life cycle. These general trends are relatively strong in the sense that they correspond to the long-term trends in the market. However, the strategies and the marketing mix decisions of the firms also significantly determine the segment sizes. In particular, the average price, the advertising expenditures, and the degree with which the products offered satisfy the needs of the segment (the average distance to the ideal point) contribute to expanding the market. This explains why the segment growth curves and the absolute sales levels differ between different runs of the simulation. Therefore, the product life cycle is partly determined by the firms' moves.

Experience Curve_____

As discussed earlier, the costs of each brand in MARKSTRAT follow the experience curve. This experience curve characterizes the production technology of the industry. However, the actual cost curves for different brands are not necessarily the same. In fact, each firm can develop a competitive cost advantage, not only by having a cumulative production larger than competition, but also by improving on their own technologies through cost reduction R&D programs. Therefore, although experience plays a role in the strategic decisions, the main sources of cost advantage are not necessarily found in market share per se. Cost reductions over time do not "just happen": the firm must work to create them.

_____ **CONCLUSION**

In this Chapter, we have described how the main decisions in MARKSTRAT are related to the performance of the brands. Although the knowledge of these relationships is necessary to make "optimal" marketing mix decisions, it is not sufficient to evaluate the marketing strategy of each firm. In particular, the relationships presented in Figure 9.1 provide little information as to the portfolio decisions that the firm must make, as discussed in Chapter 8. A good understanding of how the market responds is useful, however, in two areas of the strategic decision making process. When evaluating a marketing plan, marketing strategists must evaluate the implications of each change in the marketing activities of their firm and in those of the competitors. In addition, when finalizing the allocation of resources allocated to each brand and to each marketing mix variable, the response of consumers to these decisions is essential. This chapter has provided the basis for each team in MARK-STRAT to better understand the impact of the various marketing mix variables.

CHAPTER 9 SUMMARY _____

The Main Effects of Marketing Decisions

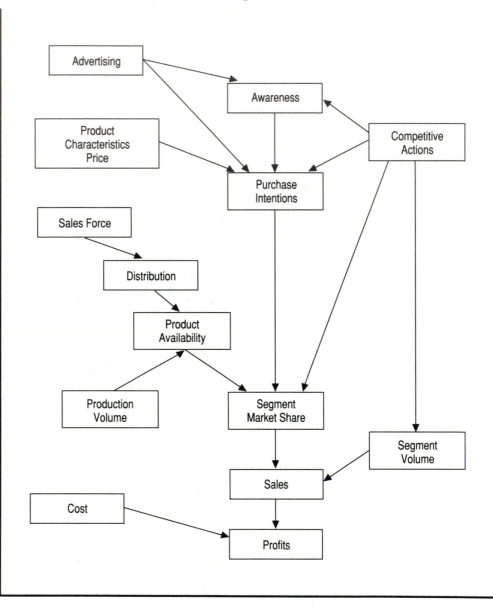

Sample Company Report
& Market Research Studies

The following represents the sample Company Report of Firm 1 in Period 5 of a MARKSTRAT simulation. The decisions of Firm 1 for the same period are specified in Figure 4.6. This is only an example, the data that it contains should not be used in making your decisions.

-------------------------- D E C I S I O N S --------------------------------

PRODUCT MANAGEMENT

Brand names	Name of R & D project	Product. planning KU	Advert. budget K$	Advert. research %	Rec. retail price $	Percept. obj. (-20 to 20 or 99) Axis 1	Axis 2
SAMA	PSALM	350	2000	10	270	-11	-5
SALT		150	1500	6	380	99	0
SALU	PSALA	150	2000	10	480	99	13
SARO		140	1700	10	345	99	5

SALES FORCE

Distribution channels	One	Two	Three
Number of salespersons	13	40	35

RESEARCH AND DEVELOPMENT

Project name	Expend-itures	--------- Physical characteristics ----------					
		1	2	3	4	5	6
PSARA	100	13	6	50	25	65	130

MARKET RESEARCH STUDIES

1	2	3	4	5	6	7	8	9	10	11	12	13	14	15
Y	Y	Y	Y	Y	Y	N	N	N	N	N	Y	Y	Y	Y

Administrator's change in exceptional cost or profit :   0 K$
Administrator's change in budget .... :   0 K$

--------------------------- M E S S A G E S ---------------------------------

MESSAGE(S) FROM THE SIMULATION

* YOU DID NOT RESPECT YOUR BUDGET CONSTRAINT.
YOUR BUDGET HAS BEEN REDUCED ON : - ADVERTISING

* OBSOLETE INVENTORIES FOR DELETED OR MODIFIED BRAND(S) CHARGED AS AN
EXCEPTIONAL COST AT 10 % OF TRANSFER COST.

-------------------   G E N E R A L   R E S U L T S   -----------------------

		SAMA	SALT	SALU	SARO
Units sold	Units	189627	111617	24497	44087
Production	Units	280000	120000	120000	112000
Inventory	Units	90373	8383	95503	139248
Retail price	$	270	380	480	345
Av. selling price	$	166	236	297	212
Unit transf. cost	$	99	98	177	147
Revenues	K$	31478	26342	7276	9346
Cost of goods sold	K$	-18773	-10938	-4336	-6481
Inv. hld. cost	K$	-775	-71	-1465	-1774
Advertising	K$	-1645	-1234	-1645	-1399
Gross marketing contribution	K$	10290	14122	-181	-314

Gross marketing contribution .	23917	K$
Research and development	-100	K$
Sales force	-1964	K$
Market research	-440	K$
Exceptional cost or profit ...	-2798	K$
Net marketing contribution ...	18614	K$
Next period budget	8061	K$

-----------------   M A R K E T I N G   R E S U L T S   ---------------------

Brands	SAMA	SALT	SALU	SARO
Market share % Units	6.8	4.0	0.9	1.6
Number of distributors				
Channel 1	634	641	658	662
Channel 2	13358	13348	13682	13640
Channel 3	1377	1379	1409	1422

-------------   R E S E A R C H   &   D E V E L O P M E N T   ----------------

Project name	Avail.	Physical characteristics						Cumul. expend.	Addition. invest. required	Minimum realistic unit cost
		1	2	3	4	5	6	K$	K$	$
PSAMA	YES	10	8	30	25	10	115	2000		
PSALT	YES	12	9	37	25	30	144	1500		
PSALU	YES	12	9	37	25	90	249	2200		
PSARO	YES	13	6	50	25	65	184	1550		
PSALM	YES	10	8	30	25	25	130	500		
PVAMA	NO	30	15	50	6	60	108	100	7603	231
PSALA	YES	12	9	37	25	90	191	900		
PSARA	YES	13	6	50	25	65	134	600		

----------------   C U M U L A T I V E   R E S U L T S   --------------------

Brand	Results since period	Units sold KU	Retail sales K$	Revenues K$	CGS K$	IHC K$	Advert. K$	GMC K$
SAMA	0	1013	272165	167408	81344	1401	11806	72678
SALT	0	473	186595	115422	51284	1194	11208	51757
SALU	4	46	22252	13725	9320	3109	3645	-2353
SARO	4	85	29443	18049	13353	2738	2899	-929
TOTAL		1618	510455	314603	155302	8443	29558	121154

Research & development expenditures (K$)   5850
Sales force expenditures (K$)   9492
Market research expenditures (K$)   1598
Exceptional cost or profit (K$)   2798
Net marketing contribution (K$)   101415

------------------------   N E W S L E T T E R   ----------------------------

```
G N P growth rate this period ..............................   4.0 %
G N P growth rate estimation next period .................   4.0 %
Inflation rate this period ................................   2.7 %
Estimated inflation rate next period .....................   3.4 %
Inventory holding cost per annum (% of transfer cost) ....   8.7 %
Cost of a salesperson next period ........................  23000 $
Cost of firing a salesperson next period .................   5700 $
Cost of training a new salesperson next period ...........   3600 $
```

COST OF MARKET RESEARCH STUDIES NEXT PERIOD (K$)

```
 1 :   70       2 :  117       3 :   70       4 :   12       5 :   41
 6 :   23       7 :   47       8 :   82       9 :   59      10 :   12
11 :   23      12 :   35      13 :   18      14 :   28      15 :   41
```

NEW BRANDS OR PRODUCT MODIFICATIONS INTRODUCED OVER THE LAST PERIOD

| Brands | ---- Physical characteristics ---- | | | | | | Retail price |
	1	2	3	4	5	6	
SAMA	10	8	30	25	25	126	270
SALU	12	9	37	25	90	186	480
SELO	10	3	50	25	20	84	170
VEVU	75	10	50	5	40	310	640
SIRO	10	8	50	20	10	93	250
VOLT	50	15	50	6	65	362	800
SUSZ	10	6	50	25	20	103	200
SUS2	17	9	50	20	50	155	280

------------------------ N E W S L E T T E R ----------------------------

INFORMATION ON SONITE MARKET

Brands	Unit sales U	Market share %U	Retail price $	Retail sales K$	Market share %$
SAMA	189627	6.8	270	51199	5.0
SALT	111617	4.0	380	42414	4.2
SALU	24497	0.9	480	11759	1.2
SARO	44087	1.6	345	15210	1.5
SEMI	273961	9.8	440	120543	11.8
SELO	34280	1.2	170	5828	0.6
SIRO	99030	3.5	250	24757	2.4
SIBI	402388	14.4	420	169003	16.6
SOLD	521276	18.6	470	245000	24.0
SONO	47744	1.7	350	16710	1.6
SOFT	360000	12.9	300	108000	10.6
SUSI	59843	2.1	170	10173	1.0
SULI	194882	7.0	350	68209	6.7
SULZ	173198	6.2	380	65815	6.5
SUSZ	120000	4.3	200	24000	2.4
SUS2	144000	5.1	280	40320	4.0
Total mkt.	2800430	100.0	364	1018941	100.0

INFORMATION ON VODITE MARKET

Brands	Unit sales U	Market share %U	Retail price $	Retail sales K$	Market share %$
VEVO	31525	26.6	810	25535	30.7
VEVU	75888	63.9	640	48568	58.4
VOLT	11265	9.5	800	9012	10.8
Total mkt.	118678	100.0	700	83116	100.0

--------------- STUDY 1 : CONSUMER SURVEY - SONITE MARKET   ----------------

BRAND AWARENESS (%)

SAMA :	61.3	SALT :	54.4	SALU :	30.2	SARO :	24.3	
SEMI :	73.4	SELO :	38.5					
SIRO :	66.0	SIBI :	72.9					
SOLD :	78.6	SONO :	62.2	SOFT :	66.1			
SUSI :	60.3	SULI :	76.6	SULZ :	54.6	SUSZ :	28.7	SUS2 : 28.7

SHOPPING HABITS (%)

Segment	Channel 1	Channel 2	Channel 3	Total
1	58.6	12.7	28.7	100.0
2	43.2	21.6	35.2	100.0
3	7.4	61.5	31.1	100.0
4	21.9	47.8	30.4	100.0
5	14.8	30.8	54.4	100.0

PURCHASE INTENTIONS (%)

Brand	Segment 1	Segment 2	Segment 3	Segment 4	Segment 5	Total
SAMA	1.3	2.6	0.1	1.2	28.3	7.3
SALT	1.9	1.1	0.4	12.6	1.5	4.3
SALU	2.4	0.4	1.6	1.2	0.4	1.0
SARO	5.1	1.7	0.3	3.1	1.0	1.9
SEMI	8.2	1.4	32.9	7.3	1.3	9.0
SELO	0.7	1.0	0.1	0.5	4.3	1.4
SIRO	1.1	1.7	0.1	1.0	12.9	3.6
SIBI	5.8	2.0	1.3	40.5	2.0	12.9
SOLD	6.9	1.3	59.6	7.5	1.3	13.7
SONO	9.0	1.4	0.6	1.7	1.2	1.8
SOFT	4.1	60.1	0.2	1.6	10.8	18.6
SUSI	1.0	1.5	0.1	0.7	6.6	2.1
SULI	39.4	3.3	1.6	7.3	2.2	6.3
SULZ	10.9	2.2	1.2	12.6	1.7	5.4
SUSZ	0.5	1.0	0.0	0.4	19.8	4.7
SUS2	1.7	17.5	0.1	0.8	4.8	5.9

---------------   STUDY 2 : CONSUMER PANEL - SONITE MARKET   ----------------

MARKET SHARES BASED ON UNIT SALES (%)

Brand	Segment 1	Segment 2	Segment 3	Segment 4	Segment 5	Total
SAMA	1.0	2.5	0.1	1.1	28.8	6.8
SALT	1.3	1.0	0.3	10.9	1.5	4.0
SALU	1.6	0.4	1.4	1.0	0.4	0.9
SARO	3.5	1.5	0.2	2.6	1.0	1.6
SEMI	8.2	1.6	28.7	6.9	1.3	9.8
SELO	0.6	1.1	0.0	0.4	4.0	1.2
SIRO	1.0	1.9	0.1	1.0	13.7	3.5
SIBI	5.8	2.4	1.3	41.8	2.2	14.4
SOLD	8.6	1.9	64.4	8.7	1.6	18.6
SONO	8.7	1.6	0.5	1.5	1.1	1.7
SOFT	3.1	54.3	0.1	1.1	8.4	12.9
SUSI	1.0	1.8	0.1	0.7	7.3	2.1
SULI	41.9	4.3	1.6	7.7	2.6	7.0
SULZ	11.7	2.9	1.2	13.6	2.0	6.2
SUSZ	0.5	1.1	0.0	0.3	19.2	4.?
SUS2	1.5	19.7	0.1	0.7	4.8	5.1

MARKET SIZE

	Segment 1	Segment 2	Segment 3	Segment 4	Segment 5	Total
Sales KU	193	545	638	854	570	2800

--------------   STUDY 3 : DISTRIBUTION PANEL - SONITE MARKET   --------------

MARKET SHARES BASED ON UNIT SALES (%)

Brand	Channel 1	Channel 2	Channel 3	Total
SAMA	3.0	5.8	10.5	6.8
SALT	2.8	5.0	3.8	4.0
SALU	0.2	1.3	1.0	0.9
SARO	1.5	1.6	1.6	1.6
SEMI	7.1	12.4	9.1	9.8
SELO	1.5	0.6	1.6	1.2
SIRO	2.1	2.9	5.2	3.5
SIBI	13.2	17.2	12.3	14.4
SOLD	9.5	26.4	17.4	18.6
SONO	3.6	0.7	1.4	1.7
SOFT	21.5	8.7	10.7	12.9
SUSI	1.8	1.6	2.9	2.1
SULI	13.2	3.5	5.9	7.0
SULZ	8.6	5.3	5.3	6.2
SUSZ	2.3	3.4	6.7	4.3
SUS2	8.1	3.6	4.6	5.1

MARKET SIZE

	Channel 1	Channel 2	Channel 3	Total
Sales KU	749	1032	1020	2800

--------------   STUDY 4 : SEMANTIC SCALES - SONITE MARKET   ---------------

* The three semantic differential scales perceived as
  most important are : 1) PRICE, 2) POWER, 3) DESIGN

* High ratings correspond to high price, high power and
  high design.

IDEAL VALUES	PRICE	POWER	DESIGN
Segment 1	4.45	6.22	5.26
Segment 2	2.92	4.76	5.72
Segment 3	5.94	5.66	5.18
Segment 4	5.30	4.02	5.68
Segment 5	2.04	3.30	5.71

BRAND PERCEPTION

	PRICE	POWER	DESIGN
SAMA	2.63	2.33	6.16
SALT	5.24	2.99	6.27
SALU	6.16	6.32	6.31
SARO	4.33	4.68	5.12
SEMI	5.91	5.53	5.57
SELO	2.30	2.59	2.32
SIRO	2.59	1.83	5.98
SIBI	5.24	4.28	6.34
SOLD	6.06	5.58	5.48
SONO	4.80	6.52	2.58
SOFT	2.52	4.46	4.88
SUSI	1.94	2.61	2.49
SULI	4.77	5.51	4.95
SULZ	4.93	4.86	5.60
SUSZ	1.90	2.57	5.03
SUS2	2.71	4.29	6.39

--- STUDY 5 : PERCEPTUAL MAPPING OF BRANDS SIMILARITIES AND PREFERENCES ---

* Study realized on a random sample of 200 individuals.
* No significant differences in perceptions have been observed between segments.
* Statistically significant results on two dimensions.
* Based on semantic scales, the most satisfactory interpretation of the axes is :
  Axis 1 : PERCEIVED PRICE
  Axis 2 : PERCEIVED POWER

		COORDINATES	
IDEAL POINTS		Axis 1	Axis 2
Segment	1	2.6	13.9
Segment	2	-8.1	4.2
Segment	3	12.7	10.3
Segment	4	8.3	0.0
Segment	5	-13.9	-4.9

BRAND PERCEPTION

		Axis 1	Axis 2
A :	SAMA	-9.6	-10.3
B :	SALT	9.2	-5.8
C :	SALU	13.8	15.6
D :	SARO	2.4	5.2
E :	SEMI	12.1	10.2
F :	SELO	-12.1	-9.6
G :	SIRO	-10.3	-14.7
H :	SIBI	8.6	2.8
3 :	SOLD	13.4	9.8
I :	SONO	4.5	15.9
J :	SOFT	-9.4	4.0
* :	SUSI	-13.8	-10.0
K :	SULI	4.7	9.5
L :	SULZ	5.9	6.2
* :	SUSZ	-14.0	-10.1
M :	SUS2	-8.3	2.9

---   STUDY 5 :   PERCEPTUAL MAPPING OF BRANDS SIMILARITIES AND PREFERENCES   ---

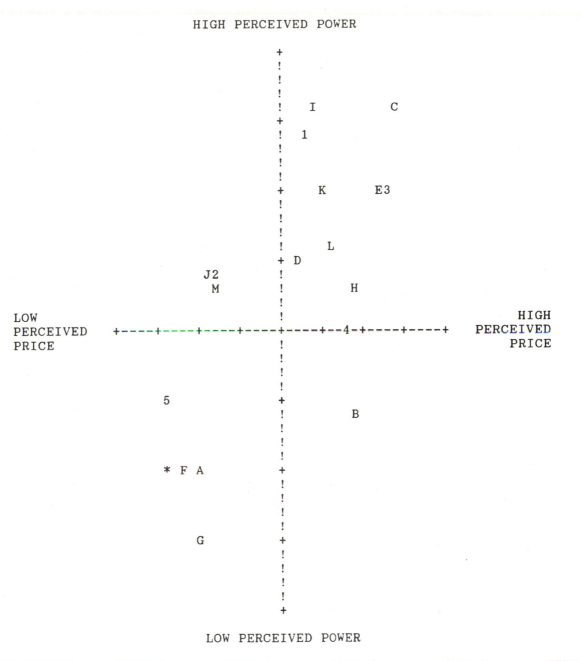

```
                              HIGH PERCEIVED POWER

                                      +
                                      !
                                      !
                                      !
                                      !      I           C
                                      +
                                      !      1
                                      !
                                      !
                                      !
                                      +      K           E3
                                      !
                                      !
                                      !
                                      !          L
                                      +  D
                          J2          !
                          M           !              H
                                      !
   LOW                                !                                HIGH
   PERCEIVED     +----+----+----+----+----+----+-4-+----+----+    PERCEIVED
   PRICE                              !                                PRICE
                                      !
                                      !
                          5           +
                                      !              B
                                      !
                                      !
                                      !
                        * F A         +
                                      !
                                      !
                                      !
                          G           +
                                      !
                                      !
                                      !
                                      +

                              LOW PERCEIVED POWER
```

IDEAL POINTS	FIRM 1	FIRM 2	FIRM 3	FIRM 4	FIRM 5
1 : SEG. 1	A : SAMA	E : SEMI	G : SIRO	3 : SOLD	* : SUSI
2 : SEG. 2	B : SALT	F : SELO	H : SIBI	I : SONO	K : SULI
3 : SEG. 3	C : SALU			J : SOFT	L : SULZ
4 : SEG. 4	D : SARO				* : SUSZ
5 : SEG. 5					M : SUS2

--------------- STUDY 6 : MARKET FORECAST - SONITE MARKET --------------

	EXPECTED MARKET SIZE NEXT PERIOD (KU)	VOLUME GROWTH RATE NEXT PERIOD (%)
Segment 1	184	-5.0
Segment 2	763	40.0
Segment 3	702	10.0
Segment 4	1110	30.0
Segment 5	684	20.0
Total	3443	22.9

-------------- STUDY 12 : COMPETITIVE ADVERTISING ESTIMATES --------------

ALL NUMBERS IN THOUSAND $

SAMA: 1684	SALT: 1265	SALU: 1669	SARO: 1366	
SEMI: 3172	VEVO: 3755	SELO: 4621	VEVU: 7254	
SIRO: 3328	SIBI: 3551			
SOLD: 6264	SONO: 0	SOFT: 6777	VOLT: 3493	
SUSI: 1535	SULI: 2852	SULZ: 2526	SUSZ: 2839	SUS2: 3021

-------------- STUDY 13 : COMPETITIVE SALES FORCE ESTIMATES --------------

NUMBER OF SALESPERSONS

	Channel 1	Channel 2	Channel 3	Total
Firm 1	13	42	37	92
Firm 2	29	26	33	88
Firm 3	24	36	42	102
Firm 4	41	36	40	117
Firm 5	32	47	43	122

------------------   STUDY 14 : SALES FORCE EXPERIMENT   --------------------

EXPECTED RESULTS IF SALES FORCE INCREASED BY 10 IN EACH CHANNEL

		Channel 1	Channel 2	Channel 3
SAMA	Number of distr.	970	14979	1595
	Market share (%)	4.3	6.4	11.8
SALT	Number of distr.	969	14959	1593
	Market share (%)	4.3	5.5	4.2
SALU	Number of distr.	993	15323	1632
	Market share (%)	0.7	1.4	1.1
SARO	Number of distr.	991	15289	1628
	Market share (%)	2.6	1.7	1.8

------------------   STUDY 15 : ADVERTISING EXPERIMENT   --------------------

EXPECTED RESULTS IF ADVERTISING BUDGET INCREASED BY 20 % FOR GIVEN BRAND

		SEGMENT					
		1	2	3	4	5	Total
SAMA	Awareness %	62.9	61.9	60.8	62.2	62.4	61.9
	Market share %	1.0	2.6	0.1	1.1	30.1	7.1
SALT	Awareness %	56.3	56.3	54.6	54.5	55.9	55.3
	Market share %	1.4	1.0	0.3	11.2	1.5	4.1
SALU	Awareness %	31.7	32.3	31.9	32.0	32.9	32.2
	Market share %	1.7	0.4	1.5	1.1	0.4	0.9
SARO	Awareness %	26.8	25.9	26.1	26.1	26.5	26.2
	Market share %	3.7	1.6	0.2	2.8	1.1	1.7

MARKSTRAT2 Software Instructions

OVERVIEW

The MARKSTRAT2 student disk, enclosed in this book, contains the software which allows you to display and print the results of your simulated MARKSTRAT2 firm, to enter your decisions and to project the financial implications of these decisions. It also contains a data file corresponding to the situation of a simulated firm in industry XYZ for illustrative purposes.

The MARKSTRAT2 student disk does not, however, contain the model which, based on your decisions and those of competing firms for a given period, simulates the competitive market activities and generates the results for this period. This simulation model is in the possession of the instructor for your course. After you have made your decisions for a given period, and saved these decisions on a data diskette, you will have to submit this data diskette to your instructor. He or she will then run the simulation model and return your data diskette to you with the results for the period. This process will be repeated for each period of the MARKSTRAT2 simulation.

The use of the MARKSTRAT2 software is very easy and does not require any specific computer knowledge. You should read the following instructions before starting to use your MARKSTRAT2 student disk for the first time. You will find after a little practice, however, that the MARKSTRAT2 software is self-explanatory and that you will no longer need to refer to these instructions.

COMPUTER SYSTEM REQUIREMENTS

Using the MARKSTRAT2 simulation requires the following minimum system configuration:

- IBM-PC, XT or AT with 256K bytes of memory
- Two 5¼ inch floppy disk drives, or one hard disk and one floppy disk drive

169

■ A monochrome or color monitor

■ The DOS operating system, version 2.0 or higher

The MARKSTRAT2 simulation has been designed to exploit different features that your microcomputer system may have. A *color monitor* provides a more attractive layout of the information, but the simulation has also been designed to run with a monochrome screen. A *printer* is also required to produce documents containing the information generated by the simulation.

STARTING WITH THE MARKSTRAT2 SOFTWARE _____

Your microcomputer system may be equipped either with two drives for 5¼ inch floppy disks (commonly called "diskettes") or with one hard disk plus one or two drives for diskettes. The instructions are different for each of these two options and you need only read the section below which corresponds to your situation.

If You Have a System with Two Floppy Disk Drives_____

Step 1. Starting Your System

   a. Insert your DOS system disk in drive A. This is the left-hand drive on most systems (or the upper one on others).

   b. Switch on your computer and wait for the MS-DOS system to be loaded. After a number of messages, the prompt A⟩ indicates that the system is ready to receive your instructions.

   c. Remove the system disk from drive A and insert in its place the MARKSTRAT2 student disk.

Step 2. Making a Copy of Your MARKSTRAT2 Student Disk

You are authorized, within the terms of the license agreement which you received, to make a copy of the MARKSTRAT2 student disk for your own personal use. It is advisable that you start by making such a backup copy, following the instructions below, in case your master disk becomes accidentally damaged.

   a. Insert your MARKSTRAT2 student disk in drive A.

   b. Insert a blank formatted diskette in drive B.

   c. Type "COPY A:*.* B:" and press the return key. Please note that there should be a space between COPY and A, and between * and B. A message will be displayed when the copy is complete and the prompt A⟩ will indicate that the system is ready to receive further instructions.

   d. Remove the backup copy diskette from drive B and store it in a safe place. Do not forget to place a label on it for proper identification.

Step 3. Using the MARKSTRAT2 *Software*

Type "MARKSTRAT" and press the return key. After the introduction to the MARKSTRAT2 software, you will see a screen asking you to indicate some parameters such as the disk unit, industry code, team number and period number. You are now in a position to start using the MARKSTRAT2 software and the XYZ illustration as explained in the next pages.

Step 4. Using the MARKSTRAT2 *Software at a Later Date*

Whenever you want to use the MARKSTRAT2 software, just repeat Steps 1 and 3 above (you will of course not need to make a further copy of your diskette).

If You Have a System with a Hard Disk

Step 1. Starting Your System

Just switch on your computer. After a number of messages, the prompt C> usually indicates that the system is ready to receive your instructions. In this common situation your hard disk drive is identified by the letter C. In some cases, a different letter may appear in the prompt if your hard disk drive has been set up with a different identification.

Step 2. Installing MARKSTRAT2 *on Your Hard Disk*

a. Type "DIR" and press the return key. This will list the files contained on your hard disk, followed on the last line by a message indicating the space remaining available. Check that you have at least 250,000 bytes free on your hard disk to install the MARKSTRAT2 software. If this is not the case, you will have to make room on your hard disk for the MARKSTRAT2 software by erasing some files or transferring them onto a diskette for backup.

b. Type "MD MS2" and press the return key. This will make a directory called MS2 on your hard disk which will be reserved for the MARKSTRAT software. Note that there should be a space between MD and MS2.

c. Type "CD MS2" and press the return key. This will change the directory used by the system to the one you have created for MARKSTRAT2. Note that there should be a space between CD and MS2.

d. Insert the MARKSTRAT2 student disk in the floppy disk drive. If your system has more than one floppy disk drive, insert the disk in drive A. This is the left-hand drive on most systems (or the upper one on others).

e. Type "COPY A:*.*" and press the return key. Please note that there should be a space between COPY and A. A message will be displayed when the copy is complete and the prompt > will indicate that the system is ready to receive further instructions.

f. Type "MARKSTRAT" and press the return key. After the introduction to the MARKSTRAT2 software, you will see a screen asking you to indicate some parameters such as the disk unit, industry code, team number and period number. You are now in a position to start using the MARKSTRAT2 simulation and the XYZ illustration as explained in the next pages.

Step 3. Using the MARKSTRAT2 Software at a Later Date

As long as the MARKSTRAT2 programs have not been erased from the MS2 subdirectory on your hard disk, you will no longer need the MARKSTRAT2 student disk. Just store it it in a safe place. Whenever you want to use the MARKSTRAT2 software, you just need to:

a. Switch on your computer and wait for the › prompt.

b. Type "CD MS2" and press the return key.

c. Type "MARKSTRAT" and press the return key.

SETTING IDENTIFICATION PARAMETERS

In the first screen after the introductory information on the MARKSTRAT2 software, you are asked to indicate four identification parameters.

a. *Disk unit for the data files.* This parameter specifies which disk unit contains the file corresponding to the MARKSTRAT2 simulated firm which you are about to manage.

If you have a system with two floppy disk drives, the MARKSTRAT2 student disk containing the software is located in drive A. The diskette containing the data file corresponding to the simulated firm, which you will manage in the context of the course, is located in drive B. In this normal situation, you should consequently enter B on this line. If, however, you are only experimenting with the MARKSTRAT2 software and want to have access to the illustrative information of the XYZ industry, you should enter A on this line, as the XYZ data file is contained on your MARKSTRAT2 student disk.

If you have a system with a hard disk, the diskette containing the data file corresponding to the simulated firm, which you will manage in the context of the course, is located in drive A. In this normal situation, you should consequently enter A on this line. If, however, you are only experimenting with the MARKSTRAT2 software and want to have access to the illustrative information of the XYZ industry, just press the return key, as the XYZ data file is contained in the MS2 subdirectory of your hard disk.

b. *Industry code.* You are managing one of five firms competing in a given industry. The instructor in charge of the course you are attending will give you the code of the industry and the number of the firm to which you have been assigned. XYZ is the industry code of the example supplied with the student disk so that you can familiarize yourself with the MARKSTRAT2 software. Just specify the industry code (maximum three characters, XYZ, for the example provided) and press the return key.

c. ***Team number.*** This corresponds to the number, 1 to 5, of the simulated firm which you are going to manage. In the XYZ example, it is firm 3. Just specify the team number.

d. ***Period for which you want the*** MARKSTRAT ***output.*** The MARK-STRAT2 simulation can be run up to Period 10. You will start with information on your simulated firm in Period 0. You will then make decisions for Period 1 and save them on your data diskette which you will then return to your instructor. He or she will run the MARKSTRAT2 simulation and give you back the data diskette with the results of Period 1. The same process will be followed for as many periods (typically from 6 to 10) as will be covered in the course which you are attending. At each iteration in this process, information on the latest period is added onto your data diskette.

After you have entered your industry code and your team number, the current period will be displayed on the next line. If you want to have access to the results of the current period, just press the return key as this is the default option. This will also allow you to enter decisions for the next period. You are also able to access the results of previous periods by entering the corresponding number and pressing the return key. You will, however, not be allowed to modify the decisions of these previous periods.

If you make any errors while entering these parameters (such as a team number not corresponding to the data diskette available to you), the software will display an error message and allow you to make appropriate corrections. You are advised to try to make such errors with the XYZ illustration to familiarize yourself with the software! A number on a previous line can be corrected by using the upper arrow (↑).

THE MAIN MENU

After having specified identification parameters, you will face the Main Menu. This is the core of the MARKSTRAT2 software and it contains all the major options open to you. When you select an option, after completion of the various steps in that option, you will automatically return to the Main Menu. The five options in the Main Menu are:

Display results: to display on the screen the results generated by your decisions.

Print results: to obtain a printed copy of the results generated by your decisions.

Input decisions: to enter the decisions which you have made for your simulated firm in a given period, and to project the anticipated financial outcome of your decisions before you actually finalize them.

System configuration: to indicate new specifications concerning the printer and display monitor in your computer system.

Exit: to leave the MARKSTRAT2 software and return to the operating system level.

You can select one of the five options by pressing the letter key corresponding to the option you wish to select, such as "D" for "Display Results." The following information will help you for each of the options which you may want to investigate.

Menus. Every screen displayed by the MARKSTRAT2 software contains a menu showing clearly each of the options available at a given stage in two different ways. Menu screens list a number of options which give you direct access to various types of information. The Main Menu is an example of such a screen. It is at the core of the software and shows all the main options available. Every other screen contains, at the bottom, a menu line with the options available at that stage.

Escape key. There is a key on your keyboard called the Escape key, usually indicated as Esc. Unless otherwise indicated, pressing the Esc key will take you back to the last Menu which you accessed, and eventually back to the Main Menu.

SPECIFYING YOUR COMPUTER SYSTEM CONFIGURATION

When using the MARKSTRAT2 software for the first time, you will need to first select the "System configuration" option to check if the default specifications match the configuration of your system. To do this press "C." The configuration screen displayed will indicate the various system parameters which you are able to change.

Auto initialization for printer. Press "Y" if you want the MARKSTRAT2 software to initialize your printer with your own paper length and form feed specifications, "N" if your printer is initialized automatically. If in doubt, indicate "Y" and specify the next two printer options as well.

Paper length. Indicate the length in number of lines of the paper pages used in your printer. Most pages are 66 or 72 lines long. If necessary, enter a new number and press the return key. If in doubt, just leave the default option. If, when you later print the MARKSTRAT2 results, you see too many blank lines at the end of each page, you can change this specification and reduce the number of lines (normally to 66). If you see that the results overflow from one page to the next, just increase the number of lines (normally to 72).

Form-feed for printer. Press "Y" if your printer requires a form-feed at the end of each page to take it to the top of the next page. Press "N" if your printer automatically generates a form-feed. If in doubt just leave the default option. When you later print the MARKSTRAT2 results, if sections of your report do not start on a new page, you can change this specification to "Y." If, on the other hand, you see blank pages in the middle of your report, change it to "N".

Color screen. This line only appears if your system is equipped with a color card. Press "Y" if you have a color monitor, "N" if not. In the latter case, selecting "N" will improve the legibility of your monochrome screen.

After having entered new configuration parameters, you will be asked if you want to save them. Press "Y" to save your specifications. If you press "N," you will leave the screen without saving any of your modifications and the configuration will remain unchanged. This option is useful when you just want to check the specifications without changing them. In either case, you will go back to the Main menu.

When you use MARKSTRAT2 again at a later date on the same computer system, the configuration that you have saved here will be operative and you will not need to specify it again. You should therefore go straight to other options in the Main Menu. Only if you have changed any element of your system in the meantime do you need to change the configuration parameters accordingly.

EXPERIMENTING WITH THE XYZ EXAMPLE

Before the beginning of your marketing course, you will find it valuable to experiment with the MARKSTRAT2 software. You can do this very conveniently by using the illustration provided on the student disk. It contains information on Firm 3 in industry XYZ in a given period of an actual simulation. To experiment with the XYZ example, just proceed as follows:

1. ***Access the* MARKSTRAT2 *software.*** Start your system and call up the MARKSTRAT2 software as described above. After the title screen, you will see the Main Menu.

2. ***Change system configuration.*** Select "C" in the Main Menu and make sure that the specifications for your computer configuration are correct, as described in the previous pages.

3. ***Display results.*** Select "D" in the Main Menu. You will then see the Display Menu with the option of displaying the Company Report (C) or the Market Research Studies (S). If you select "C," the Company Report Menu lists the various sections which you can access directly by pressing the corresponding letter, for instance "E" for R&D. On the screen corresponding to each page of the Company Report, note the menu line at the bottom indicating the options available. You can usually go to the previous page ("P") or the next page ("N") or back to the Company Report Menu ("M").

    The same facilities exist for displaying the Market Research studies, but only for those which have been ordered by your firm.

4. ***Print results.*** To obtain a printed copy of your results, check that your printer is on-line and select "P" in the Main Menu. You will then see the Print Menu with the options to print:

- A complete output, i.e. a full set containing your Company Report and the Market Research studies purchased by your firm.
- The Company Report only.
- The set of Market Research studies purchased by your firm.
- A specific Market Research study purchased by your firm.

You will be given an error message if your printer is not on-line or if you try to print a market research study which your firm did not order.

5. ***Input decisions.*** Selecting "I" for Input decisions will allow you to enter your decisions for your firm (number 3) in the next period in the XYZ example. The first time you access the Input Menu, the only option available is to enter decisions corresponding to the first part of the Decision Form. As you proceed through the input procedure, you will go through the following stages:

- *Decision Form Part 1.* This deals with the Product Management section of the Decision Form. You will see displayed default decisions corresponding to those of the previous period. As indicated in the menu line at the bottom of the screen, you can move around the screen by using the arrows, enter your decisions and confirm them with the return key or jump directly to the bottom of the screen by pressing the Escape key (Esc). You will first have to enter the names of each brand in your current portfolio, the names of R&D projects used to introduce or modify them, and other decisions for each brand. In the case of any error (such as modifying a brand with an incomplete R&D project), you will receive an appropriate message and you will be asked to correct your entry. When you have finished entering your decisions on Product Management, you will have the options, indicated in the menu line to edit your inputs ("E"), go to the next page ("N") or back to the input menu ("M").

- *Decision Form Part 2.* This screen concerns the remainder of the Decision Form dealing with the Sales Force, Research & Development and Market Research Studies. Decisions are entered in the same way as in the previous screen.

- *Marketing Budget.* The next screen displays a recapitulation of the marketing expenditures corresponding to your decisions. You will see an error message if your total marketing expenditures exceed your authorized budget. You still have the option to reduce your expenditures by modifying your decisions. This can be done by returning to Parts 1 and 2 of the Decision Form either through the Input Menu (press "M") or by returning to previous pages (press "P").

- *Warning Messages.* Messages will appear in this screen only if your decisions may result in extraordinary actions. For instance, if you have deleted a brand from your portfolio and that obsolete stocks will be disposed of at an exceptional cost. The purpose of these warnings is only to draw your attention to specific issues. They may sometimes correspond to legitimate decisions. You should check, however, if they are not the result of an error in your decisions.

- *Sales Estimates.* This module helps you to estimate total market share, unit sales and retail sales of each brand. By pressing "E" for Edit, you are able to specify the expected market shares of each brand in each segment, based on units. Total market share, unit sales and retail sales are automatically calculated using the projected size of market segments in Market Research studies 6 for Sonites and 11 for Vodites.

- *Estimate of Distribution Mix.* This module helps you to estimate the average distribution margin and average selling price of each brand. By pressing "E" for Edit, you are able to specify for each brand the expected distribution of sales between the three channels. The average distribution margin and average selling price are automatically calculated based on the distributors' margin in each channel. Please note that the total of the distribution percentages for the three channels should add up to 100%. If this is not the case, the "total" number will be flashing on the screen.

- *Projected Gross Marketing Contribution.* This module allows you to estimate the financial implications of the decisions you have entered. The numbers displayed under "quantity sold" and "average selling price" are based on the estimates generated in the previous two screens. If the sales estimates exceed the sum of the beginning inventory and of the maximum possible production (production planning plus 20%), the "quantity sold" number will be adjusted accordingly. The gross marketing contribution of each brand is then automatically computed based on your decisions. By pressing "E" for Edit, you are able to modify the expected unit sales ("quantity sold") for each brand. You may wish to use this option to test different scenarios and perform sensitivity analyses on the impact of sales levels on gross marketing contribution. You should, however, remember that these projections are based on a number of assumptions concerning parameters such as the cost experience effect.

- *Projected Net Marketing Contribution.* On the basis of the decisions entered and of the expected sales levels indicated on the previous screen, the projected net marketing contribution is calculated. You may return to the previous pages to analyze the impact of different sales levels on gross and net marketing contribution. Pressing the key for the letter "M" will take you back to the Input Menu.

When you have gone through the input procedure once, the Input Menu will display all options which you have already explored (Parts 1 and 2 of the Decision Form, Marketing Budget, Warning Messages and Financial Projections). You can access each of these options directly to change your decisions or perform additional sensitivity analyses. You also have the possibility to print a record of what you have done in the input procedure. Just check that your printer is on-line and press "P." Your decisions, the marketing budget, warning messages and financial projections will be printed. When you are satisfied with your decisions, you should save them on your data diskette by pressing "S." If you do not want to save your decisions, press "X" to exit the Input Menu. This option is useful only if you want to check decisions which you have saved before. To make sure that you do not forget to save your decisions, a warning messsage is displayed if you try to exit the Input Menu without saving your decisions.

When you exit the Input Menu, you return to the Main Menu. You can then go back to any of the options which you have already investigated: System Configuration, Display Results, Print Results or Input Decisions. If you return to the input procedure, you should notice that the decisions you have saved are now displayed. You are still allowed to change them until you return your data diskette to the instructor.

6. *Exit the* MARKSTRAT2 **software.** To exit the MARKSTRAT2 software, just press the "X" key. You will then return to the operating system level. You can always use the software at a later point in time by following the same procedure. Any decisions which you have saved will be displayed.

MARKSTRAT2 IN YOUR MARKETING COURSE

Before the first MARKSTRAT session in your marketing course, you should have carefully read the first four chapters of this book and experimented with the MARKSTRAT2 software as described in the previous pages. Your instructor will organize your class into teams of 4 to 8 students and into industries of five competing firms. Each team will be in charge of a simulated firm in a given industry with a specific name assigned by your instructor. If, for instance, you are team 3 in industry B, your firm name will be B3. At the beginning of the MARKSTRAT assignment, your instructor will give you a team data diskette

Appendix B   MARKSTRAT2 Software Instructions

labeled with the name of your team. This diskette will contain the data file with the information for Period 0 of your simulated firm. This information will be different from the one in the XYZ example. Your instructor has the option to create different MARKSTRAT scenarios. He or she will inform you of the characteristics of the specific scenario used in your course. You will have to analyze this information, make your decisions for Period 1 and save them on your team data diskette. You will then return this team data diskette to your instructor who will run the simulation model and give your team data diskette back to you with the results of Period 1. This process will be repeated for a number of periods and according to a schedule defined by your instructor. Throughout the whole MARKSTRAT exercise, the team data diskette, which contains the information on your simulated firm, will be the vehicle for communication between your team and the instructor. The student disk which you received with this book contains the MARKSTRAT2 software and should be kept in your possession.

The way in which you use the MARKSTRAT2 software in your course is similar to the way in which you experimented with the XYZ example. You should, however, be particularly careful in the following steps:

1. *Using the MARKSTRAT2 software with the team data diskette.* After you have started your micromputer system, you should:

   - if you have a system with two floppy disk drives, insert your MARKSTRAT2 student disk in drive A and your team data diskette in drive B.

   - if you have a system with a hard disk, you should check that the MARKSTRAT2 software is still present (as you copied it) in the MS2 subdirectory of your hard disk and your team data diskette should be inserted in drive A.

2. *Setting identification parameters.* The disk unit for the MARKSTRAT2 data files should be B if you use two floppy disk drives, and A if your software is on a hard disk. The industry code and team number should correspond to the industry and firm to which you have been assigned. If they do not correspond to the data file on your team data diskette, you will be given an error message. Either you have misspecified your identification (and you should correct it) or you have the wrong team data diskette (and you should contact your instructor). The period number should correspond to the latest period of the simulation, unless you want to access information from previous periods.

3. *System configuration.* After you have accessed the MARKSTRAT2 software, you should press "C" in the Main Menu to check that the specifications are correct for your computer system. The disk unit for MARKSTRAT2 data files should be B if you have a system with two floppy disk drives, and A if you have a system with a hard disk.

4. **Other options.** All other options in the Main Menu should be used as described previously with the XYZ example.

5. **Final check.** It is wise to check that your decisions have been correctly saved by going through the "Input Decisions" option a final time, before exiting the MARKSTRAT2 software by pressing "X" in the Main Menu and then returning your team data diskette to the instructor.

Finally, you should be fully aware that you are competing in the MARKSTRAT simulation against other teams in your class. Do not tempt other teams to engage in unethical activities by leaving your team data diskette unattended or by copying its contents on a hard disk accessible to others. And, throughout the whole MARKSTRAT experience, remember that, despite the competitive nature of the exercise, the real winners are those who will have learned most from the exercise!

BLANK FORMS

Blank forms printed on the following pages are easily detachable so that they can be filled in and adjusted conveniently in the course of a simulation.

    1. Decision Form (10 copies)

    2. Budgeting Form (10 copies)

        Part I: Financial Information
        Part II: Forecast for Budgeting

    3. Planning Form (5 copies)

        Part I: General Performance
        Part II: Marketing Expenditures

    4. Planning Form (5 copies)

        Part III: Strategic Analysis Summary
        Part IV: Main Strategic Options

MARKSTRAT DECISION FORM

Industry _____

Firm _____

Period _____

PRODUCT MANAGEMENT

Brand Names	Name of R&D Project (if modification) or introduction)	Production Planning (thousand units)	Advertising Budget (thousands of $)	Advertising Research (percent)	Recommended Retail Price ($)	Perceptual Objectives (−20 to +20, or 99)	
						Axis 1	Axis 2

SALES FORCE

Distribution Channels	1	2	3
Number of Salespersons			

RESEARCH AND DEVELOPMENT

Project Name	Expenditures (thousands of $)	Physical Characteristics					
		1	2	3	4	5	6

MARKET RESEARCH STUDIES

1	2	3	4	5	6	7	8	9	10	11	12	13	14	15

(For Instructor's Use)	

ec(−)   ep(+)   bd(−)   bi(+)

Modifications Resulting from Negotiations
Between the Firm and the MARKSTRAT Administrator

Source of Modification	Exceptional Profit (+) or Cost (−) (thousands of $)	Budget Increase (+) or Decrease (−) (thousands of $)
1. Additional information bought from the MARKSTRAT administrator		
_____	_____	_____
_____	_____	_____
_____	_____	_____
_____	_____	_____
2. Changes in the budget		_____
3. Fines	_____	_____
4. Other modifications		
_____	_____	_____
_____	_____	_____
_____	_____	_____
_____	_____	_____
Total		

Signature of the firm's representative _____

Signature of the MARKSTRAT administrator _____

MARKSTRAT DECISION FORM

Industry _____

Firm _____

Period _____

PRODUCT MANAGEMENT

Brand Names	Name of R&D Project (if modification) or introduction)	Production Planning (thousand units)	Advertising Budget (thousands of $)	Advertising Research (percent)	Recommended Retail Price ($)	Perceptual Objectives (−20 to +20, or 99)	
						Axis 1	Axis 2

SALES FORCE

Distribution Channels	1	2	3
Number of Salespersons			

RESEARCH AND DEVELOPMENT

Project Name	Expenditures (thousands of $)	Physical Characteristics					
		1	2	3	4	5	6

MARKET RESEARCH STUDIES

1	2	3	4	5	6	7	8	9	10	11	12	13	14	15

(For Instructor's Use)

ec(−)   ep(+)   bd(−)   bi(+)

Modifications Resulting from Negotiations
Between the Firm and the MARKSTRAT Administrator

Source of Modification	Exceptional Profit (+) or Cost (−) (thousands of $)	Budget Increase (+) or Decrease (−) (thousands of $)
1. Additional information bought from the MARKSTRAT administrator		
_____	_____	_____
_____	_____	_____
_____	_____	_____
_____	_____	_____
2. Changes in the budget		_____
3. Fines	_____	_____
4. Other modifications		
_____	_____	_____
_____	_____	_____
_____	_____	_____
_____	_____	_____
Total		

Signature of the firm's representative _____

Signature of the MARKSTRAT administrator _____

MARKSTRAT DECISION FORM

Industry _____

Firm _____

Period _____

PRODUCT MANAGEMENT

Brand Names	Name of R&D Project (if modification) or introduction)	Production Planning (thousand units)	Advertising Budget (thousands of $)	Advertising Research (percent)	Recommended Retail Price ($)	Perceptual Objectives (−20 to +20, or 99)	
						Axis 1	Axis 2

SALES FORCE

Distribution Channels	1	2	3
Number of Salespersons			

RESEARCH AND DEVELOPMENT

Project Name	Expenditures (thousands of $)	Physical Characteristics					
		1	2	3	4	5	6

MARKET RESEARCH STUDIES

1	2	3	4	5	6	7	8	9	10	11	12	13	14	15

(For Instructor's Use)

ec(−)   ep(+)   bd(−)   bi(+)

Modifications Resulting from Negotiations
Between the Firm and the MARKSTRAT Administrator

Source of Modification	Exceptional Profit (+) or Cost (−) (thousands of $)	Budget Increase (+) or Decrease (−) (thousands of $)
1. Additional information bought from the MARKSTRAT administrator		
_____	_____	_____
_____	_____	_____
_____	_____	_____
_____	_____	_____
2. Changes in the budget		_____
3. Fines	_____	_____
4. Other modifications		
_____	_____	_____
_____	_____	_____
_____	_____	_____
_____	_____	_____
Total		

Signature of the firm's representative _____

Signature of the MARKSTRAT administrator _____

MARKSTRAT DECISION FORM

Industry _____

Firm _____

Period _____

PRODUCT MANAGEMENT

Brand Names	Name of R&D Project (if modification) or introduction)	Production Planning (thousand units)	Advertising Budget (thousands of $)	Advertising Research (percent)	Recommended Retail Price ($)	Perceptual Objectives (−20 to +20, or 99)	
						Axis 1	Axis 2

SALES FORCE

Distribution Channels	1	2	3
Number of Salespersons			

RESEARCH AND DEVELOPMENT

Project Name	Expenditures (thousands of $)	Physical Characteristics					
		1	2	3	4	5	6

MARKET RESEARCH STUDIES

1	2	3	4	5	6	7	8	9	10	11	12	13	14	15

(For Instructor's Use)	

ec(−)   ep(+)   bd(−)   bi(+)

Modifications Resulting from Negotiations
Between the Firm and the MARKSTRAT Administrator

Source of Modification	Exceptional Profit (+) or Cost (−) (thousands of $)	Budget Increase (+) or Decrease (−) (thousands of $)
1. Additional information bought from the MARKSTRAT administrator		
_____	_____	_____
_____	_____	_____
_____	_____	_____
_____	_____	_____
2. Changes in the budget		_____
3. Fines	_____	_____
4. Other modifications		
_____	_____	_____
_____	_____	_____
_____	_____	_____
_____	_____	_____
Total		

Signature of the firm's representative _____

Signature of the MARKSTRAT administrator _____

MARKSTRAT DECISION FORM

Industry _____

Firm _____

Period _____

PRODUCT MANAGEMENT

Brand Names	Name of R&D Project (if modification) or introduction)	Production Planning (thousand units)	Advertising Budget (thousands of $)	Advertising Research (percent)	Recommended Retail Price ($)	Perceptual Objectives (−20 to +20, or 99)	
						Axis 1	Axis 2

SALES FORCE

Distribution Channels	1	2	3
Number of Salespersons			

RESEARCH AND DEVELOPMENT

Project Name	Expenditures (thousands of $)	Physical Characteristics					
		1	2	3	4	5	6

MARKET RESEARCH STUDIES

1	2	3	4	5	6	7	8	9	10	11	12	13	14	15

(For Instructor's Use)

ec(−)   ep(+)   bd(−)   bi(+)

Modifications Resulting from Negotiations
Between the Firm and the MARKSTRAT Administrator

Source of Modification	Exceptional Profit (+) or Cost (−) (thousands of $)	Budget Increase (+) or Decrease (−) (thousands of $)
1. Additional information bought from the MARKSTRAT administrator		
_____	_____	_____
_____	_____	_____
_____	_____	_____
_____	_____	_____
2. Changes in the budget		_____
3. Fines	_____	_____
4. Other modifications		
_____	_____	_____
_____	_____	_____
_____	_____	_____
_____	_____	_____
Total		

Signature of the firm's representative _____

Signature of the MARKSTRAT administrator _____

MARKSTRAT DECISION FORM

Industry _____

Firm _____

Period _____

PRODUCT MANAGEMENT

Brand Names	Name of R&D Project (if modification) or introduction)	Production Planning (thousand units)	Advertising Budget (thousands of $)	Advertising Research (percent)	Recommended Retail Price ($)	Perceptual Objectives (−20 to +20, or 99)	
						Axis 1	Axis 2

SALES FORCE

Distribution Channels	1	2	3
Number of Salespersons			

RESEARCH AND DEVELOPMENT

Project Name	Expenditures (thousands of $)	Physical Characteristics					
		1	2	3	4	5	6

MARKET RESEARCH STUDIES

1	2	3	4	5	6	7	8	9	10	11	12	13	14	15

(For Instructor's Use)	

ec(−)   ep(+)   bd(−)   bi(+)

Modifications Resulting from Negotiations Between the Firm and the MARKSTRAT Administrator

Source of Modification	Exceptional Profit (+) or Cost (−) (thousands of $)	Budget Increase (+) or Decrease (−) (thousands of $)
1. Additional information bought from the MARKSTRAT administrator		
_____	_____	_____
_____	_____	_____
_____	_____	_____
_____	_____	_____
2. Changes in the budget		_____
3. Fines	_____	_____
4. Other modifications		
_____	_____	_____
_____	_____	_____
_____	_____	_____
_____	_____	_____
Total		

Signature of the firm's representative _____

Signature of the MARKSTRAT administrator _____

MARKSTRAT DECISION FORM

Industry _____

Firm _____

Period _____

PRODUCT MANAGEMENT

Brand Names	Name of R&D Project (if modification) or introduction)	Production Planning (thousand units)	Advertising Budget (thousands of $)	Advertising Research (percent)	Recommended Retail Price ($)	Perceptual Objectives (−20 to +20, or 99)	
						Axis 1	Axis 2

SALES FORCE

Distribution Channels	1	2	3
Number of Salespersons			

RESEARCH AND DEVELOPMENT

Project Name	Expenditures (thousands of $)	Physical Characteristics					
		1	2	3	4	5	6

MARKET RESEARCH STUDIES

1	2	3	4	5	6	7	8	9	10	11	12	13	14	15

(For Instructor's Use)

ec(−)   ep(+)   bd(−)   bi(+)

Modifications Resulting from Negotiations
Between the Firm and the MARKSTRAT Administrator

Source of Modification	Exceptional Profit (+) or Cost (−) (thousands of $)	Budget Increase (+) or Decrease (−) (thousands of $)
1. Additional information bought from the MARKSTRAT administrator		
_____	_____	_____
_____	_____	_____
_____	_____	_____
_____	_____	_____
2. Changes in the budget		_____
3. Fines	_____	_____
4. Other modifications		
_____	_____	_____
_____	_____	_____
_____	_____	_____
_____	_____	_____
Total		

Signature of the firm's representative _____

Signature of the MARKSTRAT administrator _____

MARKSTRAT DECISION FORM

Industry _____

Firm _____

Period _____

PRODUCT MANAGEMENT

Brand Names	Name of R&D Project (if modification) or introduction)	Production Planning (thousand units)	Advertising Budget (thousands of $)	Advertising Research (percent)	Recommended Retail Price ($)	Perceptual Objectives (−20 to +20, or 99)	
						Axis 1	Axis 2

SALES FORCE

Distribution Channels	1	2	3
Number of Salespersons			

RESEARCH AND DEVELOPMENT

Project Name	Expenditures (thousands of $)	Physical Characteristics					
		1	2	3	4	5	6

MARKET RESEARCH STUDIES

1	2	3	4	5	6	7	8	9	10	11	12	13	14	15

(For Instructor's Use)

ec(−)   ep(+)   bd(−)   bi(+)

Modifications Resulting from Negotiations
Between the Firm and the MARKSTRAT Administrator

Source of Modification	Exceptional Profit (+) or Cost (−) (thousands of $)	Budget Increase (+) or Decrease (−) (thousands of $)
1. Additional information bought from the MARKSTRAT administrator		
_____	_____	_____
_____	_____	_____
_____	_____	_____
_____	_____	_____
2. Changes in the budget		_____
3. Fines	_____	_____
4. Other modifications		
_____	_____	_____
_____	_____	_____
_____	_____	_____
_____	_____	_____
Total		

Signature of the firm's representative _____

Signature of the MARKSTRAT administrator _____

MARKSTRAT DECISION FORM

Industry _____

Firm _____

Period _____

PRODUCT MANAGEMENT

Brand Names	Name of R&D Project (if modification) or introduction)	Production Planning (thousand units)	Advertising Budget (thousands of $)	Advertising Research (percent)	Recommended Retail Price ($)	Perceptual Objectives (−20 to +20, or 99)	
						Axis 1	Axis 2

SALES FORCE

Distribution Channels	1	2	3
Number of Salespersons			

RESEARCH AND DEVELOPMENT

Project Name	Expenditures (thousands of $)	Physical Characteristics					
		1	2	3	4	5	6

MARKET RESEARCH STUDIES

1	2	3	4	5	6	7	8	9	10	11	12	13	14	15

(For Instructor's Use)	

ec(−)   ep(+)   bd(−)   bi(+)

Modifications Resulting from Negotiations
Between the Firm and the MARKSTRAT Administrator

Source of Modification	Exceptional Profit (+) or Cost (−) (thousands of $)	Budget Increase (+) or Decrease (−) (thousands of $)
1. Additional information bought from the MARKSTRAT administrator		
_____	_____	_____
_____	_____	_____
_____	_____	_____
_____	_____	_____
2. Changes in the budget		_____
3. Fines	_____	_____
4. Other modifications		
_____	_____	_____
_____	_____	_____
_____	_____	_____
_____	_____	_____
Total		

Signature of the firm's representative _____

Signature of the MARKSTRAT administrator _____

MARKSTRAT DECISION FORM

Industry _____

Firm _____

Period _____

PRODUCT MANAGEMENT

Brand Names	Name of R&D Project (if modification) or introduction)	Production Planning (thousand units)	Advertising Budget (thousands of $)	Advertising Research (percent)	Recommended Retail Price ($)	Perceptual Objectives (−20 to +20, or 99)	
						Axis 1	Axis 2

SALES FORCE

Distribution Channels	1	2	3
Number of Salespersons			

RESEARCH AND DEVELOPMENT

Project Name	Expenditures (thousands of $)	Physical Characteristics					
		1	2	3	4	5	6

MARKET RESEARCH STUDIES

1	2	3	4	5	6	7	8	9	10	11	12	13	14	15

(For Instructor's Use)	

ec(−)   ep(+)   bd(−)   bi(+)

Modifications Resulting from Negotiations
Between the Firm and the MARKSTRAT Administrator

Source of Modification	Exceptional Profit (+) or Cost (−) (thousands of $)	Budget Increase (+) or Decrease (−) (thousands of $)
1. Additional information bought from the MARKSTRAT administrator		
————————————————	—————	—————
————————————————	—————	—————
————————————————	—————	—————
————————————————	—————	—————
2. Changes in the budget		—————
3. Fines	—————	—————
4. Other modifications		
————————————————	—————	—————
————————————————	—————	—————
————————————————	—————	—————
————————————————	—————	—————
Total		

Signature of the firm's representative _____

Signature of the MARKSTRAT administrator _____

MARKSTRAT BUDGETING FORM—PART I
Financial Information

Industry _____

Firm _____

Period _____

Brand Name				
Quantity Sold (units)				
Production (units)				
Inventory (units)				
Retail Price ($)				
Average Selling Price ($)				
Unit Transfer Cost ($)				
Revenues (thousands of $)				
Cost of Goods Sold (thousands of $)				
Inventory Costs (thousands of $)				
Advertising (thousands of $)				
Gross Marketing Contribution (thousands of $)				

Advertising _____

R&D _____

Sales Force _____

Market Research _____

R&D (thousands of $) . . . .

Sales Force (thousands of $) . . . .

Market Research (thousands of $) . . . .

Exceptional Cost or Profit (thousands of $) . . . .

Net Marketing Contribution (thousands of $) . . . .

Total Marketing Expenditures (thousands of $) . . . .

Total Marketing Expenditures _____

MARKSTRAT BUDGETING FORM—PART II
Forecast for Budgeting

Industry _____

Firm _____

Period _____

	Total Sonite Market (thousands of units)			Total Vodite Market (thousands of units)			Brands (Market share based on units—Sales in thousands of units)											
	Current Period	Expected Growth Rate	Forecast Next Period	Current Period	Expected Growth Rate	Forecast Next Period	Market Share	Sales	Market Share	Sales	Market Share	Sales	Market Share	Sales	Market Share	Sales	Market Share	Sales
Segment 1																		
Segment 2																		
Segment 3																		
Segment 4																		
Segment 5																		
Aggregate Forecasts																		
Retail Price																		
Retail Sales																		
Average Distributor Margin %																		
Revenues																		

MARKSTRAT BUDGETING FORM—PART I
Financial Information

Industry _____

Firm _____

Period _____

Brand Name					
Quantity Sold (units)					
Production (units)					
Inventory (units)					
Retail Price ($)					
Average Selling Price ($)					
Unit Transfer Cost ($)					
Revenues (thousands of $)					
Cost of Goods Sold (thousands of $)					
Inventory Costs (thousands of $)					
Advertising (thousands of $)					
Gross Marketing Contribution (thousands of $)					

Advertising _____

R&D (thousands of $) . . . . _____ R&D

Sales Force (thousands of $) . . . . _____ Sales Force

Market Research (thousands of $) . . . . . . _____ Market Research

Exceptional Cost or Profit (thousands of $) . . . . _____

Net Marketing Contribution (thousands of $) . . . . _____

Total Marketing Expenditures (thousands of $) . . . . _____ Total Marketing Expenditures

MARKSTRAT BUDGETING FORM—PART II

Forecast for Budgeting

Industry _____

Firm _____

Period _____

	Total Sonite Market (thousands of units)			Total Vodite Market (thousands of units)		
	Current Period	Expected Growth Rate	Forecast Next Period	Current Period	Expected Growth Rate	Forecast Next Period
Segment 1						
Segment 2						
Segment 3						
Segment 4						
Segment 5						
Aggregate Forecasts						

Brands

(Market share based on units—Sales in thousands of units)

	Market Share	Sales	Market Share	Sales	Market Share	Sales	Market Share	Sales	Market Share	Sales	Market Share	Sales
Segment 1												
Segment 2												
Segment 3												
Segment 4												
Segment 5												
Aggregate Forecasts												
Retail Price												
Retail Sales												
Average Distributor Margin %												
Revenues												

MARKSTRAT BUDGETING FORM—PART I
Financial Information

Industry _____

Firm _____

Period _____

Brand Name				
Quantity Sold (units)				
Production (units)				
Inventory (units)				
Retail Price ($)				
Average Selling Price ($)				
Unit Transfer Cost ($)				
Revenues (thousands of $)				
Cost of Goods Sold (thousands of $)				
Inventory Costs (thousands of $)				
Advertising (thousands of $)				
Gross Marketing Contribution (thousands of $)				

Advertising _____

R&D _____

Sales Force _____

Market Research _____

R&D (thousands of $) . . . . _____

Sales Force (thousands of $) . . . . _____

Market Research (thousands of $) . . . . _____

Exceptional Cost or Profit (thousands of $) . . . . _____

Net Marketing Contribution (thousands of $) . . . . _____

Total Marketing Expenditures (thousands of $) . . . . _____ Total Marketing Expenditures

MARKSTRAT BUDGETING FORM—PART II
Forecast for Budgeting

Industry _____

Firm _____

Period _____

Brands

(Market share based on units—Sales in thousands of units)

	Total Sonite Market (thousands of units)			Total Vodite Market (thousands of units)			Market Share	Sales	Market Share	Sales	Market Share	Sales	Market Share	Sales	Market Share	Sales
	Current Period	Expected Growth Rate	Forecast Next Period	Current Period	Expected Growth Rate	Forecast Next Period										
Segment 1																
Segment 2																
Segment 3																
Segment 4																
Segment 5																
Aggregate Forecasts																

Retail Price													
Retail Sales													
Average Distributor Margin %													
Revenues													

MARKSTRAT BUDGETING FORM—PART I
Financial Information

Industry _____

Firm _____

Period _____

Brand Name				
Quantity Sold (units)				
Production (units)				
Inventory (units)				
Retail Price ($)				
Average Selling Price ($)				
Unit Transfer Cost ($)				
Revenues (thousands of $)				
Cost of Goods Sold (thousands of $)				
Inventory Costs (thousands of $)				
Advertising (thousands of $)				
Gross Marketing Contribution (thousands of $)				

Advertising _____

R&D _____

Sales Force _____

Market Research _____

R&D (thousands of $) . . . . _____

Sales Force (thousands of $) . . . . _____

Market Research (thousands of $) . . . . _____

Exceptional Cost or Profit (thousands of $) . . . . _____

Net Marketing Contribution (thousands of $) . . . . _____

Total Marketing Expenditures (thousands of $) . . . . _____ Total Marketing Expenditures

MARKSTRAT BUDGETING FORM—PART II
Forecast for Budgeting

Industry _____

Firm _____

Period _____

Total Sonite Market (thousands of units)

	Current Period	Expected Growth Rate	Forecast Next Period

Total Vodite Market (thousands of units)

	Current Period	Expected Growth Rate	Forecast Next Period

Brands
(Market share based on units—Sales in thousands of units)

	Market Share	Sales	Market Share	Sales	Market Share	Sales	Market Share	Sales	Market Share	Sales	Market Share	Sales
Segment 1												
Segment 2												
Segment 3												
Segment 4												
Segment 5												
Aggregate Forecasts												
Retail Price												
Retail Sales												
Average Distributor Margin %												
Revenues												

MARKSTRAT BUDGETING FORM—PART I
Financial Information

Industry _____

Firm _____

Period _____

Brand Name					
Quantity Sold (units)					
Production (units)					
Inventory (units)					
Retail Price ($)					
Average Selling Price ($)					
Unit Transfer Cost ($)					
Revenues (thousands of $)					
Cost of Goods Sold (thousands of $)					
Inventory Costs (thousands of $)					
Advertising (thousands of $)					
Gross Marketing Contribution (thousands of $)					

Advertising _____

R&D _____

Sales Force _____

Market Research _____

R&D (thousands of $) . . . . _____

Sales Force (thousands of $) . . . . _____

Market Research (thousands of $) . . . . _____

Exceptional Cost or Profit (thousands of $) . . . _____

Net Marketing Contribution (thousands of $) . . . _____

Total Marketing Expenditures (thousands of $) . . . . _____ Total Marketing Expenditures

MARKSTRAT BUDGETING FORM—PART II
Forecast for Budgeting

Industry _____

Firm _____

Period _____

	Total Sonite Market (thousands of units)			Total Vodite Market (thousands of units)			Brands (Market share based on units— Sales in thousands of units)									
	Current Period	Expected Growth Rate	Forecast Next Period	Current Period	Expected Growth Rate	Forecast Next Period	Market Share	Sales	Market Share	Sales	Market Share	Sales	Market Share	Sales	Market Share	Sales
Segment 1																
Segment 2																
Segment 3																
Segment 4																
Segment 5																
Aggregate Forecasts																
Retail Price																
Retail Sales																
Average Distributor Margin %																
Revenues																

MARKSTRAT BUDGETING FORM—PART I
Financial Information

Industry _____

Firm _____

Period _____

Brand Name				
Quantity Sold (units)				
Production (units)				
Inventory (units)				
Retail Price ($)				
Average Selling Price ($)				
Unit Transfer Cost ($)				
Revenues (thousands of $)				
Cost of Goods Sold (thousands of $)				
Inventory Costs (thousands of $)				
Advertising (thousands of $)				

Gross Marketing Contribution (thousands of $)	
R&D (thousands of $)	Advertising _____
Sales Force (thousands of $)	R&D _____
Market Research (thousands of $)	Sales Force _____
Exceptional Cost or Profit (thousands of $)	Market Research _____
Net Marketing Contribution (thousands of $)	
Total Marketing Expenditures (thousands of $)	Total Marketing Expenditures _____

MARKSTRAT BUDGETING FORM—PART II

Forecast for Budgeting

Industry _____

Firm _____

Period _____

	Total Sonite Market (thousands of units)			Total Vodite Market (thousands of units)		
	Current Period	Expected Growth Rate	Forecast Next Period	Current Period	Expected Growth Rate	Forecast Next Period
Segment 1						
Segment 2						
Segment 3						
Segment 4						
Segment 5						
Aggregate Forecasts						

Brands
(Market share based on units—Sales in thousands of units)

	Market Share	Sales	Market Share	Sales	Market Share	Sales	Market Share	Sales	Market Share	Sales	Market Share	Sales
Segment 1												
Segment 2												
Segment 3												
Segment 4												
Segment 5												
Aggregate Forecasts												
Retail Price												
Retail Sales												
Average Distributor Margin %												
Revenues												

MARKSTRAT BUDGETING FORM—PART I
Financial Information

Industry _____

Firm _____

Period _____

Brand Name				
Quantity Sold (units)				
Production (units)				
Inventory (units)				
Retail Price ($)				
Average Selling Price ($)				
Unit Transfer Cost ($)				
Revenues (thousands of $)				
Cost of Goods Sold (thousands of $)				
Inventory Costs (thousands of $)				
Advertising (thousands of $)				

Gross Marketing Contribution (thousands of $) ....

R&D (thousands of $) .... _____ R&D

Sales Force (thousands of $) .... _____ Sales Force

Market Research (thousands of $) .... _____ Market Research

Exceptional Cost or Profit (thousands of $) ....

Net Marketing Contribution (thousands of $) ....

Total Marketing Expenditures (thousands of $) .... _____ Total Marketing Expenditures

_____ Advertising

MARKSTRAT BUDGETING FORM—PART II
Forecast for Budgeting

Industry _____

Firm _____

Period _____

	Total Sonite Market (thousands of units)			Total Vodite Market (thousands of units)			Brands (Market share based on units—Sales in thousands of units)									
	Current Period	Expected Growth Rate	Forecast Next Period	Current Period	Expected Growth Rate	Forecast Next Period	Market Share	Sales	Market Share	Sales	Market Share	Sales	Market Share	Sales	Market Share	Sales
Segment 1																
Segment 2																
Segment 3																
Segment 4																
Segment 5																
Aggregate Forecasts																
Retail Price																
Retail Sales																
Average Distributor Margin %																
Revenues																

MARKSTRAT BUDGETING FORM—PART I
Financial Information

Industry _____

Firm _____

Period _____

Brand Name					
Quantity Sold (units)					
Production (units)					
Inventory (units)					
Retail Price ($)					
Average Selling Price ($)					
Unit Transfer Cost ($)					
Revenues (thousands of $)					
Cost of Goods Sold (thousands of $)					
Inventory Costs (thousands of $)					
Advertising (thousands of $)					
Gross Marketing Contribution (thousands of $)					

Advertising _____

R&D _____

Sales Force _____

Market Research _____

R&D (thousands of $) . . . . _____

Sales Force (thousands of $) . . . . _____

Market Research (thousands of $) . . . . _____

Exceptional Cost or Profit (thousands of $) . . . . _____

Net Marketing Contribution (thousands of $) . . . . _____

Total Marketing Expenditures (thousands of $) . . . . _____ Total Marketing Expenditures

MARKSTRAT BUDGETING FORM—PART II
Forecast for Budgeting

Industry _____

Firm _____

Period _____

Total Sonite Market (thousands of units)

	Current Period	Expected Growth Rate	Forecast Next Period
Segment 1			
Segment 2			
Segment 3			
Segment 4			
Segment 5			
Aggregate Forecasts			

Total Vodite Market (thousands of units)

	Current Period	Expected Growth Rate	Forecast Next Period
Segment 1			
Segment 2			
Segment 3			
Segment 4			
Segment 5			
Aggregate Forecasts			

Brands
(Market share based on units—Sales in thousands of units)

	Market Share	Sales	Market Share	Sales	Market Share	Sales	Market Share	Sales	Market Share	Sales	Market Share	Sales
Segment 1												
Segment 2												
Segment 3												
Segment 4												
Segment 5												
Aggregate Forecasts												
Retail Price												
Retail Sales												
Average Distributor Margin %												
Revenues												

MARKSTRAT BUDGETING FORM—PART I
Financial Information

Industry _____

Firm _____

Period _____

Brand Name				
Quantity Sold (units)				
Production (units)				
Inventory (units)				
Retail Price ($)				
Average Selling Price ($)				
Unit Transfer Cost ($)				
Revenues (thousands of $)				
Cost of Goods Sold (thousands of $)				
Inventory Costs (thousands of $)				
Advertising (thousands of $)				
Gross Marketing Contribution (thousands of $)				

Advertising _____

R&D _____

Sales Force _____

Market Research _____

R&D (thousands of $) . . . . _____

Sales Force (thousands of $) . . . . _____

Market Research (thousands of $) . . . . _____

Exceptional Cost or Profit (thousands of $) . . . _____

Net Marketing Contribution (thousands of $) . . . _____

Total Marketing Expenditures (thousands of $) . . _____ Total Marketing Expenditures

MARKSTRAT BUDGETING FORM—PART II
Forecast for Budgeting

Industry _____

Firm _____

Period _____

	Total Sonite Market (thousands of units)			Total Vodite Market (thousands of units)			Brands (Market share based on units—Sales in thousands of units)										
	Current Period	Expected Growth Rate	Forecast Next Period	Current Period	Expected Growth Rate	Forecast Next Period	Market Share	Sales	Market Share	Sales	Market Share	Sales	Market Share	Sales	Market Share	Sales	
Segment 1																	
Segment 2																	
Segment 3																	
Segment 4																	
Segment 5																	
Aggregate Forecasts																	
Retail Price																	
Retail Sales																	
Average Distributor Margin %																	
Revenues																	

MARKSTRAT BUDGETING FORM—PART I
Financial Information

Industry _____

Firm _____

Period _____

Brand Name					
Quantity Sold (units)					
Production (units)					
Inventory (units)					
Retail Price ($)					
Average Selling Price ($)					
Unit Transfer Cost ($)					
Revenues (thousands of $)					
Cost of Goods Sold (thousands of $)					
Inventory Costs (thousands of $)					
Advertising (thousands of $)					
Gross Marketing Contribution (thousands of $)					

R&D (thousands of $) . . . . _____ R&D

Sales Force (thousands of $) . . . . _____ Sales Force

Market Research (thousands of $) . . . . _____ Market Research

Exceptional Cost or Profit (thousands of $) . . . . _____

Net Marketing Contribution (thousands of $) . . . . _____

Total Marketing Expenditures (thousands of $) . . . . _____ Total Marketing Expenditures

Advertising _____

MARKSTRAT BUDGETING FORM—PART II
Forecast for Budgeting

Industry —————

Firm —————

Period —————

	Total Sonite Market (thousands of units)			Total Vodite Market (thousands of units)			Brands (Market share based on units—Sales in thousands of units)										
	Current Period	Expected Growth Rate	Forecast Next Period	Current Period	Expected Growth Rate	Forecast Next Period	Market Share	Sales	Market Share	Sales	Market Share	Sales	Market Share	Sales	Market Share	Sales	
Segment 1																	
Segment 2																	
Segment 3																	
Segment 4																	
Segment 5																	
Aggregate Forecasts																	
Retail Price																	
Retail Sales																	
Average Distributor Margin %																	
Revenues																	

MARKSTRAT PLANNING FORM—PART I
General Performance

Industry _____

Firm _____

		1	2	3	4	5	Periods 6	7	8	9	10
Percentage Growth	Objective										
	Outcome										
Retail Sales (millions of $)	Objective										
	Outcome										
Revenues (millions of $)	Objective										
	Outcome										
Gross Marketing Contribution (millions of $)	Objective										
	Outcome										
Net Marketing Contribution (millions of $)	Objective										
	Outcome										
Sonite Market Share (based on volume)	Objective										
	Outcome										
Sonite Market Share (based on value)	Objective										
	Outcome										
Vodite Market Share (based on unit volume)	Objective										
	Outcome										
Vodite Market Share (based on value)	Objective										
	Outcome										
Total Market Share (based on value)	Objective										
	Outcome										
	Objective										
	Outcome										
	Objective										
	Outcome										

MARKSTRAT PLANNING FORM—PART II
Marketing Expenditures

Industry _____

Firm _____

			Periods								
		1	2	3	4	5	6	7	8	9	10
Advertising (millions of $)	Objective										
	Outcome										
Sales Force (millions of $)	Objective										
	Outcome										
R&D (millions of $)	Objective										
	Outcome										
Market Research (millions of $)	Objective										
	Outcome										
Total Marketing Expenditures (millions of $)	Objective										
	Outcome										

MARKSTRAT PLANNING FORM—PART I
General Performance

Industry _____

Firm _____

		Periods									
		1	2	3	4	5	6	7	8	9	10
Percentage Growth	Objective										
	Outcome										
Retail Sales (millions of $)	Objective										
	Outcome										
Revenues (millions of $)	Objective										
	Outcome										
Gross Marketing Contribution (millions of $)	Objective										
	Outcome										
Net Marketing Contribution (millions of $)	Objective										
	Outcome										
Sonite Market Share (based on volume)	Objective										
	Outcome										
Sonite Market Share (based on value)	Objective										
	Outcome										
Vodite Market Share (based on unit volume)	Objective										
	Outcome										
Vodite Market Share (based on value)	Objective										
	Outcome										
Total Market Share (based on value)	Objective										
	Outcome										
	Objective										
	Outcome										
	Objective										
	Outcome										

MARKSTRAT PLANNING FORM—PART II
Marketing Expenditures

Industry _____

Firm _____

		Periods									
		1	2	3	4	5	6	7	8	9	10
Advertising (millions of $)	Objective										
	Outcome										
Sales Force (millions of $)	Objective										
	Outcome										
R&D (millions of $)	Objective										
	Outcome										
Market Research (millions of $)	Objective										
	Outcome										
Total Marketing Expenditures (millions of $)	Objective										
	Outcome										

MARKSTRAT PLANNING FORM—PART I
General Performance

Industry _____

Firm _____

		Periods									
		1	2	3	4	5	6	7	8	9	10
Percentage Growth	Objective										
	Outcome										
Retail Sales (millions of $)	Objective										
	Outcome										
Revenues (millions of $)	Objective										
	Outcome										
Gross Marketing Contribution (millions of $)	Objective										
	Outcome										
Net Marketing Contribution (millions of $)	Objective										
	Outcome										
Sonite Market Share (based on volume)	Objective										
	Outcome										
Sonite Market Share (based on value)	Objective										
	Outcome										
Vodite Market Share (based on unit volume)	Objective										
	Outcome										
Vodite Market Share (based on value)	Objective										
	Outcome										
Total Market Share (based on value)	Objective										
	Outcome										
	Objective										
	Outcome										
	Objective										
	Outcome										

MARKSTRAT PLANNING FORM—PART II
Marketing Expenditures

Industry _____

Firm _____

		Periods									
		1	2	3	4	5	6	7	8	9	10
Advertising (millions of $)	Objective										
	Outcome										
Sales Force (millions of $)	Objective										
	Outcome										
R&D (millions of $)	Objective										
	Outcome										
Market Research (millions of $)	Objective										
	Outcome										
Total Marketing Expenditures (millions of $)	Objective										
	Outcome										

MARKSTRAT PLANNING FORM—PART I
General Performance

Industry _____

Firm _____

		Periods									
		1	2	3	4	5	6	7	8	9	10
Percentage Growth	Objective										
	Outcome										
Retail Sales (millions of $)	Objective										
	Outcome										
Revenues (millions of $)	Objective										
	Outcome										
Gross Marketing Contribution (millions of $)	Objective										
	Outcome										
Net Marketing Contribution (millions of $)	Objective										
	Outcome										
Sonite Market Share (based on volume)	Objective										
	Outcome										
Sonite Market Share (based on value)	Objective										
	Outcome										
Vodite Market Share (based on unit volume)	Objective										
	Outcome										
Vodite Market Share (based on value)	Objective										
	Outcome										
Total Market Share (based on value)	Objective										
	Outcome										
	Objective										
	Outcome										
	Objective										
	Outcome										

MARKSTRAT PLANNING FORM—PART II
Marketing Expenditures

Industry _____

Firm _____

		Periods									
		2	3	4	5	6	7	8	9	10	
Advertising (millions of $)	Objective										
	Outcome										
Sales Force (millions of $)	Objective										
	Outcome										
R&D (millions of $)	Objective										
	Outcome										
Market Research (millions of $)	Objective										
	Outcome										
Total Marketing Expenditures (millions of $)	Objective										
	Outcome										

MARKSTRAT PLANNING FORM—PART I
General Performance

Industry _____

Firm _____

		Periods									
		1	2	3	4	5	6	7	8	9	10
Percentage Growth	Objective										
	Outcome										
Retail Sales (millions of $)	Objective										
	Outcome										
Revenues (millions of $)	Objective										
	Outcome										
Gross Marketing Contribution (millions of $)	Objective										
	Outcome										
Net Marketing Contribution (millions of $)	Objective										
	Outcome										
Sonite Market Share (based on volume)	Objective										
	Outcome										
Sonite Market Share (based on value)	Objective										
	Outcome										
Vodite Market Share (based on unit volume)	Objective										
	Outcome										
Vodite Market Share (based on value)	Objective										
	Outcome										
Total Market Share (based on value)	Objective										
	Outcome										
	Objective										
	Outcome										
	Objective										
	Outcome										

MARKSTRAT PLANNING FORM—PART II
Marketing Expenditures

Industry ―――――――

Firm ―――――――

		Periods									
		1	2	3	4	5	6	7	8	9	10
Advertising (millions of $)	Objective										
	Outcome										
Sales Force (millions of $)	Objective										
	Outcome										
R&D (millions of $)	Objective										
	Outcome										
Market Research (millions of $)	Objective										
	Outcome										
Total Marketing Expenditures (millions of $)	Objective										
	Outcome										

MARKSTRAT PLANNING FORM—PART III
Strategic Analysis Summary

Industry _____

Firm _____

	Sonite Market	Vodite Market
Competitive Structure • Main Competitors' Advantage • Main Competitors' Weaknesses • Threats of New Entries • Mobility Barriers		
Competitive Behavior • Main Competitors' Marketing Intensity • Competitive Reactions		
Economic and Environmental Dynamics		
Company Competitive Position Assessment • Strengths • Weaknesses		
Company Allocation of Resources Assessment (Current/Future) • Portfolio • Synergies • Risks		

MARKSTRAT PLANNING FORM—PART IV
Main Strategic Options

Industry _____

Firm _____

Segmentation and positioning _____
_____
_____

Product and Brand Strategy _____
_____
_____

Advertising Strategy _____
_____
_____

Sales Force and Distribution Strategy _____
_____
_____

Research and Development Strategy _____
_____
_____

Others _____
_____
_____
_____

MARKSTRAT PLANNING FORM—PART III
Strategic Analysis Summary

Industry _____

Firm _____

	Sonite Market	Vodite Market
Competitive Structure ▪ Main Competitors' Advantage ▪ Main Competitors' Weaknesses ▪ Threats of New Entries ▪ Mobility Barriers		
Competitive Behavior ▪ Main Competitors' Marketing Intensity ▪ Competitive Reactions		
Economic and Environmental Dynamics		
Company Competitive Position Assessment ▪ Strengths ▪ Weaknesses		
Company Allocation of Resources Assessment (Current/Future) ▪ Portfolio ▪ Synergies ▪ Risks		

MARKSTRAT PLANNING FORM—PART IV
Main Strategic Options

Industry _____

Firm _____

Segmentation and positioning _____

_____

_____

Product and Brand Strategy _____

_____

_____

Advertising Strategy _____

_____

_____

Sales Force and Distribution Strategy _____

_____

_____

Research and Development Strategy _____

_____

_____

Others _____

_____

_____

_____

_____

MARKSTRAT PLANNING FORM—PART III
Strategic Analysis Summary

Industry _____

Firm _____

	Sonite Market	Vodite Market
Competitive Structure • Main Competitors' Advantage • Main Competitors' Weaknesses • Threats of New Entries • Mobility Barriers		
Competitive Behavior • Main Competitors' Marketing Intensity • Competitive Reactions		
Economic and Environmental Dynamics		
Company Competitive Position Assessment • Strengths • Weaknesses		
Company Allocation of Resources Assessment (Current/Future) • Portfolio • Synergies • Risks		

MARKSTRAT PLANNING FORM—PART IV
Main Strategic Options

Industry _____

Firm _____

Segmentation and positioning _____

_____

_____

Product and Brand Strategy _____

_____

_____

Advertising Strategy _____

_____

_____

Sales Force and Distribution Strategy _____

_____

_____

Research and Development Strategy _____

_____

_____

Others _____

_____

_____

_____

_____

MARKSTRAT PLANNING FORM—PART III
Strategic Analysis Summary

Industry _____

Firm _____

	Sonite Market	Vodite Market
Competitive Structure • Main Competitors' Advantage • Main Competitors' Weaknesses • Threats of New Entries • Mobility Barriers		
Competitive Behavior • Main Competitors' Marketing Intensity • Competitive Reactions		
Economic and Environmental Dynamics		
Company Competitive Position Assessment • Strengths • Weaknesses		
Company Allocation of Resources Assessment (Current/Future) • Portfolio • Synergies • Risks		

MARKSTRAT PLANNING FORM—PART IV
Main Strategic Options

Industry _____

Firm _____

Segmentation and positioning _____

_____

_____

Product and Brand Strategy _____

_____

_____

Advertising Strategy _____

_____

_____

Sales Force and Distribution Strategy _____

_____

_____

Research and Development Strategy _____

_____

_____

Others _____

_____

_____

_____

_____

MARKSTRAT PLANNING FORM—PART III
Strategic Analysis Summary

Industry _____

Firm _____

	Sonite Market	Vodite Market
Competitive Structure • Main Competitors' Advantage • Main Competitors' Weaknesses • Threats of New Entries • Mobility Barriers		
Competitive Behavior • Main Competitors' Marketing Intensity • Competitive Reactions		
Economic and Environmental Dynamics		
Company Competitive Position Assessment • Strengths • Weaknesses		
Company Allocation of Resources Assessment (Current/Future) • Portfolio • Synergies • Risks		

MARKSTRAT PLANNING FORM—PART IV
Main Strategic Options

Industry _____

Firm _____

Segmentation and positioning _____

_____

_____

Product and Brand Strategy _____

_____

_____

Advertising Strategy _____

_____

_____

Sales Force and Distribution Strategy _____

_____

_____

Research and Development Strategy _____

_____

_____

Others _____

_____

_____

_____

_____